Songs of
Toby Gad

Complete Lyrics

Cherry Lane Music Company

ISBN 978-1-60378-161-9

Visit our website at www.cherrylaneprint.com

5TH AVENUE

Your curly hair
Brown eyes, I remember
Your deep voice
Your luscious lips, I surrender
You were here, it felt so good
Now you're gone and I

CHORUS:
I saw you on Fifth Avenue
That's where I fell in love with you
Walking in the dark
Wondering where you are
Hoping I'll find you
On Fifth Avenue

I couldn't breathe
The way you smiled, I was taken
I couldn't speak
Felt so weak, I was shaken
Face to face, time stood still
Everything was spinning

CHORUS

CHORUS

CHORUS

On Fifth Avenue, etc.*

*The word "etc." indicates multiple repetitions of a line or phrase.

9 TO 5

Early in the morning clock hits quarter to five
I could use the extra sleep but if I'm late I know I'll get fired
Everyday I bust my ass tryin' so hard to please
When I come home late at night I'm so God damned tired

CHORUS:
I'm a 9 to 5, doin' what I do to survive
I'm a 9 to 5, with my nose to the grind
I'm a 9 to 5, watchin' my life pass me by
And if I don't do something about it gonna be here 'til I die

Every dime I earn has already been spent
If I buy me a pair of socks, then I won't have enough for the rent
Big man keeps me small so I won't get any ideas
I used to have a dream, but it drowned in the beer

CHORUS:
I'm a 9 to 5, workin' 'til the sun goes down
You might be king, but it's me who makes the crown
I'm a 9 to 5, watchin' my life pass me by
If I don't do something about it I'm gonna be here 'til I die

Killin' every weekend at the OTB
One of these mornings I know luck will smile on me
I'll make a million dollars and buy the whole damn land
And never suck up to that motherfucker again

CHORUS:
I'm a 9 to 5, folks like me make the world go 'round
You better think twice before you stab me down
I'm a 9 to 5, watchin my life pass me by
If I don't do something about it I'm gonna be here 'til I die

ABSOLUTELY ADORABLE

Baby I love loving you
You make me come closer to the woman that's inside of me
The wild child that I never knew
Till I met you
You make me immune to the troubles of this crazy world out there
When you say that I'm your girl
And oh

CHORUS:
You're absolutely adorable
Simply unbelievable
Baby I want to be what you are to me
So beautiful
And absolutely adorable

One of a kind of the kind I need
You feed my soul when I crave your body and your strong embrace
You touch me like no one before and I want more
You take me away
From this crazy world out there
When you say that I'm your girl
Oh

CHORUS

I feel the rhythm, feel the rhyme
Your love's like poetry to me
It's in your touch it's in your voice
It's just as deep as love can be

CHORUS

CHORUS

ADMIT IT

Hanging in the booth, giving me the eye
I got the message why you gotta act shy
Looking at you noddin' your head
I can read your mind you really want it bad
I can tell by the look on your face that you're really, really, really into me

PRE-CHORUS:
Is it me or is it hot in here
Burning up, adrenaline rush, can't get enough
Is it real or am I just imagining?
Do I want it too much? Am I making it up
I try to ignore you babe
But I keep coming back for more

CHORUS:
Just admit it, I know you want it
Why you're over there when you could be right here
Come and get it, you know I got it
Can't you read the signs, why you wasting time
When you could be mine
Just admit it, admit it, etc.

Trying to impress caught me acting like a fool
Don't want you to see me but I really do
'Cause I'm the type of girl who's used to playing it cool
If you wanna win me over it's up to you
Yeah babe, c'mon and make your move

PRE-CHORUS

CHORUS

PRE-CHORUS

CHORUS

ALIVE

CHORUS:
What would you do if someone told you you were going to die today
Out of the blue, but you knew it was true what would you do that day

Would you confess your love to your secret crush
Call your boss and tell him off, pretend he hurt you so much
Would you give away everything you have to somebody in need
Or rob a bank, strike it rich, get everyone down on their knees
Steal a really fast car, head for the freeway
    a hundred sixty miles and hour and counting

CHORUS

Would you shut off your phone
Spend your last day alone in peace
Or would you meet with all your friends
Kiss them goodbye as you leave
Would you go wild, throw a party
Have the time of your life
Or would you break down and cry
Or would you get a preacher
Pray and confess all your sins
So you won't go to hell

CHORUS

Would it give you the courage to do everything you were afraid to try
Would it set you free to say all the thoughts you've been holding inside

Hey, but you're still alive, etc.

Why would you wait until it's too late? Someday we're all gonna die
Just follow your heart, say what's on your mind and do what you like

While you're still alive, etc.

ALL I HAVE

I was missin' you
You were miles away
He was close to me
I let him stay
Then I closed my eyes
He almost felt the same
But when the morning broke I cried out your name
If I'd only known it would break us
I'd done anything just to save us

CHORUS:
'Cause you're all I have
When the world comes down on me
You're the one I love
And I'm begging you to see
You're all, you're all, you're all I have
You are, you are the one I love
You are, you are, you're all I have

You've forgiven me
But it doesn't change
The guilt I feel when you mention his name
No more innocence
How to trust again
Wanna believe that you won't do the same
And every time we fight we're getting closer
I slowly die inside, I'm scared it's over

CHORUS

Your love for me was always there
Maybe too much for me to care
Now that I know I messed it up
I'd give my all to take it back

CHORUS

ALL I THINK ABOUT IS

For seven years you were my friend, always asking for my hand
I never let you get too close to me
Until that lonely summer night when we both lay side by side
I don't know why you looked so good
I guess I'd drunk more than I should
Four years later here we are
How did I let it go this far

CHORUS:
You are my Friday night when finally work is over
You are my pillow when I wake up feeling sick
A night without you is like a party with no forex
When I'm around you all I think about is

I felt so sorry for the girls
Who let a boy control their world
Well, I was happy being free
With all the boys in love with me
But look at me now
Before I knew it I'm locked down
Feeling sorry for myself
Being framed up on a shelf
Now I don't know how to breathe
When you're not here with me, yeah

CHORUS

You're like the jelly to my peanut butter sandwich
And if you were a dog I would wanna be your

CHORUS

ALL THE BOYZ

All the fellas got me goin' insane
Want to know my number want to know my name
Tell me why these players always sound the same
Swinging them chains talking that game

All the real ladies lookin' for a real man
Lookin' for somebody who will understand
Something like a 7 on a scale of 1-10
Holla at me if you can

CHORUS:
What's up boys around the world?
Show me if you know how to court a girl
What you give is what you get
Triple threat can you handle that
All the boyz around around the world, etc.

Boys, can't leave us alone, boys follow us home
They can't tell us apart when they get us on the phone
Keep messin' up our names cause they think we're all the same
We play our little games and we put the boys to shame

CHORUS

CHORUS

All to Myself

As I'm getting ready for our date
  tonight
I take a look in the mirror,
  something's just not right
You are the one I just know that
  inside
But I've got to draw the line
I decide tonight's the night to tell
  you how I feel
Gonna tell you everything and keep
  it real
There's no other girl that can ever
  love you the same
Even though it's hard for me to say
I just can't have it any other way

CHORUS:
I want you all to myself
Boy you know I'm not the
  jealous type
If we do this we're gonna do it right
If not then don't bother to call
I want it all or nothing
Don't you take my love for granted
or we're better off just ending it
  right now
I want you all to myself
All to myself

Heard about the girls that seem
  to always come around
But if you're with me that's
  something I can't allow
I refuse to be treated just like
  any other girl

I need to be your world
If you want me baby all you really
  have to do
Is to love me and me only and
  always be true
There's no other girl that can ever
  love you the same
Even though it's hard for me to say
I just can't have it any other way

CHORUS

Real love is just so hard to find
I don't wanna waste my time
If I'm not gonna be your only one
Then I'll be gone tonight
But I really think that we've got
something special
You'd regret if you let this go
So make a choice, make up
  your mind
'Cause you know that I

CHORUS

CHORUS

Always on My Mind

We say hello, kiss on the cheek I know
Something there I try so hard to hide
So I walk away to escape the pain that I must face when I look in your eyes
It's so hard to pretend you're only a good friend
'Cause you and me are meant to be walking hand in hand
So I try to resist but I'm burning for your love
I can't get myself to give it up

CHORUS:
I'm not supposed to love you, but I can't help it
I'm not supposed to want you, but I can't fight it
I'm not supposed to show you my feelings hiding every sign
But I can't lie you're always on my mind

I can't deny you're always on my mind
Always on my mind, yeah

Hopelessly try to escape what the feeling's not supposed to be
But something happens every time that you're close to me
Tension building when you're approaching me
More than friends is what I hope to be

When you pass me by I can feel the fire
Try to keep it down but everybody knows
When we hug goodbye you hold on so tight
It feels so good I don't want to let go
I try so hard to pretend I'm only your good friend
Who am I deep inside? You want it to the end
So we try to erase a love we cannot face
But it's impossible to make it go away, go away

CHORUS

I can't deny you're always on my mind

C'mon, yeah, bring your fire girl,
C'mon, yeah, uh huh, I cannot, I cannot
'Cause you're always on my mind
My mind, I can't help it, here we, here we go

CHORUS

You're always on my mind

CHORUS

I can't deny you're always on my mind
Always on my mind

Can't stop thinking about you
Why you always on my mind

ANGEL OF THE DARK

He once was a hero who fought in ancient wars
He thought he was better so he challenged the gods
The gods grew angry and put a curse on his life
They made him an angel yet a killer inside

CHORUS:
The angel of the dark
Preying on the strong
His wings are tainted black
He's waited for so long

To all of the mortals only a shadow could be seen
A silent assassin like a whisper in the wind
He's slayed the rulers, presidents, and kings
Who challenged the gods in struggles they couldn't win

CHORUS

He saw the kingdoms rise, watched the empires fall
At the mercy of gods forced to heed their calls
Weary of his purpose he begged for his release
If only he could die and find his peace

ANYTHING

She was my everything, she's all I had
She was everything I needed in my life
And I was her world
I knew when I meet her
I would die a thousand times and make it right

I would give anything, and I mean anything
If I could have her back in my life

I tried to go my way
I left you all alone never knowing that you really were the one
There's nothing that you did, but I was just so wrong
And now that I'm awake the damage has been done

I would give anything, and I mean anything
Just to have you back in my life

CHORUS:
Late at night I would run away
I guess I was afraid to think about forever 'cause I never loved this way
I didn't wanna lose the freedom that I had but I lost everything
And now I want you back

CHORUS

I would give anything, and I mean anything
If I could have her back in my life

Average Joe

Take a trip to Malibu on the weekend so me and you
    can get away and just kick it
It's quite alright, do what you like
If you want it baby you can get it
We can cruise all night in the Rover
Walk on the beach with my arm around your shoulder

CHORUS:
Would you be there even if I didn't have a Benz
Ain't got a lot of money to spend
Don't get along with some of your friends
Won't you tell me would you be there
I just wanna know, would you hold a nigga down or would you let him go
If I was nothin' but an average Joe, won't you tell me

So you're gonna stick around cause you're open
Got up in your mind and now you're hoping
You can wear my ring, we can share these things
Oh you can have it if you want it
But only if you prove to me that you don't want me for my things
I got to know

CHORUS

Is it material or spiritual
Is it emotional or sexual
Is it physical, natural
Gotta keep it, shorty whatcha gonna do
You could be with me, I could be with you, etc.

CHORUS

Is it material or spiritual
Is it emotional or sexual
Is it physical, natural
Gotta keep it, shorty whatcha gonna do
You can be with me, I can be with you

BACK TO EARTH

Girl you're having your lazy days
Wasting all the time away
What's the matter with you lately
I don't know you this way
You used to be unstoppable
And it's better for what you do with your days
I used to see this light inside of you
But now you're dark in your old mood

CHORUS:
Oh I Turn the TV off get up and take a look around
Put on some clothes get outta the house
I don't see how such an amazing girl
And this crazy bird just let it go
Come back to earth

Thinking about the times when your middle name was Joy
With all the outside noise it's hard to hear your voice
You used to be creative, appreciative, innovative
But now you're negative, insensitive and offensive
And I wonder if you can kick it

CHORUS

French fries, pizza, Haagen Dazs, Ben and Jerry's with your favorite show
You switch the channel to the second rerun though you, I don't know
That's about the time for a new episode in your life
What are you waiting for
Baby, what are you waiting for

CHORUS

BAD DAYS

Couldn't find a reason to get out of the bed
Then I woke up to those nasty things you said
But when I heard my shoes knocking at my door
It's only 9 a.m. and I can't take no more

CHORUS:
But bad days don't last forever, etc.

I need some sunshine but it's just pouring rain
Got to the platform and missed my subway train
Bought a coffee but just spilled it on my skirt
It's the third time this week that I'm late for work

CHORUS

Now the boss is screaming
I just laugh right in her face
Told him I'm not crazy I've had it for today
You can't be serious it's not even known
It's got to get better 'cause it sure can't get no worse

CHORUS

Another precious day has gone passing by
It all happened so fast that I didn't realize
All my frustrations have got me so boxed in
That's just how the day begins
But not how I let it end

'Cause bad days don't last forever
Don't last forever

BAD HABIT

Did you ever have a bad habit that you just couldn't quit
Well here's mine

I can't sleep, I can't eat, can't get you off my mind
It kills me to need you
This is only my first time
Being in love with someone, feeling so strong for someone
Heaven help me, I don't know what I'm doing

I love you but I hate you for how you make me feel
You're not seeing me, but ironically, I'm at home
    waiting for that phone to ring
Hoping to hear from you
Make believe that your feelings are true
Why do I keep believing your lies
It's like I need them to survive

CHORUS:
It feels good every time you say that you love me
I find myself hoping that you're thinking of me
It makes me sick to my stomach
Boy, you're like a bad habit that I just can't quit
I never wanted it to be like this
Never wanted to be so dependent
But I need it and I have to have it
I've got to get rid of this bad habit

It feels so good

Pinch me, I need to know, is this still my life
How I dedicated everything to only making you feel right
Keep proving my love to you
There's nothing above you
It's hard to picture my life before you
Look at me, just speak to me

Can't you see my tears
I need you to tell me the little words I want to hear
Like, forgive me for treating you like I don't really love you
I'll take you over and over again no matter how bad it gets at the end

CHORUS

Got to get away from all of this madness
I can't be letting you create all this sadness
I'm standing in the middle feeling helpless
Love is so crazy
One moment I'm on top of the world
And I regret ever being your girl
I love you and I hate you but I can't let go of you
It feels so good, it hurts so bad
It's about time, but I need it and I had to have it

CHORUS

I love to hate you baby and I hate to love you baby
I hate to hate you baby
You're just like a habit to me
I love to hate you baby and I hate to love you baby
But I need it and I had to have it
You're just like a habit to me

BADUNKADUNK

It's a natural fact that
We live in a time where a dime used to carry a fatback
Ain't no if and's, believe it
I saw a girl the other day calling a butt crack new cleavage
I mean what's with this obsession
Just on TV spend two hours measuring celebrity ass dimensions
You think it's crazy down in Brooklyn
I got invited for a party where your ass could be the guest of honor
Could not believe it when I saw it
At the front of the line I heard a man talkin' bout it like

CHORUS:
Badunkadunk, dunkadunk, dunk
Girl you ain't getting' in the club
But your dunkadunk, dunkadunk
Girl you could step right up
But your dunkadunk, dunkadunk, dunk
Naw, you ain't gettin' past me
But your dunkadunk, dunkadunk, dunk
Girl, you can get in for free

These dudes is ranking asses, no joke
Some man in black told me to lift my jacket up and poke
Now I'm a feminist like hell
But the party was lookin' hot so I gave him the best wiggle I could sell
I know I felt like a chicken
But why should politics get in the way of the five people I could be meetin'
The power of the fatty
It's amazing what a girl can do even with no tatties
And I know that shit ain't right
But finally I can benefit and that shit is so tight

CHORUS

All the ladies who was feeling their self-confidence
On a high cause they know that they're fly
Whether you got on some shit from last year
Or you're rockin' new gear it's your world so it don't matter
And all the guys who look beyond the outside
Who like a girl for their mind but recognize a nice thigh for you
Ain't nothing wrong with knowing what you want and lovin' who you are
'Cause I love every single part

All the ladies who was feeling their self-confidence
On a high cause they know that they're fly
Whether you got on some shit from last year
Or you're rockin' new gear it's your world so it don't matter
And all the guys who look beyond the outside
Who like a girl for their mind but recognize a nice thigh for you
Ain't nothing wrong with knowing what you want and lovin' who you are
'Cause I love every single part

I know you're lookin at me funny like
Why she let him see her booty? She knows she ain't right
But now ladies let's keep it real
What's the point of tight jeans if a look nobody even steals
I'm just sayin' that I'm proud
Of every asset I was given and I'll say that shit mad loud
So if you feel me, if you don't
It's all good cause they're listening
And you can feel how you want

CHORUS

CHORUS

He was like
Turn around, stick it out
Let me just see what you workin' with
And I got a nice little fatty
I mean I can't front
Like I may as well put it to work every now and then

BAND AID

When I met you I didn't really like you
First impression was you were somebody who'd
Walk right by when I wave at you and say Hi
But they say bad beginnings make happy endings
Now that I know you I begin to understand things
It's turned around 180 degrees
I found my missing piece

CHORUS:
There's something about you that's like the sun
You warm up my heart when I come undone
You're like my soul mate and on those days
When I hurt, when I break
You are my band-aid

When I get caught in the rain and it feels like
There is no one in the world who understands my
Complications that I'm facing certain days I
Talk it through with you
No matter how I try to hide you see straight through my disguise
You know how to fix me you are my therapy baby

CHORUS

You are, you are my band-aid
You are, you are
You are, you are
When I hurt, when I break, you are
You are, you are
You are, you are

CHORUS

BATTLEFIELD

You're so ugly it shatters the mirror
I'd be happy if I didn't see
   you around
Lately you've been kind of creepy
Everything you say is freaking
   me out
You've got a violent nature
One can only love or hate you
Don't keep getting in my face
Just go and take the highway
You think you're bad ass but you're
   really not
You wish you had class, don't have
   a shot
La La La La La La La La and and and
You think you impress me go,
   dream on
You don't wanna test me bring it on
You might've should've though twice
   before she took of her pants

CHORUS:
How could I ever fall for you
I've got nothing but scorn for you
I loved you, adored you, I gave my
   heart for you
But now it's just a battlefield

I can't seem to shake you off me
I'm really getting scared of you
   trying to intimidate me
It doesn't matter what you do
I'm gonna draw the line
This is your territory, this is mine
If you ever again come near me

I'll make sure that you serve
   juvy time
You think you're bad ass but you're
   really not
You wish you had class, don't have
   a shot
La La La La La La La La and and and

CHORUS

Please get away from me
Did I ask you to touch me, no
And I don't wanna talk right now
So shut your dirty mouth
I'm about to lose control
Don't push me over the edge
Move and get out of my way
Before you wish you never met
   me right now

CHORUS

CHORUS

BE WITH YOU

There's something about you that I'm liking, girl
More than just your body
I have a real good feeling that I should get your number baby
I must admit I'm feeling insecure
Somewhere deep inside I know for sure that you're the one
I can't let you get away

CHORUS:
I love it when you come around my way
Sometimes I want to tell you just to stay
I've never been the one who at a loss for words, but it's true
Don't know why I feel the way I feel
But I gotta let you know that this is real
Why is this so hard
All I wanna do is be with you

Girl I wanna be with you
Oh I wanna be with you
Be with you

I ain't lying you're so beautiful
Girl I want to flaunt you
I have a real good feeling that you should have my number
So come and holler at me baby girl
There's something I got to tell you
You're the one
I can't let you get away

CHORUS

Gonna get my thoughts together baby to let you know what's on my mind.
Cause I would hate to see you walk away when I know you could be mine
Trying to be the fool that tells you, I'd be a fool to let you go
So before this day is over baby I got to let you know

CHORUS

BE WITH YOU

I noticed every time that we're
   out together
And you see some hottie passin' by
You quickly turn your head
You try to shake it off say
Whatever baby, I'm not blind

Cuz I'm not tryin to blame you
   (no, no)

PRE-CHORUS:
What's on your mind
What turns you on, cuz baby it's ok
You know I love you and tonight
   we're gonna play

CHORUS:
I wanna be with you
Turn the lights down low bring my
   shirt up slow
Open the buttons one by one
And watch it come undone
I wanna be with you
From my skin tight jeans to
   my lingerie
Tonight I'm gonna be every woman
   in your fantasies

So put your two-way off and light
   the candles
Put the slow jam on
Cuz all there is is you and me
Baby sit back make
   yourself comfortable

Take your shoes off, loosen your tie
Cuz you ain't goin' nowhere tonight

PRE-CHORUS

CHORUS

Let me be, etc.

Let me cook a little somethin'
   for you
It's my gift then you know what
   I'm gonna do
Work the dough with extra care
Add a little spices everywhere
Steam the meat with wine and juices
Turn the heat up no excuses
Whip the eggs, prepare the canvas
Taste the flavors make sure it's best

CHORUS

I wanna be with you
I swear I do

BE YOURSELF

I was happy then, I was happy then
    doing nothing
Then he came along
He looked into my eyes
I'm going to make him fall in love
No you won't, yes I will
The way he looked at me, no he
    looked at me
I got that feeling
I know I'm going to get him
He's not your type of guy, so why
    won't you just let it go
No I won't, yes you will

Ooh, ooh, ooh, ooh, ooh, ooh just
    let it go, etc.

CHORUS:
Why you try to copy what I've got
Everybody says it's obvious
It's all about you no matter what
    and you won't give up
You'll always think you know what
    I should do
But just as long as it's right for you
You try to be me but what the hell,
    just be yourself

We were happy then, yeah we were
    happy then doing nothing
And then you had to walk in
Well, I didn't know that you had
    gone behind my back
No I didn't, yes you did

You think that every boy I want to
    date is crazy for you
But when they just ignore you
You have to get in my face and try to
    bring me down
Before he comes around

Ooh, ooh, etc.
Just let it go

CHORUS

We were happy then, yeah we were
    happy then doing nothing
Ooh, ooh, ooh, ooh, ooh, ooh just
    let it go, etc.

CHORUS

Ooh, ooh, ooh, ooh, ooh, ooh just
    let it go, etc.

THE BEACH SONG

We do what we want to
Whenever we want to, etc.

I twist my hair with my finger when
 you're next to me
And when you call my name I get
 weak in the knees
Write your name in my notebook
 over and over again
Daydreaming and wishing you and
 me could be

PRE-CHORUS:
Dancing in the rain
Sleeping in until noon
Being on the beach and
Writing new tunes
Watching the moon
Under the blanket
In a cocoon
See you at the beach house, sounds
 like a plan
We can spend the night out in
 the sand
Maybe stay the weekend and then

CHORUS:
We do what we want to
Wherever we want to, etc.
Getting lost in the breeze
Hanging out at the beach

Some people tell me that you are
 not that one for me

But what they don't understand is
 that we got chemistry
No matter what they say I can't deny
 what I feel
I just like you being around, can't
 wait until

PRE-CHORUS

CHORUS

That would be my perfect fantasy
But let's get back to reality
All I can give you is my love
And I hope that's good enough

CHORUS

See you at the beach house sounds
 like a plan
We can spend the night out in
 the sand
Maybe stay the weekend and then
Getting lost in the breeze
Hanging out at the beach
Getting lost in the breeze
At the house on the beach

BELIEVE

This song is dedicated to everybody
 out there that's struggling
I've been there

Growing up in a shelter
Not a lot of food to eat
All I wanted was a warm home
At night I'm afraid to sleep
Never really knew my father
My mom says I have his name
But I don't really want to know him
I'm sure he feels the same
Mama didn't feel responsible
Had problems of her own
Didn't know who to talk to when I
 felt all alone

CHORUS:
But I still believe in me
I've got to believe in me (I believe)
If I don't believe in me
Nobody will, nobody will believe

Brother hustles around the corner
Ended up at NYC (Damn shame)
All he wanted was a good life and
 a decent family
Sister started prostituting and
 nobody gave a damn
Must be hard having two kids when
 you can barely stand
Mama didn't feel responsible
Had problems of her own (I'll do
 it by myself)

Didn't know who to talk to when I
 felt so alone

CHORUS

How can you stand when the world
 is against you
You don't know where to go, who to
 trust with your life
Don't get no love from your family
No one's there, they don't care if
 you're dead or alive

CHORUS

CHORUS

BETWEEN THOSE LEGS

It's your childhood friend from church always offering you a ride to work
Picks up your laundry, carries your groceries never asks anything in return
Says he only wants to be your best friend but you forget he's still a man
All along all he's tryin to do is get

CHORUS:
Oh, between those legs, etc.

Just the nerdy guy at school who does your homework for free
Except for the looks at your cleavage to spice up his fantasies
It's the boss who raises a toast to the deadline he didn't blow
He says there's something I wish you would before he could promote you

CHORUS

It's the trainer at the gym who forgets he's acting civil
But he turns into a dog the moment he hears you're newly single
It's your boyfriend's best friend's brother whose compliments
    are always on the verge
It's your super, your bank teller, your high school teacher
All they wanna do is get

CHORUS

It's the testosterone
A code in their DNA
They try to make it happen
It's just the way they were made
It's circles in their head
Our walks that makes them crazy
We can't help that we're choosey
It's just the way we were made

BIG GIRLS DON'T CRY

The smell of your skin lingers
  on me now
You're probably on your flight back
  to your home town
I need some shelter of my own
  protection baby
To be with myself instead of clarity
Peace, serenity

CHORUS:
I hope you know, I hope you know
That this has nothing to do with you
It's personal, myself and I
We've got some straightenin'
  out to do
And I'm gonna miss you like a child
  misses their blanket
But I've got to get a move on
  with my life
Its time to be a big girl now
And big girls don't cry
Don't cry, don't cry, don't cry

The path that I'm walking
I must go alone
I must take the baby steps 'til
  I'm full grown
Fairytales don't always have a happy
  ending, do they
And I foresee the dark ahead
  if I stay

CHORUS

Like the little school mate
  in the school yard
We'll play jacks and Uno cards
Ill be your best friend and
  you'll be mine
Valentine
Yes you can hold my hand
  if you want to
'Cause I want to hold yours too
We'll be playmates and lovers and
  share our secret worlds
But it's time for me to go home
It's getting late, dark outside
I need to be with myself and center
Clarity, peace, serenity

CHORUS

BIGGER THAN YOU

Thought I was weak
For a minute I was stuck on you
Built my day around your mood
Thought it was me incapable of
   keeping you
Felt unworthy no matter what I do
You fed off my positivity
Thought you took it but there is
   more to me

CHORUS:
You're not my world, you don't
   know this girl
I still hold the power and I choose
Purpose and known, room left
   to grow
My life is so much bigger than you

You're not my happiness

How I tried to let you be apart
   of me
You were kind but that just fueled
   your jealousy
How I cried every time you
   punish me
Just for having fun when you
   couldn't be the one when I was
   in need
You fed off my passion and
   my dreams
And I'm still alive there is more
   to me

CHORUS

You're not my happiness

I reached within, shut you out
My life begins here and now
Open sky rain down
God knows my heart and knows
How long it's been since it smiled
I'm young, beautiful, smart, true
Personality's funny, cool
Big heart, I give my last
Good friends don't have to ask
Gifted, blessed, healthy, ooh
I'm gonna be wealthy soon
Did you miss it when I said I'm cool
Why'd I even care for you

CHORUS

CHORUS
Whether you love me a lot, whether
   you love me or not
I'm gonna be happy

BLACK CAT

Black water road
Looks a bit shady
Don't bother now
I've gone crazy
Lingering thoughts
In my head so
Don't touch, I don't
Feel that healthy
Feel that healthy

CHORUS:
Don't say you're sorry
Too late you crossed me
You've done it this time
And that's the last time
There's a black cat waiting
And I won't be saving you now

Moon glows, who knows
What I'm capable of
Mistake - it's your fault
For takin' her clothes off
These pins I'm sticking
In your rag doll
You should have known after all

CHORUS

The night is falling
The thunder's coming
You'll be sorry
There's no saving you

There's a black cat waiting
Bad luck's coming

CHORUS

BODY LANGUAGE

I don't speak Portuguese, Chinese, Lebanese, Arabian
Bulgarian, Italian, French, or German
But I know what you mean, yeah I know what you mean
Eyes locked, buns move, jellies jumping one, two
My way, your way, I like the way you do it boy
You know what I need, and you know what I need

CHORUS:
Talk to me with your body language
Move with me, rock me if you can
Baby, tell me all your secrets
From A to Z, let me see you dance
Talk to me with your body language
Move with me, I'll show you who I am
Baby, I'm gonna leave you breathless
Talk to me, let me see you dance (talk to me)

Rocket letter, T.O. hump back, what's that
That I've got you runnin' hard, shake my feather that past
Follow me, baby follow me
Take you to a corner, I'm Dora the Explorer
You can be my Monkey Boots, let me teach you something new
You won't forget, won't forget

CHORUS

CHORUS

Bootie Call

See I try to be a really good girl
Pretend I'm happy with a simple,
  simple world
Everybody says we're the perfect fit
  but something's wrong with this
  picture and I can't quite point
  my finger at it

Cause he's too short for a shorty
  like me
I'm getting bored every time he
  gets excited
And I can't ignore this desire I feel
If a girl's got to have it you can't
  blame her
If she's waitin' for it

CHORUS:
Bootie call, 3 a.m. at night
When my man's asleep and I know
  it ain't right
Try to fight it but my mind it keeps
  me wondering if I should
I don't want it but I got it 'cause it
  feels so good
Bootie call
Try to fight it but I'm lying keeps me
  wondering if I should
I don't want it but I got it 'cause it
  feels so good

The guy I got is kinda nice
  and sweet
But I can't wait until I fall asleep

Yeah he got the brains but he don't
  bring what I like
He always got the romance covered
  but he don't got that spice
The other guy never leaves my mind
  he takes control
He makes my body feel so good it
  makes me hot like whoa
He keeps me feigning when I'm
  leaning on my man
So good I'm getting dizzy when I
  think of that

CHORUS

Alex, mmn I love you. Jordan?
  Ah, shit.

CHORUS

Let's keep this between us

BOTTOMS UP

CHORUS:
Move your hips, do your thang
Get off the wall, don't matter what
they think
From your fingertips, to your toes
You know you hot, so let
everybody know
Gotta take it low, to the floor
From the hills to the streets
of the ghetto
Hips don't lie, so move 'em up
We ain't gon' stop, till we see
everybody's bottoms up
Bottoms up, Bottoms up, etc.

Miss KeKe P, looking extra glossy
Gotta rep your style, lookin'
extra flossy
"I'm bossy!" But I keeps it cute
With my stunner shades on, and a
tree in my roots
I got the Chi-Town swagger and I
rocks it full
"Yes, Mudville!" baby, we don't take
no bull
We keep it rockin' when we move
our hips
Do that old school stunt when we
make it dip

CHORUS

Keep it movin', man, make it
poppin', man

I'm making the rules, gotta catch
me when you can
Might see my face on the
movie screen
Hypnotize you, frame by frame,
scene by scene
Staying fly while I keep it fresh
Only thirteen- and I ain't even
close yet
Sittin' back, saying this a hit
While you swing side to side, and
move your hips

You got some swagger, better
let 'em know
You got some swagger, better
let it show
Take your swagger with you to the A
then bring it back up to the bay

Now bob your head, then
look away, etc.

CHORUS

You got some swagger? Better
let 'em know
You got some swagger, better
let it show
Take your swagger with you to the A
then bring I back down to the bay

Now bob your head, then
look away, etc.

BOUNCE

PRE-CHORUS:
We be bouncing, flipping, jumping, jazz funking, just do something
Bounce, bounce, bounce, bounce
Move ya booty to the Boogaloo Beat
Use your moves no don't refuse it just feel the music and
Bounce, bounce, bounce, bounce
To the rhythm of the Boogaloo Beat

CHORUS:
Get busy baby kick the funk with me
I'm ready do you want to rock with me
Yeah shorty only if you're giddy with me
Bounce, bounce, bounce, bounce
Move your booty to the Boogaloo Beat

What you hear is a testa
To get you to move your chesta
Bounce your body like a seizure
Make you lose all your respi-
Ration
Ain't no hating
We came to party and shake it (don't stop)
The crowd is breaking, pop-locking, swinging, rotating
We getting physical with it, when you grooving so sexy smooth baby
When you do like you move, show me how you move baby (dance, dance)
I'm feeling how you move boy (bounce, bounce)
Get crazy what you do boy

PRE-CHORUS

CHORUS

People dancing freaky everywhere
Try my hardest baby not to stare
Moving groovy in your funky shoes

Daddy I love those sexy things you do show me how you Boogaloo
Keep this party jumping all night
Shake my fatty just the way you like
Oh baby you do it so right
I think your coming with me tonight

PRE-CHORUS

CHORUS

I wanna know (I wanna know)
Do you like the funk (I feel the funk, oh I feel the funk)
I wanna know do you feel the funk (I feel the funk, oh I feel the funk)

(I wanna know)
Vamos a bailar, aqui toda la noche
Vamos a bailar, hasta la manana (I wanna know)
Vamos a bailar, aqui toda la noche
Vamos a bailar, hasta la manana

PRE-CHORUS

CHORUS

I wanna know (I wanna know)
Do you like the funk (I feel the funk, oh I feel the funk)
I wanna know do you feel the funk (I feel the funk, oh I feel the funk)

CHORUS

Bow Down

I don't know what you've been told
But you should know that you're too old

You've seen these walls for all of your life
This room is laughing at you
You heard this voice too many times
Don't you ever wonder why you're still here

Change comes so slow
For all that you know
Things would always stay the same
You do as you're told
You just play along
While your life passes you by
Before your eyes

CHORUS:
Spread your wings, face the sun
Take your chances, before they're gone
Ask your questions, hold your ground
'Cause life is too short to bow down

It's in your hands
All that you need is the confidence to speak
For yourself do what you feel
Just go ahead and lead the way

CHORUS

I don't know what you've been told
But you should know that you're too old

CHORUS

Boy Drama

I had no intentions on company
Just wanted to learn how to love me
But then you came with love leading
    me astray
Said that maybe I should try
    another day
So I dropped my plans, take a ride
    with you
Took a chance, 'cause no telling
    what love might do
'Cause I dream there's a man for me
But boys like you always get
    in the way

CHORUS:
What's wrong with me
Is there something that I need
    to change about myself
Cause I believe what you give is
    what you get
And who you are is what you attract
'Cause I can't stand this boy drama
    no more
And what you see is not always
    what you get

Now I try conversation
But every time we talk it's the
    same thing
What you doin'? What's goin' on
Is there a broken record playing the
    same old song
I'm really getting into you, think
    about you all the time

But there is nothing that you said
    that will make me change
    my mind
I want a man who understands how
    to treat a lady like me

CHORUS

Girl I know you tired
I know you tired of the same old
    lines over and over again
'Can I come to your house? I
    like you
You should be my girlfriend, come
    on now
Women, it's alright
If you want to love yourself, take
    yourself out to a movie
Do something special for you
Enjoy you, love you, be yourself

'Cause I cant stand this boy drama
    no more
And what you see is not always
    what you get

I'm gonna buy me some flowers
Stay up and watch a late night movie
    with me
On my own 'cause I love me

BOYFRIEND

An average day in my life
Rush, rush
So little time
For all the things I like to do
It's a glamorous world but it
    gets to you
All this doesn't mean a thing if you
    can't share with somebody
Shopping sprees won't keep a smile
    if you already got it

CHORUS:
I wish I had a boyfriend
(wish I had a, wish I had
    a boyfriend)
Could it be you
(wish I had a, wish I had a)
Cuz L-O-V-E don't come easy
(wish I had a, wish I had
    a boyfriend)
Could it be you
(wish I had a, wish I had a)
Cuz L-O-V-E don't come easy

Don't get me wrong I do enjoy
Traveling tours I can't wait
To think about
How it could be
If that somebody
Made me happy

All this doesn't mean a thing if you
    can't share with somebody
Shopping sprees won't keep a smile
    if you already got it

CHORUS

Send me a message if you think
    you're the one for me
If you can make me smile and know
    what I want baby
I'm just a simple girl not asking
    for the world
So tell me, come on tell me
Are you what I'm looking for

CHORUS

BOYFRIEND

Everybody's got a boyfriend but me
It's like they try to rub it in on TV
And my best friend just called
    me up
And guess what she just fell in love
He's everything that she's been
    dreaming of
Like Romeo and Juliet
Jen and Brad and the newlyweds
Cleopatra and what's his name
So cute together it makes me sick

CHORUS:
I need a guy that's six foot tall
Tan skin, blue eyes, and loves
    his dog
And he buys me a hot convertible
Or anyone who's available
Every girl's got a boyfriend,
    a boyfriend to love but me
When God gave out boyfriends
    he must have forgot about me

Long blonde hair and he just
    don't care
Wears his clothes for weeks
    and I swear
He just might be the one for me and
    we have perfect chemistry
But he's already found his destiny
Like Romeo and Juliet
Jen and Brad and the Newlyweds
Cleopatra and what's his name
So cute together it makes me sick

CHORUS

Are you anywhere out there
Will you send me a message, baby
Cause I'm getting lonely
Watching everybody fall in love
Like Romeo and Juliet
Jen and Brad and the Newlyweds
Cleopatra and what's his name
So cute together it makes me sick

CHORUS

Boys Boys Boys

Corey whispered in my ear what
    a shorty want to hear
Cute as heck, yo Corey had me open
But he really got me vexed when
    he lied about his ex
Cause all he wanted
Ty couldn't keep his fingers
    out my hair
Acting like he care, but I'd always
    catch him stare
He'd fantasize when I wasn't
    by his side
Had his eyes on another girl's thighs

PRE-CHORUS:
Let's talk about boys and all the
    things they say to you
Let's talk about boys, most of it
    ain't even true
Let's talk about boys and what's
    really on their minds, yeah
Let's talk about boys, don't you fall
    for every lie

When they say

CHORUS:
Baby baby, ride with me, I promise
    you I'll never leave
Baby baby, let's be friends
When all they really want is to get in
    your pants
Baby baby I'm down for you, ain't
    nothing that I wouldn't do

Shorty you know that I only got
    eyes for you
First they make you want them then
    you gotta dump them

Justin wanted to be my man but he
    couldn't understand
That I'm young and thugs don't last
Always coming around the block
    showing off what I got to his boys
So I put him off last

PRE-CHORUS

CHORUS

Why do we all the time, put up with
    foolish boys messing with
    our minds
Why do we still believe, when we
    know in the end we'll
    get deceived
Why do we still give them a chance
We just can't be friends
Foolish boys know not what they do

CHORUS

PRE-CHORUS

First they make you want them, then
    you gotta dump them

BRANDY

You said we needed space
We could date who we want to date, hey babe
So you're hanging with miss beauty queen
You gotta be kiddin' me, please
You always want what you want
When you've got what you need
And you get what you want
And you run back to me

CHORUS:
Brandy, she's got to go
She's nothing but a waste of time
She's got you and you know I'm not
Brandy, she's not what you need
She may have an angel face
But I'm not gonna be replaced by
Brandy, she's got to go

Everybody knows you don't know
You're just the fling of the week, poor baby
You were so into her
Tell me what do you see in Brandy
Sweet dreams to wake up
And see what you lost
Find all you've got, baby
Like it or not

CHORUS

Go Brandy, go Brandy, go, etc.

CHORUS

She's got to go, etc.

BUFF TINGALING

It's not our party but we're
   going anyway
Pretend we know somebody so they
   let us through the gate
High in fashion and fashionably late
All us Conti girls we don't care
   what you say
Turning heads every time we
   hit the floor
Spinning tunes from 1984
God is rocking when we turn it up
   some more
We're doing what we came here for

CHORUS:
Oh whatever's gonna happen tonight
   stays on the dance floor
It's only between you and I and
   I won't tell a soul
As long as we can see eye to eye
Whatever's gonna happen for sure
   stays on the dance floor

Buff Tingaling Ya

We get it down as the volume
   goes up
Guys talkin' 'bout us, tryin to
   chat us up
We're shakin' it, livin' it up
It's Saturday night, so what
Bass is kicking 'til the
   speakers blow
Girls get jealous 'cause their
   fellas go

Lookin' at us as we're
   stealing the show
We just dancin' low

CHORUS

Heart beats faster, beat hits harder
Crowd goes crazy, chemistry,
   you and me
Non-stop dancin', strobe
   lights flashing
In slow motion, intense emotion

CHORUS

Buff Tingaling Ya

CHORUS

CHORUS

Buff Tingaling Ya

CADILLAC HOTEL

Crazy man's preaching in the street in the morning
Sayin' white man's corrupted the world and Jesus ain't coming
The seagulls are laughing and I finish my coffee
In a little café on the corner of Rose and Dudley
Sand falls from my hand as I pick up my guitar
I lay out a blanket, kiss the sun, and I sing words from my heart
You'll make your way to the place where I am,
    and I'm like "Hey, won't you come listen to me play?"

CHORUS:
I wanna see the sun rise on the roof of the Cad-Cad-Cadillac Hotel
Spend the whole night under the stars, singing to you until
I melt in your lips; taste your sweet kiss of candy caramel
I wanna see the sun rise on the roof of the Cadillac Hotel, with you

The evening sun falls into the ocean of the Malibu skies
And I can't help but drown in the blue of your emerald eyes
Your small lips say, "Hey baby, won't you come up to my room?"
But I'm like, "Just come with me, I know a place with a better view"

CHORUS

The moon lights your face in the dark of the night
I pull you in with my sweet lullaby
The city is sleeping, I'm melting inside
La, la, la, la, la, la, la

I wanna see the sun rise
With you
Taste your lips, taste your lips

CHORUS

La la la, la la la, la la la, la la, etc.

CALL ON ME

Hey, you can't hide it anymore
You're wearing at the threads
You're walking on the edge
Hey, I can see through your smile
You refuse to trust yourself
You refuse to take my help
It kills me inside to see you this way
I wish you would try

CHORUS:
When you feel lost
Don't hold it in, don't be a stranger
Call on me when you feel down
Just come around, I'll be there
To let you know that you are loved
You are loved, you are loved

Did you really think I would let you lose yourself
You know me better than that
Did you really think that I couldn't tell
Because I know you better than that
It kills me inside to see you this way
I wish you would try

CHORUS

CHORUS

CHORUS

CAN I KICK IT WITH YOU

Can I kick it with you
Come on baby tell me your name
I've been wanting your attention all night
Can I kick it with you

Baby you
You got that mysterious smile
I don't know just what it is that you do
I wanna know your name
Is it true? You are really one of those guys
The type that never wants to make the first move

Guys like you never give a woman what she wants to give
But always get what they want from her
Guys like you never tell a woman what she wants to hear
Never straight about the way they feel
Guys like you never holler at a girl when she's looking fly
But still they catch her eye
Guys like you ignore a girl just to get her to come over and be like

CHORUS:
Can I kick it with you
Come on baby tell me your name
I've been wanting your attention all night
Can I kick it with you?
Don't tell me you ain't feeling the same
Saw you check me from the corner of your eye
Baby, baby, every time I try to get with you
You just keep on getting me confused
Why do I fall for guys like you?

Chauntelle I don't kiss and tell
You like an angel that fell
Or my name is hell
I spell razor with z-a-h

Live in the states
BK, NY, where the love is blind
And to me the virtuous woman is hard to find
One of a kind
With heaven in your twinkling eyes
Most guys catch butterflies thinking they live
Too much pride when you tongue-tied sometimes inside

Guys like you got the girls always guessing why you do what you do
What's going on inside your mind
Guys like you act like they just ain't thinking 'bout you
So you think about them all the time
Guys like you pretend that they just don't understand
Just to see how bad you want 'em to be your man
Guys like you question our answers with answers that are questions
So we come back again

CHORUS

Even though you make a beautiful bride
If love is a crime, I speak from a prisoner's mind
Hand-cuffed to that touch of a woman I trust
You know it's much more than lust from them princess cuts
King Tut, got a queen now makin' him smile
And we gotta pure love like a Hebrew child
It be guys like me that be feelin' your style
Meanwhile can't find a way to say it out loud
It be guys like me need a girl like you
So if it ever hit the fan she gonna know what to do

CHORUS

CAN'T TAKE IT BACK

Don't know where to begin, I just can't pretend
I've been holding this in, afraid to lose a friend
But I let it slip when I fell all over you last time we met
And now the word is out

CHORUS:
I can't take it back, no, no
It's out in the open
I told you everything
Now I wait till I know how you feel
Don't ask me to act, go on
Like nothing has happened
Now that I gave my heart away like that
I can't take it back

Well it's out of my heart and in your hands
As the hourglass drops its final grains of sand
I'm holding out hope that stars in your eyes are gonna fall for me at last
I take the chance

CHORUS

I let down my guard
And I have to carry on
I've gone too far

I can't take it back, no, no
It's out in the open
I told you everything
Now I wait 'till I know how you feel

Don't ask me to act, oh no
It's out in the open
I told you everything
Now I wait 'till I know how you feel, etc.

CAR WINDOWS

Shoulda, coulda, woulda said a hundred things to you, I didn't
God, I wanna try but when I do I come unglued in a minute
And I'm still waiting for the waiting to end

CHORUS:
I write your name in car windows when it rains
My fingers slide imagining your face
By now I've left a million clues
Told you everything except the truth
A confession I can't make to you

Knowing in a split second everything could change drives me crazy
Wishing you had ESP to connect with me oh baby
I'm still waiting for the waiting to end

CHORUS

I'm lovesick and only you can save me
You're the cause
You're the cure
You're the remedy
I wish you knew, etc.

CHORUS

I write your name in car windows when it rains
My fingers slide imagining your face

CATWALK VOGUE

In the dressing room getting
   ready to go
Mascara, lipstick,
   powder on my nose
Touch up my hair,
   curled and sprayed
In the mirror I see that look
   on your face (high fashion)
I-I-I-I (do I make you nervous)
I-I-I-I (jealous)

CHORUS:
Meet me at the catwalk
   (jealousy is my fuel)
At the catwalk (you won't see
   me lose my cool)
Lights on, cameras, looks on me
I make the front page of
   every magazine
V-O-G-U-E, my legs make
   'em go crazy
Meet me at the catwalk
   (V-O-G-U-E, etc.)

Slip in my dress, zip it tight
Ready to get out there, ready to fight
Secret whispers behind my back
But it doesn't hurt, it only makes
   me laugh, 'cause (high fashion)
I-I-I-I (know I make you nervous)
   (high fashion)
I-I-I-I (jealous)

CHORUS

I feel the beat of my heart
I'm ready for the show to start
The music is loud,
   I can see the crowd
Only VIP's around
Everywhere the stakes are high
Dollar signs in their eyes
They came to choose,
   now here's my cue
The moment of truth

CHORUS

(V-O-G-U-E, you know me, etc.)

I make 'em go crazy

CHANGE OF HEART

I know we had plans, things that we wanted to do
But something in the feeling is changing my mood
Sorry to say, I hope that you understand
I can't be with you right now
I need time for myself

CHORUS:
And I ain't sayin' I don't love you
Maybe tomorrow is written in the stars
But I can't lie it's just that I
I just had a change of heart

I was told to always be clear, go after what you believe
Suffocating in my soul, find it hard to breathe
And this ain't been easy for me
Lord knows it ain't been easy on me
Tryin' to figure it out and stay true to myself

CHORUS

Please don't take this the wrong way
I'm tryin' to do what's best for me
It might not be clear to you

Cause I had a change of heart
Change of heart
Change of heart, etc.

CHEATING / THANK YOU

Thank you for never calling back
Thought yesterday you told me you would call me before you go to bed
Thank you for all the misery
That you had me going through since the last time we met
Thank you for never being there
For making me feel lonely every time I need someone to care
Thank you for always making sure
Whenever I felt good you somehow manage to get me insecure

And I don't know if I love you or hate you more
'Cause right now I can't tell for sure

CHORUS:
If you're cheating on me while I'm waiting at home
I keep trying to call you but you don't answer the phone
Are you lying to me when you say nothing is wrong
'Cause I got a feeling you're wasting my time
Maybe I should move on

Thank you for bringing me that rose
Back when I was sick in bed and I just got to know you
Thank you for making me believe
That if I only trusted you, you would fall in love with me
Thank you for kissing me that way
Till you got what you wanted and you'd be sure I'd stay
Thank you for telling all my friends
That we would have a future when this is the beginning of the end

And I don't know if I love you or hate you more
'Cause right now I can't tell for sure

CHORUS

CHORUS

CHEER ME UP

You get me out of my seat
It's like I've been in bed for a week
I've been slipping and sliding
   all over the place
And no body cares and I'm
   such a disgrace
You get me out of my mood
That's something only you can do
'Cause I feel like I'm home when
I'm in your arms
And that's why I need you to

CHORUS:
Cheer me up
Come and dance with me
   and you take my hand
Cheer me up
Even if we're the only ones dancing
Cheer me up
Please won't you
Cheer me up
Even if we're the only ones dancing

Gimme a reason to smile
The kind that would last for a while
Like only you know how,
   make it okay now
You got your ways how to make
   this girl's day
It's the magic that's in your touch
It makes everything mean so much
The poetry in your eyes
Is enough in itself to take me
   to a high

You gotta cheer me up

CHORUS

You turn my frown upside down
My smiles lost and found
When you are around
You cheer me up
You turn my frown upside down
My smiles lost and found
When you are around

CHORUS

Only you got the magic
Only you got the key
   to my heart, etc.
Happiness can last forever
I want a part of it
   even just a little bit, etc.

CHILLS

The sunlight smiles
Faithful everyday for you
No one can come close to the
Joy you bring to me
Whispers like a summer breeze
To put my mind at ease
When I look into your eyes
I envision you and me
On love's journey
So I wrote this melody
To show you that you send me

CHORUS:
Chills, running through my body
Shiver down my spine
Keeps me quiverin' for you
So happy that your mine
I'm shaken, I can't control myself
Cause you
You send me chills
Chills, you send me
Chills, chills

Come whisper in my ear
Tell me what your heart desires
Girl I feel that you're the one
That I could spend forever with
You give me that sensation
That no other love can give
Boy what you do for me
Goes far beyond my wildest dreams
Say you'll never leave
Girl when you look at me
I get this feeling inside of me

CHORUS

Cold as the winter breeze,
    makin' my heart freeze
Hot as the summer flame,
    when you say my name
Sparkling like Perrier, calm and
    easy like chardonnay
I feel chills when you look at me,
    chills when you touch me
Chills runnin' all over my body, hey

CHORUS

CHRISTMAS

Snowflakes, Christmas lights
Presents underneath the tree
All that I am waiting for is for you to come home to me
You work hard all year but
Still, it never seems enough
Saving to give me everything
When I'm just happy to feel your love

CHORUS:
All I want for Christmas is to be with you
To have you here next to me
See your smile light the room
Out of all my wishes
Only one has to come true
And that is to be with you

I imagine every second that you're walking through that door
You touch me with your sweetness
How could I ask for more?
Your kiss, your warm embrace
Those butterflies I feel within
When you hold me in your arms again
Baby, you're my everything

CHORUS

At Christmas time, everybody's asking for the sky
Thinking about all the things money can buy
Never knowing the best present lies
In the love of those who stay by your side

CHORUS

Out of all my wishes, only one has to come true
And that is to be with you

Cocquetta Bonita

CHORUS:
All my cocquettas in the house
Raise your hand
And to all you other girls
You better watch your man
'Cause we're comin' and we're comin'
Ain't no stoppin' us
Your boys are runnin' yeah they're runnin'
Tryin' to get with us
There ain't no messin' with
A cocquetta bonita
A cocquetta bonita

Boy take my hand, you know you want to
Boy take my hand, you know you got to, etc.

Raise your hand
Watch your man

CHORUS

Boy take my hand, etc.
Boy take my hand, you know you want to
Boy take my hand, you know you got to

COME BACK

It's so hard to say goodbye
Can't believe you're out of my life
And the words can't describe the pain
Can someone please stop the rain
Why is this world so cruel
Life had just barely begun for you
Your memories break my heart
And life has torn us apart

CHORUS:
Come back to me
I need you in my life
Why'd you leave me
Just know that I love you
I wish you were here with me

Can't tolerate the thought
Of you never coming back
What I'd do to see your face
No one can take your place
I remember back in the day
You brought me so much joy
Just promise when you're looking down
You'll pray that I can get through this

CHORUS

It's so hard to say goodbye
Can't believe you're out of my life
Just promise when you're looking down
You'll pray that I can get through this

CHORUS

COME OVER

Like a rain drop from the sky that wakes a rose in the desert sand
When I look into your eyes I believe in love again
If I could find a way to build a bridge between our hearts
I would lay it down today so you'd listen when I'd say

CHORUS:
Come over here, come over here and make me feel good
I wanna hear something so real to make me feel so good

I can be a reason to wanna make you stay until the morning come
Share a beautiful moment then another one
Before you know it you know it this is what you want
Say I love you I love you like I'm your number one

Gets so cold in the city, I need someone to hold me tight
If I could find a way to build a bridge between our hearts
I would lay it down today so you'd hear me when I say

CHORUS

Don't treat me like no stranger 'cause I could be your sugar
Would love to be your dinner, but first I need to know you

CHORUS

I can be a reason to wanna make you stay until the morning come
Share a beautiful moment then another one
Before you know it you know it this is what you want
Say I love you I love you like I'm your number one

You make me feel so good

CONTROL

I understand that you couldn't call me back
I understand that you had other plans
I try to understand that you wouldn't hold my hand
Last night at the game when we were chillin' with your friends
I understand when you say you need some space
I believe when you promise things are going to change
But now we're standing here and things are still the same
I can't pretend any longer it'll be okay

CHORUS:
I'ma take control
I can only love somebody who's in love with me
And it's obvious that you ain't got what I need
I'ma take control
I've been wasting all my time trying to make believe
Get away from me
I got to break free

Felt I was lost every night waitin' for your call
Felt I was ugly you didn't say I was beautiful
I was afraid I even believed it was true
When you told me I would never find someone like you
I was wrong thinking you were always right
I was so wrong I didn't want to end up in a fight
I didn't see that everything I really need
I had it all along inside of me

CHORUS

Now I'm moving on, picking up the pieces
Thinking why it had to take a broken heart
Before I finally found the strength to go my way

CHORUS

'Cos I Said So

Put on your high heels, lip stick, mini skirt
Come on lets go
Into my car, turn the radio on up high
I said high
At the red light, boys trying to get the digits but we said bye
Buh buh bye
'Cause we're heading to the club
Nothing's going to stop us now, let's go

CHORUS:
Are you ready, are you ready
Are you ready, let's go, etc.
'Cause I said so, I said so, etc.
Are you ready, let's go

Hey baby
So we're flirting with the dude at the door 'til he says we're okay
Move the velvet rope back and get out of our way
All the guys got their eyes on us as we're moving onto the floor
Grabbing us with drinks, but we're doing what we came here for

CHORUS

'Cause when I say so then I mean it
There's no excuse
I know you're shy and I'm not trying to tell you what to do
But we just wanna rock out and I know you want to too
So baby what's the matter with you

CHORUS

Are you ready, are you, etc.

Are you ready, let's go

CRAVE YOU

I need you tonight
Why don't you come save me
Wanna feel you inside,
    it's driving me crazy
I know that it's weak and I wish
    I could hate you
But there's something about you
    that's making me crave you
Why will you go
Do I have to follow
A bittersweet pill that is
    so hard to swallow
All I can think of is you in my veins
Running the sanity out of my brain

When my cravings show my mind
    screams no
Able and normal, but I can't refuse

CHORUS:
You're calling
Can't stop the noise inside my head
I'd come running
And I'd die to have you back
I can't hate you
I crave you
I wish I could erase you

I'm getting through rehab but they
    couldn't save me
Even tried therapy but, fuck, who
    could phase me
I'll stick to self-destruction that I
    just can't abide

Tells me I need you but I know
    it's a lie

When my cravings show my mind
    screams no
Able and normal, but I can't refuse

CHORUS

I can't stand the way you always
    rule my feelings
You're sand to me that stops these
    wounds from healing
I got to break free from
    the chains on me
And get back the guy you used to be
And ignore you when

CHORUS

I can't hate you, I crave you
I wish I could erase you

CRUISE CONTROL

I met this young man just
   the other day
He set my world on fire in
   a special way
He had the prettiest smile that
   I ever seen
Had me feeling like a daydream
Hey are you goin' my way, baby can
   I take you there
It was the first night of spring and
   love was everywhere
I didn't think twice as I jumped
   into his ride
Street lights flashin' by, this I
   whispered in his ear

CHORUS:
Put the ride on cruise control
In the drop top singing to that
   old school soul
Baby, close your eyes and kiss me
Then she made me lose control
She was so hot couldn't keep
   my eyes on the rode
Then she touched me (baby, baby)

Smooth, cool ride down
   the road side
Underneath the starlight sky,
   I'm beside you
Relax sit back enjoy the ride
   I'll put it in auto-drive
Are you down to be my boo

Baby, we can take this where
   you wanna go
Baby tell me what you really like,
   there's no wrong or right
And that's just what we'll do
Let me ease your body baby
   from head to toe
Gently moving closer, take it
   nice and slow
I couldn't resist such a sweet
   and tender kiss
Time stood still and it felt
   like paradise

CHORUS

(Car crashing sounds)

Keep cruisin', keep cruisin',
   keep cruisin'

CHORUS

Keep cruisin', keep cruisin',
   keep cruisin'

CRUSHED

Cold blooded, devious and cruel
You finally did it
The sheep turned into the wolf
I was longing for protection
Let down my guard
Gave you my heart, went against
   all my rules
Now I need protection from you

Bare-naked, I tore off all my clothes
Trying to shower off this pain
   inside my bones
Tears all over my face falling
   like the rain
Drowning my life and
   memories of you
And nothing can chase them away

CHORUS:
I'm crushed like a tin can
   on the street
Crushed, I never felt so weak
It's like a bottomless hole
Nothing but darkness in my soul
I just don't understand
I love you so much
I'm crushed

Spreading cancer infesting my flesh
I hear the rats feasting in the trash
All we created, all our
   beautiful dreams
Destroyed by a cloud of demons
   you set out on me

CHORUS

Like a prisoner released by mistake
I'd trade all this freedom just to get
   back inside my cage
I didn't see it coming I was so blind
I believed in your trust, believed
   in your love
How could you hurt me so much

CHORUS

CYNICAL

Look at them they'll never make it
Girl's got no talent
Guess she'll have to fake it
He didn't work as hard as I did
Who's she trying to kid

CHORUS:
Jaded observations, little accusations
Nothing's good enough
So full of pride and satisfied
Well, I could be that way on any given day
See the road as the enemy
But I don't want to be so cynical
I don't want to be so cynical

I'm not saying that I'm perfect
I'm just saying that it isn't worth it
To always see the glass half empty
Dwell on all that's missing
And what's wrong in my life

CHORUS

What's this world coming to

CHORUS

DADDY

I've seen pictures of you and your new family
That stranger's little girl, she looks a lot like me
It hurts to think someone else may call you daddy
But I guess it's good to know you're finally happy

I remember when you said we were where you were supposed to be
I remember when you said you promised me you would never leave
In the end all you cared about was being free
But I guess it's good to know you're finally happy

There are days that I can say
My heart just can't forgive
But I know deep down inside
If I give this heat alive
I'll never fully live

I can't tell you how many times I would've made you proud, daddy
If only you could see me and the woman that I am now
I miss you, I love you, and you best believe
It's really good to know that you're finally happy

DADDY

Daddy, are you askin' for trouble
Cuz this family is gonna fall apart
Tell me who can I turn to
If I can't turn to you
You should know better
You've been in my shoes
You're crossin' the line
If you want me to let it go
I wont fall in love
Just cuz you say so
You tell me not to be foolish, selfish
or prejudice in this house
But that's the way that you're
    actin' now

CHORUS:
Daddy – listen to me just for once
    with your heart
I don't think that you quite
    understand me
I made up my mind can't you see
    you will lose me
If you don't stop being
    so demanding
I love you to death but you'll make
    me hate you for life
If I have to chose between
    him and you
Is that what you want me to do

Daddy, I'm sorry
You're just making this hard
So hard for us
I know that you love me
You'll always want me to stay

But now it's breaking your heart
To see your baby girl taken away
But I can't walk away from the
    feelings I have
I don't wanna run from
    the family I love
Love means understanding
And accepting someone
    for who they are
And daddy you don't
Accept what I feel in my heart
Whatever you do you can't
    keep us apart

CHORUS

Daddy I love you, but you're not
    makin' sense
Please I don't wanna lose you
I still wanna be friends
But for once in your life you
    have to admit
You're makin' a big mistake
You're tryin' to hold me
But you're only pushing me away

CHORUS

CHORUS

No, no please, daddy I love you
Don't make me go away
Daddy please don't do this

DAMN (BE YOUR GIRL)

Is it a chemical reaction
    a magnetic attraction
Or a game of seduction I don't care
    I like it
A tremble in my thighs makes me
    feel so alive
When I look in your eyes I just stare
    I can't fight it

PRE-CHORUS
Ain't nobody moves my body like
    yours it's out of control
Heart is jumping blood is pumping
    got me shaking my soul

CHORUS:
Damn, boy I want to be your
    number one
Want to be the one to turn you on
I'm gonna go crazy if I don't tell you
    how you rock my world
Damn, I want to be your girl

Do you want to be my man
Or do you want to spend
    the rest of your life
wondering what might have been

It's taking over my senses
    I feel defenseless
It's so intense come on baby
    can you feel it
Is it my imagination should I try
    to be patient
Or give into the sensation,
    it feels so good

PRE-CHORUS

CHORUS

I said Aloha, Aloha
It's Raze and Lola
I roll a mocha inside the Copa
Grey goose straight no chaser soda
With a smile like that Mami must
    get closer
So type your number in
    my Motorola
So we can have a nice time and
    talk this over
And you can be my queen bee and
    I can be soldier
With his and her Rovers without
    the chauffeur
If opposites attract Ma heaven
    and hell
Is it Gucci you got on or is it Chanel
Anyway you got a smell got me
    under a spell
That Absolut and ginger ale got me
    ringing your bell
4 o'clock at your doorstep
    get in the Corvette
So we can see the sunset
    eventually raw sex
Verbal intercourse ma you ready
    to come next
My wisdom I'm giving her is making
    her more wet

CHORUS

DANCING IN THE NUDE

Sweet obsessions – giving in
I surrender to the call of your skin
Imagination – uncensored
Let your body do all of the talkin'

PRE-CHORUS:
Lets get scandalous, reckless
My desire for you is bottomless
No boundaries
I know what you need tonight

CHORUS:
Let's get wet
It's gonna get wild
I wanna see you sweat until your
    shirt slides
Baby come close
As close as dancing in the nude
Just me and you

Uncontrollable – unashamed
All my instincts runnin' wild for
    you to tame
Flyin' hunger – hails your name
You're the blood that is pumpin'
    through my veins

PRE-CHORUS

CHORUS

Everything you want
Is what I'm gonna be
What you really are baby
Is everything I need

PRE-CHORUS

CHORUS

CHORUS

DELIRIOUS

All the boys get the girls in their
   ride at night
To find a car with a headlight out
They gotta hit the roof then
   the clothes come off
And it all starts goin' south
It's getting hot in the Buick in
   the big backseat
Where the party's goin' on
I'm just a good girl most of the time
Who's to say it's wrong

CHORUS:
Let's get delirious
Let's do it, let's go crazy
Let's get delirious

Everyday we do what we gotta do
And we've had it up to here
Now it's time to do what
   you wanna do
So stop and pop your mirror
To the super woofer till the
   neighbors call the cops
I smile at the man in the sexy blue
Say officer take it off

CHORUS

Everybody's getting crazy
Everything's getting out of hand
Do you want to be my baby, etc.

Come here mister policeman

So we move the party to
   the local jail
And we'll bump 'til we make bail
We've got the drunk offenders and
   the male pretenders
And us, we're raising hell
Oh my goodness every time we party
It's like we're doing
   something wrong
Why don't you keep your money?
Just calm down Mom
I'm gonna stay here all night long

CHORUS

CHORUS

DIAMOND

It's your smile I sing about
I close my eyes you're all I see
It's this kiss I dream about
Every night you're here with me

CHORUS:
I just came to let you know
You're like a diamond in the snow
And you are the sun that warms my soul
You are the half that makes me whole

You're the rain that clears the air
So soft and so pure
All this time you were right there
I never noticed before

CHORUS

Just one look in your eyes and I know
That I'm such a lucky girl
Each day with you in my life
Wish I could rewind and live it
Over and over again

CHORUS

CHORUS

I just came to tell you
And I just came to show you
And I just came to tell you

DISEASE MIX 1

CHORUS:
When you're gone it feels like my whole world's gone with you
I thought love would be my cure but now it's my disease
I try to act mature but I'm a baby when you leave
How can I ever get used to being without you

Don't say you got to break away
That look in your eyes is making me nervous
You slide like silk through my arms
I'm trying hard not to feel helpless
When you first put it on me
I was hooked undeniably
But if you take that away from me
I won't know how to breathe

CHORUS

Every time I lose myself in your head I close my eyes, don't want to be found
ever again
And now you got to leave me here when I just got so addicted to that sweet
feeling

CHORUS

Here's what I'm going through when you're gone
Showing serious symptoms of withdrawal
Talking all night to my stupid pillow
Curling in my bed like an armadillo
Waiting for that call it makes me crave for your voice
When I get you on the phone I only want you boy
The longer we talk the more I feel incomplete
I just can't get what I need

CHORUS

DJ, DON'T PLAY THIS SONG

DJ don't play this song
Don't play this song
Don't, etc.

Don't say I didn't warn you
Once this beat goes on
There's no stoppin' on and on
Did you get that
Hip hop be bop
Non-stop around the clock
Getting hot, speakers bump
Feel the beat in my body, body

We must be doing something right
   'cause the party's rockin'
Got to get down low to take it high
   and it's not my fault

CHORUS:
People in the club go wild and
   keep it jumpin'
Gets 'em moving crazy beggin' DJ
   keep on bumpin'
Can't control their feet, no
Just follow the music flow
Stop this madness, hit the gong
DJ don't play this song
Don't play this song
Don't, etc.

Told you what but
You just had to push your luck
Now you're jump struck

You should have listened
Once it starts up
We have to wind it up
DJ better turn it up
So we can move our bodies

We must be doing something right
   'cause the party's rockin'
Got to get down low to take it high
   and it's not my fault

CHORUS

Actions speak louder than words
Now you got 'em rockin' through
   the doors like herds
People goin' crazy takin'
   over the spot
Like a Jerry Springer when he
   was on top
The FCC tryin' to shut down the club
Sure no, ain't gonna be done
Guess you never thought these
   things could go wrong
Next time you better listen
   when I tell you
Not to play this song

CHORUS

CHORUS

Do It to You

In my room I'm all alone
Got your pictures staring back at me
Where you were I should
   have known
It's not where you said you'd be

PRE-CHORUS
Your fingers on my naked skin
Don't make me feel a thing
Empty words and broken dreams
Is all you left for me

CHORUS:
But now it's you that's all alone
Is it killing you, boy, to see the truth
As it's laughing back at you
No, you never thought I could
   do it too
No, you never thought I could
   do it to you

I love the taste of sweet revenge
It makes me want to smile
Your lies have brought me
   to the edge
Now just watch me go wild

PRE-CHORUS

CHORUS

Feel it burning deep inside of you
And you got a taste of your own sins
And now we're even
Don't tell me what it's like to lose
I can't find no sympathy
You're just another memory

CHORUS

CHORUS

DO THAT THING

CHORUS:
Do that thing to me one more time
Feel your body lying next to mine
On my carpet take a ride
Make me feel like a queen tonight
Do that thing to me nice and slow
Feel your body going with the flow
Boy you know that you're
    blowing my mind
Make me feel like a queen tonight

I'm on fire
I'm crazy with desire
Your love, it takes me
    higher and higher
I don't want to come down
I'm flyin'
There can be no denying
Your love is mystifying, surprising
There's enough to go round

CHORUS

Do that thing to me, etc.

I like the way you work it
Let's take our time it's worth it
You know we both deserve it
Don't rush it, time is never enough
Let me taste it
It's much too good to waste it
So let's get down to basics,
    don't fake it
Give me all of your love

CHORUS

Do that thing, etc.
Do that thing to me one more time

CHORUS

DO YOUR THING

A little girl grew up in a tough town
Had some friends always
   putting her down
Hairbrush was her microphone
Favorite song came on and
   she'd sing along
You shouldn't even try to waste
   your time
Get your head out of the clouds was
   her favorite line
She waits on tables makin'
   money somehow
Wondering how she'll ever get out

CHORUS:
Girl, just do your thing
Doesn't matter what they say
Keep on doing your thing
Don't let your dreams slip away
Let your heart sing
You've worked too hard to let
   them confuse you
Just do your thing

Nothing's good enough,
   can't do anything right
But she still feels the fire inside
No one cares about a young
   girl's dream
But she keeps believing, as hard
   as it seems
Wanting to break out and prove
   them all wrong
Never fit the mold all along

She always knew she could
   do better
Promised herself she'd always
   sing her own song

CHORUS

Faith and trust was hard to find
But one day she put her fears aside
She moved out and she moved on
Found herself and grew strong
Ignoring what they all used to say
Deep down she always
   knew her way
Singing to herself

I know it gets hard at times
When you find you're the one
   left behind
Seems everyone's always leaving
They keep on deceiving
   instead of believing
Got to wake up, forget all
   that fake stuff
Get up and sing

CHORUS

CHORUS

DON'T BE A STRANGER

Lately I've been running away from you
Maybe just 'cause I'm scared of losing you
Hiding out somewhere just to find out
How much you love me
Testing boundaries of our relationship
Hurt you a little to see if you can forgive
Just enough to know that in spite of it
You'll come looking for me

CHORUS:
Oh, don't be a stranger
Oh, don't be a stranger
Help me tear down the barricades and the steel and armor that I've made
If anyone can do it it's got to be you

I found solace in these peaceful waters
But I'm wondering what's going on with us
And I'm longing for you to put
My feet back on the ground
Last night I had some strange dreams about you
Got me worried about what you been up to
Hope that you're not feeling overwhelmed
By my emotions

CHORUS

Am I destroying what's left of us
Are you coming back to save us
Is it your fault, is it mine
If we fall apart over time

CHORUS

Oh, it's got to be you, etc.

Don't Give Up On Me

I'm so sorry for acting so selfish
Never saying thank you
For you were there for me
Through good times, bad times
Hard times, sad times
So if I seem ungrateful to you
I hope you knew
That I didn't mean to

CHORUS:
Don't give up on me
Don't give up on me, not now
'Cause when the tears are falling down my eyes
I need you right by my side
Don't give up on me

I remember when we first met
I was on the edge of my seat
We were on the verge of becoming enemies
But you kept trying
Till I stopped hiding
Now no one knows me better than you do
Can't you see I need you

CHORUS

I just couldn't sleep at night
Can't ignore if this ain't right
Why was I too blind to see
You only saw the best in me
I've been stubborn, refused your help
But you know me much too well
Gotta be patient with me, please

CHORUS

DON'T GO LOOKING FOR ME

You don't ever give up
No you're never going to give up
Will you?
I think you get the message
But you don't want to hear it
Do you?
You're like my jealous ex-boyfriend
But you never were my boyfriend
Don't you get it, get it, get it
You won't get it, get it, get it

CHORUS:
Don't go looking for me anymore
'Cause you won't find what
    you're looking for
Don't go holding your
    hopes up high
'Cause I couldn't love you if I tried
Some other girl would be lucky
    to have you
But it won't be me, it won't be me

You always ask me over
You're trying to win me over
Don't you
You call me for no reason
You wish you had a reason
Don't you
You're like my jealous ex-boyfriend
But you never were my boyfriend
Don't you get it, get it, get it
You won't get it, get it, get it

CHORUS

Gotta stay away, gotta stay away
If you cant be my friend
You gotta stay away, gotta stay away
Don't you understand?

CHORUS

DON'T LOOK BACK

I look in your eyes and I see the dreams I'm about to destroy
It breaks my heart because I love you, this is something I cannot afford
You put your arms around me but it's like I can't breathe
I'm feeling numb to your touch, boy I missed it so much

CHORUS:
Maybe it's best you leave, pretend that you never loved me
Forget all the memories from the first kiss to our anniversary
I gotta be alone, I gotta find myself and find the strength to move on
Don't look back

I pick up the phone and there is silence, but I know that its you
I want to say something but I pause 'cause there is no use
And perpetuating this heartbreaking mistake
Living this life when I know I'm dying inside

CHORUS

Maybe it'll take a lot of time to get over you
Maybe right now I'm just confused
But I feel like this is what I got to do
Help me to let go of you

CHORUS

CHORUS

And don't look back

DON'T SAY GOODBYE

I'm lying here
Thinkin' 'bout you
No more tears
Fighting for you
So don't throw it in my face, in my face
I know what I did to you
And don't make me feel guilty
Keep blaming me
I still want you

All cried out
Pleading with you
Dying now
Don't say that we're through
I'd rather you hate me than break me
You're all I ever knew
Now hold on cause
I'm trying to save us
I'm still in love with you
(Still love you still love you)

Don't say goodbye
Don't, don't say goodbye, etc.
(Don't say, don't say it now)

DOORMAN

About 5'5", pretty little eyes
Always smell good and I kinda like
    your style
See you in the morning and I see
    you late at night
And the time in between you are
    on my mind
I met both your parents and most of
    all your friends
A few of them even said
    I'm a gentleman
I know you so well but we're
    worlds apart
And I got to find a way to your heart

CHORUS:
I'm just a doorman, opening doors
For you when you come in, bet
    you didn't know that
I think about you late at night
When my shift is over, having
    thoughts about me being
More than your doorman, walking
    down these Harlem streets
While we hold hands, visualizing
    me and you
While we slow dance
Everybody's watching and I never
    wanna let go

Boy ain't no way, you're wasting
    all your time
That's what they say when I tell them
    you'll be mine

But I'll be crazy if I never even try
I know I have a chance I
    feel it inside
Today I'm gonna make my move
This is what I got to do
I'll tell you what you mean to me
This feeling is so strong that it
    must be real

CHORUS

It's 5 in the morning
Got me waiting outside of your
    elevator hold
The rain is pouring
Couldn't get it together so I wrote
    you this letter, girl
But I didn't have the nerve to give
    it to you
But here's what the letter said

CHORUS

CHORUS

DRIFTING

We were best friends
Now we don't talk anymore
We were soul mates
Now we feel completely ignored
You say we've grown apart
We should go our separate ways
It's not really working out with us
And we were just wasting our days
But I think it's just a phase

You don't say hello
You don't look at my face anymore
I hear you're an emo
I wonder what you're standing for
They say you found yourself
Your world has changed with you
But everything around you was
    black and white
Do you think you found the truth
'Cause I think it's just a phase

CHORUS:
It's like the rain falling in your eyes
Don't you miss the sunshine
Big clouds hanging in your sky
And it's like you don't mind
    where you're drifting
While your life is drifting away

Like the weather
Seasons will come and go
You're like winter
When I look at you I'm
    freezing cold

You used to make me laugh
You'd even laugh about yourself
We'd chase late nights after boys
    on MySpace
We talked endless hours
    by ourselves
Girl, don't you miss that too

CHORUS

DRIVE MYSELF CRAZY

I never imagined someone could
    make me feel
Like I'm falling so deep I wanna
    believe it's real
Have you lost ya mind, has your
    conscience gone away
Just take your take your time, cause
    puppy love will end someday
Well, sometimes you meet someone
    that makes you feel so complete

CHORUS:
I drive myself crazy over you
I'm drownin' my sorrows
    cause of you
I drive myself crazy over you
I'm falling in love
I'm falling in love

See lately, I feel like I don't know
    what to believe
Nothing that you say can take away
    this void inside of me
Listen to me sister, I know
    the games they play (sista)
It may sound like love, but he may
    not want the same
    (want the same)
Girl you gotta do what you feel is
    right for you
If it's love don't let it pass you by

CHORUS

Every time that I see you
    I'm driven crazy
And when you're not near me
    it hurts to even think about
All the times that we shared
    like yesterday
I'd be wrong because I know
    I've never felt this way
This is love and I can't deny it
My friends don't understand ask me
    why I can't hide it
Sometimes I wanna pinch myself
Cause this love's for you,
    and nobody else

CHORUS

I drive myself crazy over you
    (I'm goin' crazy, baby)
I'm drownin' my sorrows cause
    of you (I'm goin' crazy for
    you, baby)
I drive myself crazy over you
    (I'm goin' crazy baby)
I'm falling in love (I'm goin'
    crazy for you baby)

I'm goin' crazy, baby
I'm goin' crazy for you, baby, etc.

DRIVEN

I'm driven by something
   inside of me
When you tell me that I can't
I'll show you I can

I'm not afraid to risk it all
Take a chance and hope
   I'll miss the rain
That's just who I am

Cause I've seen the finish line
Nothing can stop me now
I can feel it down inside

CHORUS:
I'm driven by the voice within
I'm giving it my everything
I'm taken by the biggest dreams
Nothing can stop me
I'm driven by the odds to beat
And everybody who believes
It's impossible, undoable for me
Just wait and see

You know it when you feel it
And it feels unlike
   anything you know
You know what I mean

Like staring at the poster on the wall
One day I will have it all
It's waiting for me

'Cause I've seen the finish line
Nothing can stop me
I can feel it down inside

CHORUS

Darkest clouds or brightest day
High to low will come my way
I'm living for the hope to seize
   every possibility
Should I take it off take it for a ride
I got what it takes to be strong
To get back up and then
   I'll try again

I'm driven by something
   inside of me
When you tell me that I can't
I'll show you I can

CHORUS

DROP IT ON ME

CHORUS:
Drop it mami, drop it mami
Drop it on me, hey hey
Drop it on me, drop it on me
Drop it on me, hey hey
Muevete duro, muevete duro, etc.
Muevete duro, hey hey

Tonight's a special night, to get you by my side
I've been waiting all week long to get it on with you
Sometimes we hit the floor, dance like we never did before
I'm going to put it on you Boricua style

CHORUS

Let the music take control, once we start you can't say no
Move your eyes and follow me, te muestro mi amor
Make me feel oh so nice
While you whisper something
My hands on your hips, do what you came here for

CHORUS

(Rap)

CHORUS

Este canto es tuyo, corazon es tuyo
Quieres que sea tuyo, dame amor puro
Asi, asi, asi, etc.

(Rap)

EACH OTHER

I know you're mad at me but there's nothing I can do
And I'm sorry, I'm sorry's just not good enough for you
You can hate me all you want to and pretend that you don't care
We can fight until we crumble but it won't get us anywhere
Don't you know me better at the end of the day

CHORUS:
All we really have is each other
In this crazy world in this short life we live
Try to leave the past in the past where it belongs
And hold on

'Cause all we have is each other

You know I said some things I did not mean
And I know I hurt you but you mean more to me than anything
It kills me when I see the way you look so sad
But please don't give up on the love we had
We're so good together at the end of the day

CHORUS

CHORUS

'Cause all we really have is each other
In this crazy world in this short life we live

EASIER SAID THAN DONE

Wakin' up from a sleepless night
Was it me who was wrong
Was it you who was right
I don't wanna open my eyes
I don't wanna stop dreamin' that
    you're still mine
Ask myself girl why you actin' crazy
Wishin' you were here to
    call me baby
Baby, baby

CHORUS:
All of my friends tell me, "Move on"
I'm better off now that you're gone
They say my new life has just begun
But it's easier said
Easier said than done
Easier said, easier said than done

Wanna call just to hear your voice
But I promised myself not to spoil
All the progress I've made so far
But just the thought of you is still
    tearin' up my heart
Seein' pictures of you and me
It's like we're installed in a wound
    that never heals
Yeah yeah, and maybe it never will

CHORUS

And I've perfected the art
Of acting like I don't even care
I smile when I cry inside

But my heart doesn't really have
    a place to hide
And I know that I'll be alright
But I still miss you like crazy
Maybe it's just the loneliness that's
    playing with my head
But I wish you were holdin'
    me instead

CHORUS

CHORUS

EAT DIRT

Found a piece of candy on the floor
And I couldn't resist but taste it
Mamma wanted to smack me
And that's when I made up my mind and I ate it
And I have to admit it tasted better
Than the ones in the kitchen cupboard

Every night I look out the bedroom window
Wondering what it's like to run away
And daddy told me he would hit me if I did it
So I made up my mind and I ran away
And I have to admit it wasn't as scary
As I thought it would be

CHORUS:
What doesn't kill makes you sick
And if you're sick you learn a lesson
And with every lesson you'll get wiser, wiser
So I figure that it pays to cross the line
And eat a little dirt sometimes

I found a book about mystical things
My mamma said it's against our religion
So late at night I'd read it anyways
And that was the last time I asked for permission
And I have to admit that I don't regret
Telling her lies 'cause it opened my eyes

CHORUS

I won't let my years go to waste living in a cage
This prodigal child will always stray
I got over the stomachache, wiped the mud off my face
'Cause this world belongs to the brave

CHORUS

EXPLANATION

Want to hear your voice, but I'm drowning in silence
Half hearted smile, think I don't see the difference
I want to touch your hand, but I don't know if you want me to
You don't understand, just what you put me through

Why did you say that you loved me
When you don't act that way
I really believed you

CHORUS:
I need an explanation
Get me all excited then you go and pull away
When I want you by my side you don't seem to want to stay
But around your friends you treat me like your favorite accessory
I need an explanation
You invite me over, just to make me wait all day
But when I leave you know the perfect words to say
Pulling on my heart, acting just like I am your everything

Every time I call, one-sided conversations
You don't say a word, avoid the confrontations
I'm holding on, but I can't find the signs
That you are in love, when I read between the lines
Why are you so indecisive, 'cause I still believe you
But I feel so deceived

CHORUS

How can I love you when you won't make up your mind
You say you love me, but you're too afraid to try
I can't go on living, with my heart out on a string
Let me know what's inside
Baby tell me

CHORUS

CHORUS

90

Fame (The Game)

CHORUS:
Fame makes a fool out of anyone
Fame takes you back to the golden childhood
Fame makes you think that you're having fun
Fame - the game

Get on the plane and
Get off into the limousine
To the early morning show
Everyday routine
Make up fake up get a manicure
Five minute autographs, grab a picture, yes or no
All the same answers to the same questions
Create a scandal with your reaction
What's that you say, take it or leave it
Paparazzi wanna see you bleeding

CHORUS

Late suit days, hair extensions
Botox faux-forced interventions
Nude job, boob job, all nouveau
It ain't what, but who you know
Uncalled perjury, cosmetic surgery
Dirty secrets frame your glory
It'll get the cover story

CHORUS

Everybody wanna be a star
It's all about who they think you are
Pulling up in a crazy car
The front door is your garage
Everywhere an entourage
Play like you've been living large
Someone got your credit cards
Lend me your blah blah blah

(Be careful
Be careful what you wish for)

Since I was a child of three
I'd watch old movies on the silver screen
Kate, Bette and Marilyn were the reigning queens (do you wanna be a star?)
I know if I can make it out
Out of this sleepy town then I could go real far
I could, I'd really work so hard
And I could do it and do it and do it 'til I become a star

CHORUS

Miami, London, Paris in a week
Lying in private, catching up sleep
Celebrity parties, politic profits
Rock'n' roll bully boys walk the red carpet
Getting in VIP through the velvet rope
Shake hands, photograph and you gotta go
Little black book pools with the CEO
Smile and tell' em what they wanna know
And tell' em what they wanna know

(Be careful
Be careful what you wish for)

CHORUS

Everybody wanna be a star
It's all about who they think you are
Pulling up in a crazy car
The front door is your garage
Everywhere an entourage
Play like you've been living large
Someone got your credit cards
Lend me your blah blah blah

(Fabulous, fantastic)

FASTER

The pressure's getting higher
I'm feeling this desire
I try to catch my breath, it's hard to breathe
I'm lit up like a fire
Angel like a fire
Addicted to the rush it's giving me

Move, get out of my way
Oh I'm not afraid

CHORUS:
Faster
I'm on the edge I wanna go
Faster
Push it to the edge I wanna go
Faster
I want it all I want it now
Don't slow me down

Driven by the danger
The challenge is my savior
My legs are going numb I'm feeling weak
It gets me so excited
I'm shivering inside
I can't resist the thrill it's giving me
Move, get out of my way
Oh I'm not afraid

CHORUS

Don't slow me down

CHORUS

Don't slow me down

FATAL

Why do I get so excited whenever you're near
What is it that makes me so nervous whenever you're here
With every breath you're on my mind
It's like you're with me all the time

CHORUS:
I guess it's fatal
Like a disease without a cure
I've never felt this way before
Don't want to admit but you know it's true
I'm falling for you

Everywhere I go is like nowhere without you
But somewhere is a place where there's always something new
You mean everything to me
Wherever I look it's you I see

CHORUS

I'm falling for you

There is no description for when my heart skips a beat for you
There is no prescription for what you do to me

CHORUS

I'm falling for you
I'm falling for you
I guess it's fatal

Fatty Koo

Ooh, ooh, ah, ah, ma, ma, ma, ma
Let me get a taste of your sweet potato pie
Ooh, ooh, ah, ah, ma, ma, ma, ma

Yo, it's Fatty Koo (ah, no, no, no, no)
Keep it hot, got black, Cajun, cabana models
Sweet candy sensation, you give me all that I need
Up in the club, mami, you bouncin' and shakin' like you don't care
You in your see through Victoria's Secret underwear

Girl, you so hot, you make me doo wop
When you shake your fatty, eyes turn, mouths drop
I wanna see you shake your fatty, please don't stop
(Don't stop, don't stop) Crazy

CHORUS:
Ooh, ooh, ah, ah, ma, ma, ma, ma
You the mommy and I'm the daddy
When you feel the rhythm, lose control
Move your body and get on the dance floor
Fatty Koo! She's freakin' her fatty koo
Fatty Koo! She's freakin' her fatty koo
Fatty Koo! She's freakin' her fatty koo
Fatty Koo (hey!)

Ay, sexy daddy
I know you like it when I shake my fatty, fatty
I see your eyes lookin' at me
If you want me, you can have me
Tell me if you want to freak with me
I can be your little fantasy
You know I like it when you undress me
(Baby, we can do it) follow me

CHORUS

You already know who's hot and who's not.
You hot, sizzlin' in the drop
Belly dancin' don't stop
Let's get it on, you on top
So many reasons we got
No schemes, what I need with a plot
This is pelle all day, ma
So what you actin' bashful for
Go on and shake and give me your encore
You damn right we want more
Let's leave the club and go on a detour
We can make love as we cruise on the seashore
Givin' it up real nice up on the dance floor
Follow me, be sure
I got a thing for you, ma, but keep it on the low
And maybe we can creep after the show
You like that

CHORUS

Belly dance for me
Mmm, etc.
Don't stop
Mmm, etc.

FEARLESS

Everybody's got a place for me
But where do I fit in?
If every morning is a brand
   new canvas
What colors will I use today to
   fill it in
And I've got tendencies
To want to draw outside the lines
So will you still love me
Even if my castle ain't built
   by your design

All of this ego I see in the mirror
It's so disconnected, but that's
   if I let it
All of the demons that I'm
   fighting daily
I won't let them get me
No, no, 'cause

CHORUS:
Life is for the fearless
Nobody wants to hear this
It's all about the madness
You make beautiful
If love is what you're afraid of
Then it's time to get creative
Just you and that old paintbrush
Make it beautiful
Make it beautiful

I don't like Mondays
I'd rather lie in bed
Sometimes it's safer under
   my blanket

With the dreams inside my head
And I've got tendencies
To see things black and white
But that gray area
Is the most frightening and exciting
   part of life

All of this ego I see in the mirror
It's so disconnected, but that's
   if I let it
All of the demons that I'm
   fighting daily
I won't let them get me
No, no, 'cause

CHORUS

Bold strokes, strange shapes
Don't make sense all the time
Bright shades, let your
   imagination run wild
All of these choices, but which
   one to make
And all of these boundaries
   I'm breaking away
And I can't wait, I can't wait

CHORUS

FEELIN' LIKE YEAH

I'm just sittin' here wondering
   what to do
On this boring Saturday night
Daddy's out of town why don't
   you come around
And take me for a ride
No matter where we go or
   what we do
Just crank the radio
Roll the windows down, we'll just
   mess around
I'm ready now let's go

Let's go crazy, it don't matter
What we look like at the red light
This would never put together
It just feels so right

CHORUS:
I'm feelin' like yeah, yeah
Gimme some of that oh, oh
Need some of that
Right here tonight
I'm feelin' like yeah, yeah
Gimme some of that oh, oh
Need some of that
Right here tonight

Checking out the backyards
   of the houses we drive by
Seeing if somebody has a party we
   could crash for the night
Sweet-talkin' as we're walkin'
   by the fatty at the door

Let's show them how to party and
   rock it out on the dance floor

Let's go crazy, it don't matter what
   the DJ's brought along
Cause we've got beats and
   we've got heaps of those
   booty shakin' songs

CHORUS

We've got all night, got all the time
So relax and let things fly
Let you hair down let it loosen, babe
Just let it slip away

CHORUS

FIGHT FOR ME

Every time you call me
I'm your only one
You said you'd never leave me
The next day you were gone
Is there someone between us
I gotta know the truth
Boy it drives me crazy
To imagine being without you

CHORUS:
Fight for me
Promise you will change
Show that you're strong enough
You're man enough
Whatever it will take
Fight for me
Don't make me walk away

If we belong together
Why are we apart
Boy you're playing games with me
But don't you use my heart
Can't you see I'm hurting
My back's against the wall
Let me know you're worth it
And you will give your all

CHORUS

I want to believe you
You promised you won't let me down
With all that we've been through
How can you leave me alone
This way

CHORUS

Find Me

Cold feet, sweaty palms
Out of place, feeling wrong
All alone in a crowd
Wish somebody would save me now

It's a lovely day but there's clouds
   in my head
I want to shout out loud but
   I'm quiet instead
I feel the sunshine on my skin
Something wont let it in

CHORUS:
I wanna lose myself in you
Ooh, ooh, yeah, yeah
Can't think of nothing else to do
But first I got to find me

Shoop, shoop, shoop, etc.

Every time you're at my door
I get to know myself a little more
This crazy girl never knew
Life could be so beautiful

It's a lovely day but there's clouds
   in my head
I want to shout out loud but
   I'm quiet instead
I feel the sunshine on my skin
Something wont let it in

CHORUS

Shoop, shoop, shoop, etc.

There's no turning back now
I can't let myself down
So for now let's take it
   one day at a time
And we'll see

It's a lovely day but there's clouds
   in my head
I want to shout out loud but
   I'm quiet instead
I feel the sunshine on my skin
Something won't let it in

CHORUS

Shoop, shoop, shoop, etc.

FIND MYSELF

19 years gone by
She's dying for a change
She feels she has a purpose
And that it's taking her away
Tempted by the promise
Tempted by the unknown
She wants to leave this town
And so she says

CHORUS:
I don't know where I'm going
I don't know what I'm looking for
But I'll know it when I see it
And I'll tell you when I find it
Don't try to hold me back now
Why can't you just let go of me?
I know that you mean well
But I'm trying to find myself

A father loves his child
Doesn't want to hold her back
But he cannot say goodbye
Because she's all he ever had
All she's got on her mind
Is how to escape
She sees him as the problem
That's standing in her way

CHORUS (2X)

FIRE 3

What's your name where you're
   goin' where you come from
My name's Shaliek and it's you
   that I'm wantin'
I like your style and the way
   that you're struttin
The scent of you and your
   sweet smellin' perfume
Got me fantasizin' bout you being
   in my bedroom
Come over here before I have to go
   and get you

CHORUS:
I feel the burning when you look at
   me baby and it won't stop
No matter what I do maybe
   we should hook up
The way you move your body getting
   hotter (fire, fire, fire, fire)
Got you sweatin' like you just got
   out of the hot tub
Grindin' grindin' grindin' move
   your body closer
Burnin' like the heat in a toaster

You move your body like waves
   in the ocean, slow motion
I know you want it baby girl
   I got that potion
You know I'm thinking that it's time now
Feeling like we should go ahead
   and wild out
Show them how it supposed
   to be done now

CHORUS

I know you feel this dance
Girl I know it beats like that
Tips off Jack, wine goes down
   then she throws it back
Just take it easy it hurts to see
   that you're willing
To do whatever just to flirt with me
I see you mirroring my style you're
   clocking my step
Then we watch you go down
   like a merry go round
But Stats not no player and
   I know you hate it
And I'm rough on paper and
   you got to face it man

Yeah you see his cash you know
And he could ride that stick
   like a rodeo
Your back's shot shaped girl
   like a bottle of Hypno
Something that could turn me
   into a freak oh
Got to have you in the bedroom
   with the ohs and ahs
Five five yeah girl with my face
   and your thighs
When it comes down to love
   you know Caskerada
My brothers with Shaliek
This so fly and now

CHORUS

THE FIRST OF A MILLION KISSES

For the longest time you didn't even talk to me
When I walked by
Giving you the eye
You would look the other way

And every week I would be waiting in the car by the back door
    for you to notice me
And then one day you were sitting at the table with a slingshot
And I asked you if I could give it a try
And you went laughing at me saying you look so cute girl
The way you try to pull that back
Are you sure you can handle that?

CHORUS:
And that was the first of a million kisses
I got out of the car but you pulled me right back in had me wondering
Everything about me was spinning
Then you looked into my eyes
I felt something inside
That was undeniable

Didn't hear from you for three nights and endless days
I drove myself crazy wishing you would call me to tell me you were okay
Till finally one day I saw you waiting in your car at my school
Asking me if you could drive me home
Then we were sitting in the back seat and you said you wanted to be with me

CHORUS

Unbelievable

CHORUS

FLAVA FLAVE

I talk about him day and night,
  his name is—
I see you standing right there
  with your crew
Now baby we can kick it
  what you want to do
Won't you come on up and
  just talk to me
I don't care what you say
  if we got chemistry

Tell me what's your name tell me
  where you're from 'cause
  your so cute
Let me look at you, just turn around
  cause I'm in to you

CHORUS:
Flava Flava Flav, etc.
Whatever you want
Whatever you need
You know I got it
I got it with me
Flava Flava Flav

What you want to do
If you want to go with me
  I'm rolling with you
I'm down with your crew
It doesn't matter we can do
  whatever, 'cause baby I can't wait
Here's my number just hit me later
So you and I get together again

All I think about all day is Flava Flav
All my people say he's not
  good enough for me
But I'm going to play my game
  the way I want to play
I can't stop he's too hot,
  don't care what they say

Tell me what's your name tell me
  where you're from 'cause
  your so cute (so cute)
Let me look at you just turn around
  cause I'm in to you

CHORUS

What you want to do
If you want to go with me
  I'm rolling with you
I'm down with your crew
It doesn't matter we can
  do whatever
Cause baby I can't wait
Here's my number just hit me later
So you and I get together again

CHORUS

FOR ALL THE WRONG REASONS

For all the wrong reasons
 I fell for you
For all the wrong reasons
 I'm still holding on
Though I know it's wrong
Don't belong in your arms

For all the wrong reasons
 we've gone too long
For all the wrong reasons
 I fell in love
And I wait for that day
When you want me to stay anyway

CHORUS:
You're just like a tattoo, I wish
 I could erase you
If you only knew how much
 I try to hate you
You're everywhere no matter
 what I do
Face the truth
I can't get rid of you

For all the wrong reasons
 I trusted you
For all the wrong reasons
 I can't undo
All the love I gave
But you'll never change

For all the wrong reasons
 you fell for me

For all the wrong reasons
 we made believe
That we'd be fine
But we cross that line every time

CHORUS

For all the wrong reasons
 I fell for you
For all the wrong reasons
 I'm still holding on

CHORUS

For all the wrong reasons
 we fell in love
For all the wrong reasons
 it's not enough

FORGIVE MYSELF

It's been a long time in this stubborn world
And I'm, I'm fading fast
I never said I was unbreakable
Or I was, was built to last
And you, you are so alive
You never questioned once
The reason why I throw it away
But that won't happen today

CHORUS:
I would never forgive myself
If I let you walk away
There's another condition
That my head is trying to say
It's been empty days and manic nights
Since I, I let you go
And it's impossible
To forgive myself again

Another cold hour in another town
And you're so far away
I've got to move fast to the other side
Before it's all too late
I'm running down a crowded street
With rescue on my mind
As I pass by a familiar place
A place where I once died

CHORUS

I don't have the answers to your questions
I don't want to wear to your frustrations
I am golden this time
I am golden this time

CHORUS

CHORUS

THE FORMULA

Sometimes it seems like everybody knows
Everyone but you
Just how to deal when you're practically almost
Sure he feels it too
Every simple look gets so confusing
That you don't know what to do

CHORUS:
But there's a formula
When you're crazy in love
And you're so obsessed you can't catch your breath
A formula when you start to blush
You pretend you don't care then you care too much
Don't think he thinks you think he doesn't know
'Cause I know if he knows you know he can't say no
It's for you to know and for him to find out
And I think you know what I'm talking about
Ooh na na na, etc.

Day after day you overanalyze
Everything you hear
You can't escape he's running through your mind
And every time he's near
Every simple look gets so confusing
And you still don't have a clue

CHORUS

Three steps to happiness
But no one ever wants to go first
You're at a standstill but when you're face to face
There really is no need for words

CHORUS

FREAKS

I wanna hear the Freaks song

Got my pick of all the guys in town
But the one I want doesn't care
   that I'm around
Every other guy falls in love
   with me, it's so crazy

This one guy won't stop stalking me
One guy wants my sympathy
Feels like I'm on reality TV,
   all eyes on me

CHORUS:
Those freaking freaks are freaking
   trying to freak me
Freaking geeks are freaking dying
   to meet me
Dum da da da, etc.
What's a girl to do?

This one says he'll make it
   last forever
I roll my eyes at him and
   say whatever
Blah blah blah, etc.
All I want is you

You can call in the middle
   of the night
We can do whatever you'd like
But you're like I'm all
   down with her

What's your problem? Here I am
Can't you take me like a man
Don't be hating and dissing on me
You're not Slim Shady

CHORUS

CHORUS

Guys they like the way
   I work my booty
But I'm much more than just
   your average cutie
Ha ha ha ha, etc.
All I want is you

CHORUS

They really like the way
   I work my booty

FRECKLES

I used to care so much about what others think about
Almost didn't have a thought of my own
The slightest remark would make me embark
On the journey of self doubt
But that was a while ago
This girl has got stronger
And if I knew then what I know now
I would have told myself don't worry any longer it's OK

CHORUS:
'cause a face without freckles is like a sky without the stars
Why waste a second not loving who you are
Those little imperfections make you beautiful, lovable, valuable
They show your personality inside your heart
Reflecting who you are
Who you are, etc.

I wondered if I could trade my body with somebody else in magazines
Would the whole world fall at my feet
I fell down, worthy, and would blame my failures on the ugliness I could see
When the mirror looked at me
Sometimes I still feel like the little girl who doesn't belong in her own world
But I'm getting better at reminding myself

CHORUS

Reflecting who you are, etc.

CHORUS

FREE

You told me, "Put on a face and join the race"
You taught me not to fight back
For years I surrendered 'cause I was afraid
Denied where my heart is at
Now I see you pushed it to the back of my mind
Too scared of what I might find

CHORUS:
Goodbye to a girl who didn't belong in your world
My dreams, my life
Now that I've made it right
Don't let me make a promise I know I can't keep
Got to make my own decisions
Find out what it's like to be free

And so I've walked through the knife for half my life
I don't care if I'm naked home
And suddenly I'm taking my life in my own hands
I don't care if it's not what you had planned

CHORUS

Here I am on my own
I see you through my eyes
Take a breath, I look around
And leave the past behind

CHORUS

FRIENDSHIP WITH BENEFITS

We both on the same page
Makin' the most of our younger days
Won't rock the boat we don't want the waves
I don't wanna get soaked I want the sun rays
Never think about her dumpin' me
She just wanna keep me company
A lotta other chicks stay front and see
I can already tell what they want from me

CHORUS/RAP:

I ain't looking for relationship
Just a friend with benefits
Tell me if you're cool with it
And we can hit it off (Come on)
I'll keep this verse slim, girl
I gotta get fried
And there's three little words
I try to live by
Don't want no commitments
Don't want nothing serious
I'm twenty, sexy, single
Wanna live it up, I'm ready let's go
Hell yeah, I'm wit it
Wouldn't say it if I didn't
I ain't kiddin I admit it
You get flyer by the minute
You look good, I look good
Lookin' good like we should
Together we look even better
What'cha what'cha waitin' for
Nothin' girl the time's right
We up in the limelight
If I invite anyone
To my place it's you tonight
You want me, I want you

We know what we're gonna do
We're too young for this relations-shit
Strictly friends with benefits

I come and go as I please
We just friends
You ain't my squeeze
Why wear my heart on my sleeves
When I can just breeze
And leave with such ease

No pressure
We fresher
Than most
Close
But no extra
Catchin' of feelings
See the ceiling, it's made of glass
And that, that's appealing

CHORUS/RAP

See neither one of us ever mislead
Or send mixed singles so we succeed
I ain't goin' claim we never disagreed
Or been in the wrong lane
Had to switch the speed
Still I can't say that I haven't wondered
If we could surpass our level of comfort
It is what it is (But it is what it is)
So here's to friendships
With them benefits

CHORUS/RAP

Friends with benefits, etc.

Its no secret we keep it casual
Anything else might feel unnatural
We get right, and we get fly
There's three little words I try to live by

G'ON GIRL

Now you know you need to get
   on the floor
To get on the floor
All the ladies in the place, come on

I want to see the sweat dripping
   from your body
And I want to feel your heart
   vibrating my body
Move to the rhythm of the jamming,
   jumping, funky band
And hear the last call for everyone
   to get out and dance, so

PRE-CHORUS:
Come on, come on,
   come on, come on
Come on the dance floor's filling up
   so come on, come on
(Then sing it again) come on,
   come on, come on, come on
Come on the dance floor's filling up
   so come on, come on

CHORUS:
G'on girl
Let me see you do your thing
Get your ass on the dance floor
Let me see you do your thing
G'on girl
Let me see you do your thing
Get your ass on the dance floor
Let me see you do your thing

I gotta get a little taste of your love
You got me feelin' I don't
   wanna give up
I knew you felt me when I walked
   in the room
You dazed me like zoom
I feel it in my hands, I feel it
   in my feet
I feel it taking control of me

PRE-CHORUS

CHORUS

Shake that thing girl
Come on, come on
G'on girl
Now you know
You need to shake that thing
Cause I'm feelin what you're doin'
I just want you to shake that thing

CHORUS

GEISHA TRACK

CHORUS:
Walk like a geisha
Talk like a geisha
Look like a geisha
Love me like a geisha

CHORUS

CHORUS

GET BETTER SOON

Mamma tell me why do
We move around so much
Why is there only one bedroom
When there's five of us
My shoes are hurting
They're tight on my feet
I'm kind of hungry
But there's not much to eat

CHORUS:
Baby you don't have to worry
I will find a way to provide for you
You mean everything to me
There's nothing that I wouldn't do
Times are hard but we will
    get through
With all of my heart I promise you
Things will get better soon

Mama tell me why
It's so cold inside
Why do we have a heater if
It's off all the time
Why are my clothes used
Is it wrong that I want more
My friends have brand new
Things you say we can't afford

CHORUS

There are people less
    fortunate than us
To some we may not have much
But we have love

And that's something that
    money can't buy
So wipe the tears from your eyes
I'm never leaving your side

CHORUS

Things will get better soon
I promise you they'll get better soon

GET WEAK

Yesterday I saw you eating your lunch in the changing room by yourself
I tried to get in, you lock yourself in, how can I help
You thought that I wouldn't notice you're wearing baggy clothes and
Trying to hide those bruises but I'm not stupid

You're not around anymore you call in sick with all your fabricated excuses
I try to call you up but you don't answer the phone,
    to be honest this is useless
It's obvious that you cry but you say there's something in your eye
Things are going to go south if you don't open your mouth

CHORUS:
Don't let him get into your head don't let him bully you like that
When you fast-forward five years you'll be laughing off those tears
Now they use their fist to win but when life kicks in they'll move rubbish bins
Though the struggles made you stronger
You won't any longer get weak

I see you walking up and down the stairs pretending you are busy
Letting nobody know you want to be alone covering up your story
I wish I could rescue you and talk it through
    but you think everybody's out to get you
But that's not true

CHORUS

Don't let him get into your head
Don't let him get into your head
Brush them off your shoulder
If your friends try to change you maybe it's time to change your friends

CHORUS

GIRL AROUND THE CORNER

They see her standing there with frizzy hair
They laugh and walk by
She feels invisible, fakes a smile
But inside she cries
They think she's sort of weird, she's not from here
That girl is strange
Nobody talks to her or even cares
To ask for her name

CHORUS:
That girl around the corner
That girl around the corner
This is how I feel sometimes
Sometimes I feel a little like
That girl around the corner

Nobody really knows what really goes
On in her mind
She thinks the deepest thoughts she hardly talks
Just look in her eyes

CHORUS

She's like a butterfly that grows inside her cocoon till it's time
Saving her fragile wings, her precious dreams till the day she flies

CHORUS

That girl around the corner

THE GIRL YOU DON'T WANNA KNOW

Did I disappoint you baby
Did I turn out to be that girl
That you don't even want to talk to
Am I corrupted baby
Do you see the devil in disguise
Where once an angel stood?
I'm sorry it took you so long
    to figure me out
But if you only see what
    you wanna see
How will you know what
    I'm all about

CHORUS:
I'm the girl you don't want to know
I'm a flirt, I'm a tease
A little rough but I'm sweet
And I ain't putting on no show
If you love me, you love
    me untaintedly
With the eyes of a woman wronged
Guys trip, fit the script
Make the girls feel they're wrong
But you know I just want to have
A little fun too, just like you
Hypocrisy

Am I still your mama baby
Do you still look at me with those
Same baby eyes like you used to
Or is my skin bitter now
When you taste me with
    your tender lips
Do you want to just spit it out
You get mad when you find out

I've been having fun without you
But you better get mad at yourself
I'm just doing what you always do

CHORUS

When a guy gives it up on the block
To everyone, he's the man
But let a girl get too friendly
No one will understand
No I didn't go half as far as you did
But you bitch cause you think
        there ain't no room
For the both of us to act
    just like you

CHORUS

Sincerity
Hypocrisy
Sincerity

GO GO DANCER

Pink laces, lights electric blue
Leather stockings, yellow pleather boots
Black mascara running down her cheek
Most promiscuous she flirts with me
Then she grabs my hand rushes through the crowd
To the ladies room, puts her duffle down
She looks a hot mess, slips out of her dress
Sparkly pasties this girl is shameless

CHORUS:
She says I'm not a stripper I'm a go go dancer, dancer
She says I'm not a stripper I'm a go go dancer, dancer
Friday night is my night
That's when you'll always find me here
Ask the guys at the bar for Chastity and I'll meet you here
I will wait for you

She digging through her purse, looking for her fix
Xanex, blow, K, Tina
She runs a pharmacy offer's some to me says it's almost free
But there's something you got to do for me
Pulls out another load, passes it to me
Sweat rolling down her face, look of urgency
On your way home would you promise me to deliver this to 24 Avenue E

CHORUS

She's gone off to work again and I've got this envelope in my hand
While there's panic breaking out in the crowd.
The music stops, house lights go on
Police rush in there's something wrong
I see her lifeless body as they carry her out

She says I'm not a stripper I'm a go go dancer, etc.

CHORUS

GOD

One day I was walkin' down the street and I met God
The two of us sat down, I shook his hand
We had a long, long talk
I didn't notice how time flew by
It was in the middle of the night
When I looked around we were sittin' there all alone
One day when I was feelin' really let down
And I wanted to know

CHORUS:
Why when I pray it's like talking to myself
Why don't nobody care about anybody else
Why do I keep failing when I try my best
Why do I need money to feel like I'm blessed
What are my sister and me always fighting for
Why does my country solve every conflict with war
Why when you have the power to change everything
Am I still singing the same song my parents used to sing

There was a long moment of silence
I was on the edge of my seat
I thought any second he'd just say something
But he just stared back at me
Then my eyes started peepin' his gear
I noticed a peace sign danglin' from his ear
Some sandals that exposed manicured toes
Saggin' jeans with large gapin' holes
He cleared his throat and he asked me
Is this not what you expected to see
I said, "Don't change the subject on me"

CHORUS

He shook his head and he said, "Yo, you think you got it bad
Look around, I did all this work and you see what's come out of that
Everybody comes to me with all their problems thinking, I've got a plan
Then they get mad at me if I don't right away give 'em a hand
And when I give you something you say, No, I want it all
But it's like the more I give you, the less you wanna call
Do you really wanna know what I think?
Just think about what you already know

Why when you pray it's like talking to yourself
'Cause you got the answers but listen to someone else
Why do you feel like a failure when you try your best?
'Cause all you know is money to measure your success
What do you and your sister keep fightin' for?
When you criticize other people for going to war
I've given you the power to change everything
You just prefer to sing the same song your parents sang

GOOD DAY

Hey there, how are you
I know it's been awhile
Yes, I'm fine thank you
What's that? No not this time
Don't, stop, please don't
Go there just let me talk
I'm trying it's not easy
We've been there before

CHORUS:
It's like we're only living for those few happy moments
When things are better
When I'm your little princess and you act like you wanna know me
And we're safe together
And nothing in the world can come between us
And take the love away
I hope I catch you on a good day
I hope I catch you on a good day

Yes I'll come visit
As soon as I can get away
No I won't forget
To take pictures so memories don't fade
Sorry there are all these
Things that we can't change
I'll do my best to
Stay strong when you break

CHORUS

When you smile and you really mean it
When you're genuine and I can feel it
When there's joy and you don't steal it
It makes it all worth it

CHORUS

Good Morning America

Cruising down the highway
The radio is singing along with me
The morning sun is rising
It's 6 AM it all seems easy
Threw my dreams in the backseat
I'm on my way to sunny L.A.

CHORUS:
Good good morning America
I'm gonna be a star
Spend all my savings on an old guitar
Good good morning America
Isn't it great to be
Living the American dream
Good good morning America

Can't wait for my audition
Got a job for the day and a room for the night
This is it, I won't believe in
No turning back till I'm in the spotlight
The highway lights are slowly fading
Hollywood hills are calling my name

CHORUS

CHORUS

GOOD WOMAN

Now I know it's hard sometimes being a man in this society
But let me tell y'all ain't nothing harder than being a woman
   if you know what I mean
A woman's got to do everything, go to work, cook, and clean
All the while every song y'all sing be talking 'bout how it's just one thing

CHORUS:
If you want a good, good woman
You better be a good, good man
You better hold me tight and treat me right
Or ill find someone who can
'Cause I'm a good, good woman
And I deserve a real good man
If you don't hold me up
I can't hold you down
We need each other
Don't you understand

So many times you look around complaining 'bout what you got
Don't even notice who I am, only focus on the things I'm not
I do everything I'm supposed to, but it's never good enough for you
You always thinking that I'm up to no good every time that we're apart

CHORUS

All your boys say if you're a real man
Don't fall for no lady, just let a lady fall for you
But now don't you find it funny that all your boys are lonely
Wishing they were in your shoes

CHORUS

All my sisters out there feeling me
All my brothers out there feeling me
If you a real man holler at me
If you a good man holler at me, etc.

GOOSEBUMPS

Teachers say you're lazy
Parents call you crazy
They just can't seem to fit you
   in the mold
Preacher says you're gifted
Grandma calls you misfit
The way you dance little brother
You touch my soul, I get

CHORUS:
Goosebumps
Give it all you got
The way you let your body talk
You got nothing to prove
It's all in you boy
You're misunderstood
Boy you're much too good
Don't you question what
   you're gonna do

Just 'cause they don't see it
Don't mean you ain't got it
Anybody that's in the biz
Knows that you're the shit
It's all you've ever wanted
Some would kill to get it
You're one in a million boy
Don't you quit now

CHORUS

When you crank up a boom box
   baby boy
You're on stage, backflip,
   you're a superstar

You're to the crowd what fire is
   to the art
It's undeniable you're unbelievable
Stay unbeatable

CHORUS

When you break up a boom box
   baby boy
You're on stage, backflip,
   you're a superstar
You're to the crowd what fire is
   to the art
It's undeniable you're unbelievable
Stay unbeatable

THE GREAT DIVIDE

I'm waking up, you're
   going to sleep
And I wonder are you
   thinking of me
I'm getting ready for another day
   without you
And you're just starting to dream

It's hard to let it go
To make it through the day
It's hard to hold on
When we're both so far away
Maybe we should just move on
And get on with our lives
But how can we survive

CHORUS:
When our hearts are so connected
That we'll die when you
   take them apart
And when one half of me is missing
If I can't hold you here in my arms
Can we overcome the distance
Make it through time
Can our love bridge the waters
Overcome the great
The great divide

I'm soaking up the sun you're
   underneath the moon
And I wish that I could share it
   with you
You live your life and I'm
   living mine

Somehow we've got to find a way
   to get through

It's hard to let it go
To make it through the day
It's hard to hold on
When we're both so far away
Maybe we should just move on
And get on with our lives
But how can we survive

CHORUS

I keep waiting for the day when we
   find a place to stay
And we'll always be together
And I keep waiting for a time when
   every single night
Belongs to me and you and we'll
   never have to move again
We can spread our roots and grow

CHORUS

GREW UP TO BE MY BABY

Weren't you just the girl next door
Never noticed you before
But time's been on your side
Have you always had that pretty smile
If you did I don't recall
How'd I miss those blue eyes
Ain't it funny what a little distance can do
I had to stand back to see the real beauty in you

CHORUS:
You grew up to be my baby
Look at you now
You woke me up and saved me
I almost didn't see what was right in front of me
I must have been crazy
You grew up to be my baby

Been around the world and came back home
And found how much this girl has grown into a woman
A woman who is everything I need
Who's the star of all my dreams and waking moments
It's so amazing what your love makes me do
Like making a promise of forever with you

CHORUS

Looking back I can see how we've wasted our time being just like strangers
But you just never know what the future will hold until you get there.
And tonight as I lie by your side, still awake, and I watch you sleeping
I can't believe

CHORUS

GYPSY

You got me
My life is in a suitcase
My heart is in a box
My smile is on a TV
I feel a little lost
Like a bird I fly around the block and by
I'm lower than the blimp up in the purple sky

PRE-CHORUS:
You got me, you got me
You got me where you want me, you want me
You want me wrapped around your finger

CHORUS:
But I'm free like a gypsy trying to strut my stuff
Feeling a little tipsy, high off of this love
I can feel you in me don't want to give it up
But I can't get enough

I'm homeless but I'm happy
I'm broke but I feel rich
Cause I got rid of all my shit that used to make me itch
Like a dream you came crashing in my life
You gave me every reason not to run and hide

PRE-CHORUS

CHORUS

I'm homeless but I'm happy
I'm broke but I feel rich
Cause I got rid of all my shit that used to make me itch

CHORUS

CHORUS

CHORUS

HAPPY

Landlord's knockin' at my door
Cussin' me out
Got laid off my job the night before
I can't figure how
I'm gonna fix tomorrow when
Yesterday's still a mess
Can you tell me what's
    the point man
It all seems meaningless

Wish that I could step away
    and breathe
This world's tryin' to swallow me
Clear away the clouds
    inside my head
Someone just tell me

CHORUS:
That it's okay now
What are you worryin' about
Got my dreams, got my life,
    got my love
Got my friends, got
    the sunshine above
Why am I makin' this
    hard on myself
When there's so many beautiful
    reasons I have to be happy

People lie, people hide, people cry
And they don't know why
If fear is all that we should fear
Then what are we so afraid of
Cuz fear is only in our head
So why do we let it control us

Fear makes me forget how
    sweet and simple
Things in life really are
Fear makes me believe
    that I'm alone
Someone please say

CHORUS

Any day I'll go mad thinking that
Everyone is against me and
    the world wants to fight me
Preparing to battle an enemy unseen
During my stressing I'm blinded
    to the lesson that could be a
Blessin' if I'd be confessin'
    that the enemy
I'm tryin' to beat
Is hidin' inside of me

CHORUS

HARDCORE

Lips, chains enjoy the pain
Let's play, get into my domain
Be on top and in control
Won't let you dog me out no more
The first time it really hurt
I was innocent, so naïve
But no more nice girl
Won't let you deceive me anymore
Her body was your plaything
    just for pleasure
Until you pulled the leash too tight
    and stole her treasure
Tired of gettin' treated like
    your possession
She was strong and tough inside

CHORUS:
Now I'm hardcore
Try to test me I got the floor
I'm hardcore
Used to be sweet and
    willing to please
Been through the fire
    won't take it more
That little girl's matured
It's gonna be my way or
    no way at all

Handcuffs, cameras, get in the scene
Who said cute girls
    couldn't be nasty
Giving you what you deserve
Can you smile but you're
    looking so disturbed

When a guy pimps he's the shit
But when a girl plays
    she's just a bitch
Don't take it personal
I learn from the best don't act
    like you don't know

CHORUS

At guys I'm like snakes with
    poisonous venom
Still I got in the grass just to
    wiggle with them
It felt so good till it went so bad
When I know you lied about
    all the chicks you had
All the sleepless nights
    that I spent alone
Now I'm hardcore right now
    to the bone
You think you're so sweet
    but I flipped the scene
    make you scream
Strip down now, dance for me
It's my time

CHORUS

HE GOTS THE LOOK

CHORUS:
He's got the look
Turning heads when you
   see him walk by
Make you weak when he's giving
   you the eye, what
Trying to hide but you
   can't turn away
Never seen a fellow looking so good
He's got the look
Feeling shivers running
   down your spine
God, I think about him all the time
Wanna talk but you getting all shy
Never seen a fellow looking so fine

I know you don't know my name
But it's just something that
   I can't proclaim
Been dreaming about you
   for so long
And the way you walk listenin'
   to your headphones
And then way back
   when I was young
Used to watch you play 'til
   the day was done
Ain't trying to come off crazy
Just letting you know I just
   became a lady

CHORUS

I felt like I was complete
When I watched you chill
   on Cooley Street
I can see you from the front
   of my window
Instead of findin' gold one,
   you my rainbow
Grew up and moved away
But in my thoughts you'll always stay
Cuz when I'm home thinkin' of you
In my wildest dreams,
   you're thinkin' of me too

CHORUS

Oh he's got the look
Oh he's got the look
When I see him walking by from
   the corner of my eye
Got me saying, "boy you're fine,"
   the way you catch a shorty eye

Yeah he's got the look
Yeah he's got the look
Got me sayin' "My, my, my"
   baby boy you're looking fly
Fashion - you're the latest thing
Thinking about you make me sing

CHORUS

HELLO GOODBYE

I found myself in a dead end street
Looked in the mirror but it just wasn't me
So I packed my bags, moving on
Grabbing just some of my things, and I'm gone
One foot in the past, one foot in the sky
One eye smiles while the other one starts to cry

CHORUS:
Hello, goodbye
It was good to meet you, nice try
Hello, goodbye
Before I can even make it last
It's already passing me by

Free as a bird once again don't know where I'll land
Tired of the hurt every time I change my plan
I want to be somewhere I can call my home
This time around do it right and let my roots grow
One love sweet enough to make it through whatever comes
One heart strong enough to hold me back when I say

CHORUS

One foot in the past one foot in the sky
One eye smiles while the other one starts to cry

CHORUS

HEY BOYZ

Stuffing all my pillows so it looks like I'm asleep
Supposed to be a good girl but there's another side of me
Climbing out my window, sneaking out the gate
No one's supposed to know 'cause they think I'm well behaved

CHORUS:
Hey boys see you checking on me
Want to come and check this out
Hey boys I like what I see
Yeah that's what I'm talking about
Mama told me not to call boys but I do
Mama told me not to give it up too soon
Mama told me not to, ooh

I feel kind of rebellious, hope they don't find out
I do it for the hell of it yeah it feels good no doubt
Sometimes I get busted, don't know what to say
Daddy was disgusted but I do it anyway

CHORUS

See I really want to be a good girl but sometimes I can't help it
They really try hard but no matter what they do they just can't stop me
I don't mean any harm when temptation is strong
I got to do what I want

CHORUS

HEY KITTY KITTY

Hey kitty kitty my cat nip is silly

Here kitty kitty come bounce
  and dance with me
I'm blowin' on that sticky
  straight from New Guinea
Catch me up in Europe,
  clubbin' in the city
With three sweet atomic cats
  with nine mili's
I war like Achilles, dare you
  come get me
Hey kitty kitty my catnip is silly
Hip, hop and diamond rocks
Lick my body like a lollipop
Stop, drop and check ya watch
The party stay hot 'til
  whatever-o'clock
Sexy, sexy Henny and Jenny
New York Ranger, the black
  Wayne Gretzky
Hell raiser, with chicks
  on the Jet Ski
International – you already met me

CHORUS:
Wanna make love
Feels so good to be back
Now there's no turnin' back
Is it love, is it lust
I don't care, it's just us
There's no wrong, there's no right
Your desire is your guide
So let's break every rule
What is mine now is yours

Hey kitty kitty my catnip is silly

My bank's stolen money
It's razor, dinero
Even if its yen, pesos, Euros
Two commas, seven zeros
We no widows
We came from chicken wings
Potato chips
It's Jenny from Atomic Kitten
And gun kissin'
You can't catch us in a club
  that ain't hittin'
You won't catch me with a kitten
  that ain't whippin'
And look finger lickin' (And Imma
  smack the beat written)
It's love boys lux
In the most high we trust
Rollin' up a Dutch
While we on the tour bus
With the Ghetto Government
  logos on the truck
With Red Bull, Grey Goose
  spillin' from a cup

CHORUS

Hey kitty kitty my catnip is silly, etc.

Act like Jenny the coat-flasha, etc.

Hey kitty kitty my catnip is silly

HEY MAMA

Hey mama?

Yes Baby

Can you tell me the story of how
   you and daddy met back then?

Well it started in high school I met
   your father sitting all by himself
My heart just melted,
   he smiled at me

But mama, but how did daddy know
   you were the one if he
   didn't even know you?

You see we had chemistry that we
   share from him to me
Filled me up with so much joy
It was love, love at first sight

How did you feel? And what
   did he say?

He said "I love you,
   love you, love you"

Hey mama, how did daddy
   get you to move with him
   and start a family?

When he proposed to me he
   promised that we would
   be together always, always

And daddy, when did you and him
   decide to have me?
   And how did you do it?

See we raked the soil, planted the
   seed, gave it love and all it needs
Hoping it would flower into
   a beautiful tree
It was love, love at first sight
He took my hand and he said
   "I love you, love you, love you"

When a boy loves a girl he buys
   her flowers and takes her
   to see the world
Showers her with affection and
   guides her in the right direction
All the joy and happiness
   that she needs

Sittin' here all day
Daydreaming
Hopin' for the day you say
   "I love you love you, I love you"

His Hands

I was captured by the features of his face
I never even asked his name
It was obvious what we felt inside
Attraction between him and I
Everyone around us knew what this was leading to
I couldn't hide the thoughts within my mind
I was sitting there killing time

CHORUS:
Until everyone left the room
I stayed behind and we already knew
What his hands were about to do
So we put down the shades and it felt good
All of this we didn't plan
But we kept it going on and then
It started to become intense
And we knew it would have to end

I couldn't keep my focus anymore
Got a little hazy and I had to have more
I couldn't fight what was going on
The feeling was just too strong
Even though I said I wouldn't go there
All of my inhibition went up in the air
I had a hard time it was going to fast
And I couldn't wait for the hours to pass

CHORUS

CHORUS

HOLLYWOOD

Things are so different here
Old truths seem to disappear
And who you were doesn't matter
My point is a better view
Make me look beautiful
And every face, same old story

CHORUS:
In Hollywood, Hollywood
Every sunrise, you get so close
Every sunset, an overdose
No one cares, but everybody knows

Bask in someone else's fame
Live off of the family name
And who you are is all that matters
It's so hard being young today
Do your ads
You go far for doing nothing

CHORUS

Everybody wants to be someone
Everybody wants to be someone else
And if you're down they'll hand you a shotgun
Just get me out, just get me out

CHORUS

Get me out, get me out, etc.

HOUSE OF FATTY KOO

Yeah! I'd like to welcome y'all all out to the wonderful house of Fatty Koo
Starring: Marya, Gabrielle, Joshua, Valure, young Chappelle, and Eddie B

Ooh, you're in the house of Fatty Koo
House of Fatty Koo
You're in the house of Fatty Koo
(Fatty Koo)
Ooh, you're in the house of Fatty Koo
House of Fatty Koo
You're in the house of Fatty Koo
(Fatty Koo)
Ooh, you're in the house of Fatty Koo
House of Fatty Koo
You're in the house of Fatty Koo
(Fatty Koo)
Ooh, you're in the house of Fatty Koo
House of Fatty Koo
You're in the house of Fatty Koo.
(Fatty Koo)
Ooh, you're in the house of Fatty Koo
House of Fatty Koo
You're in the house of Fatty Koo
(Fatty Koo)
Ooh, you're in the house of Fatty Koo
House of Fatty Koo
You're in the house of Fatty Koo
(Fatty Koo)

Let's go, cheddar fries, cheddar fries

How Could I Get Lost

How could I get lost, etc.

I feel like I'm with you even
    when I leave
I can feel your touch in every step
And every breath I breathe
You're my whisper of hope
The smile on my face
The quiet in my soul
You're the bright of my day
The star in my night
That guides my way

CHORUS:
How could I get lost
Now that I found you
It's like I was born just
    to be around you
Something tells me deep in my heart
Home is wherever you are
It doesn't matter what you do
I'll always find my way back to you

I can feel your heartbeat right
    in time with mine
I can see forever waiting
    in the sparkle in your eyes
You're the fire that feeds me
The one who believes me
Even when I'm wrong
You're my sweetest temptation
My one inspiration
That keeps me strong

CHORUS

'Cause that's where I feel safe
When my world falls
    down around me
When I crave a soft embrace
When I need your love
    to surround me

CHORUS

How U Do It to Me

I'm a busy girl and I've been all around the world
And I've seen so many things
But nothing comes even close to you
Many go left some go right
And it's possible that I might
Get swept away with the tide but I've got you

CHORUS:
You shut out the crazy world
I am your baby curled up in your arms
Never wanna leave ya
Only wanna be here
Your hands are magic baby when you touch me
I don't hear the masses, the noise of the traffic
How'd you do it to me, etc.

I look into your eyes automatically mesmerized
We're in a bubble just you and I
The things I love about you multiply, multiply
You take me away it's like a permanent holiday
So many tricks up your sleeve

CHORUS

Many go left some go right
And it's possible that I might
Get swept away with the tide but I've got you
Cause I'm a busy girl and I've been all around the world
And I've seen so many things
But nothing, nothing comes even close to you

CHORUS

How You Won Me Over

Said I wasn't lookin', I don't need no man
I ain't got no time to play around
Said that I was happy, I'm my own best friend
But you were cool, said either way you're down
So you played it smooth babe
How'd you know I'd like that

CHORUS:
You were careful not to seem too keen
You flirted with such subtlety
That's how you won me over
That's how you did it
That's how you won me over
You kept me dancing on my feet
While you were scheming secretly
That's how you won me over
That's how you did it
That's how you won me over

You didn't waste a moment to get me on my own
But made it look as if it wouldn't change
You'd always keep me laughing and you always had a shoulder
Knew everything I'd say before I told you
So I began to like you
Till I couldn't be without you

CHORUS

Sometimes I think 'bout what it'd be like
If I never found you
You've won my heart and now
I can't picture my life without you

So you played it smooth babe
How'd you know I'd like that

CHORUS

HUMAN

I've said sorry over
  a thousand times
Is there anything to say to you
  to help you dry your eyes
I would make it all better if I could
I hope you realize

PRE-CHORUS:
I cry, and you cry
I hurt, and you hurt
I make mistakes
But I can turn back time

CHORUS:
I'm only human (Forgive me)
I'm only human (Love me)
I'm only human (Save me)
Save me from myself
I'm no superwoman (Embrace me)
I'm fragile and broken
  (You're just like me)
I'm perfectly human
  (I might just tell a lie)
I'm perfectly human
  (But I'm an angel in disguise)

I'm staring in the mirror and
  a stranger's looking back
What are you afraid of girl,
  the future or the past
If you wanna see inside of me all
  you have to do is ask

PRE-CHORUS

CHORUS

Maybe what tears us apart
Is what brings us back together
And everything that
  makes us different
Really brings us closer
Could you hold me
  (For a little while)
Could you love me
  (Without a doubt)
I need you, I need you

CHORUS

I'm perfectly human
We're all angels in disguise

HUMBLE

It's about time to show the real me
Take off this mask and let you know
   who I am
Gotta tell the truth
It's about time to share my secret
I have to come clean
Can you keep your lips sealed
And I'll be honest with you

All of this time I've been
   playing a role
Hope you still love me now
   that you know

CHORUS:
When it all comes crashing down
When there's no way
   to turn it around
When there's no one
   to blame but myself
When I start to pick up the pieces
And you still help me
   clean up the mess
I feel humble

Never really meant to be ungrateful
So glad you stuck it out with me
Even when you brought
   me happiness
And I brought you misery
Never really meant to be unfaithful
So happy that you're still around
Even though it might seem like
   I let you down

All of this time you were the one
   I turned to
But I didn't know what
   you went through

CHORUS

Found out the hard way
I was running so fast
But I had to stumble
The world had to crumble
It's a long ride to the top
The fast way down
Please don't count me out

CHORUS

HUMM ALONG

The moment you walked in
I could see it on your face
You must have had a crazy day
You don't want to talk about it
Don't worry it's okay
'Cause you know I love you anyway
Little sister listen up
I know sometimes you think
    that you've had enough
But you just can't give up

CHORUS:
When things are going wrong
I find a happy song
I put it on and humm along
Don't let life get you down
Find a way to turn it around
Put on that song and humm along

When you don't get what
    you think you need
Maybe it wasn't meant to be
And something better will
    come your way
There's no need to get frustrated
The best things happen when
    you least expect it
So put that smile back on your face
Little sister listen up
I know sometimes life can
    get so tough
But when you fall get right back up

CHORUS

I know it hurts every time
    you get neglected
Nobody wants to feel rejected
Everything happens for a reason
Every day it makes you stronger
Every heart it makes you wiser
Let the worries go and humm along

CHORUS

HUNG UP

I say something wrong
And you get so upset
A little too far
And you get so mad
Can't we find a way to deal with this
All we do is go around in circles

CHORUS:
We get so hung up
On things that don't really matter
Can't we just brush them aside and move on
And move on

CHORUS

All our attention
Is going to waste
Leaving us empty handed
When it's time to pay
All these thoughts
Are itching under my skin
Creeping up like insects from within

CHORUS

CHORUS

Don't let our nothings
Blind our vision
Be understanding
Spite our frustration
Learn to listen
Listen with caution
Before these problems
Get out of proportion

CHORUS

HURT NOT BROKEN

I wanna kick you in the face and throw your clothes out my window
But I wont do what you've done no
I keep tearing photographs just so I can glue them back together
Sure I can forget but it won't make it better

CHORUS:
Cause I'm hurt but as long as I'm not broken
I won't stop giving us a try
But I don't know what were gonna build this love on
If the trust we had is gone
Gone gone gone... is gone

Why cant we be done with this don't you see it isn't working
All the time we spent from here to hell and back again
And why do we make promises knowing well never keep them
Sure I can pretend its easier then leaving

CHORUS

I Am (Because You Are)

Sometimes I'm breaking in pieces
Scattered on the ground
In these moments of weakness
You turn me around
When I am in your arms
It feels like I am home
No matter what
I won't be alone

CHORUS:
I am because you are
The answer to my why
The courage when I'm shy
The voice when I'm in doubt
The whisper in the wind
The strength to start again
When I fall apart
I am because you are

Sometimes sadness turns into
A blessing in disguise
Sometimes loneliness helps me
To clearly hear your voice
When I look in the mirror and see my troubled face
You appear and give me grace

CHORUS

The one who holds me in the night
Who's there to tell me I'm alright
You're everything in times when I can't see
The one who guides me when I'm scared
When I need someone to care
That's why I believe

CHORUS

I Am Who I Am

People tell me all the things that they want me to be
But I try to walk on my own two feet
Everybody here seems to know where they're going
But I'm still figuring out where do I belong
I'm trying to picture myself in a year or two from now
Being that business girl on Wall Street
But no it doesn't feel like me
Or the pretty fashion model flashing her designer shoes
Living in a fantasy world
But that's not who I really wanna be

CHORUS:
Cause I am who I am and I don't know where I'll end up someday
But I'll tell you when I feel it
Cause it is what it is and I'm trying my best to make everybody happy
But I got to start with me

I'm sorry that I had to lie but I didn't have the strength to tell the truth
But I hope you'll forgive me anyway
I know you really want to say what's best for me
I know it's hard to let go but I will be okay

CHORUS

Say no if you really don't think so
Let go if your conscience says no no
It's your life and nobody knows better than you do
What's right for you
Don't do it if you know you can't preach it
Don't touch it if your heart can't feel it
You got big dreams go ahead and live them

CHORUS, etc.

I Don't Miss You at All

It doesn't hurt when I think of you
And all the things we'll never get to do
I don't dream at night about the way we were
I tore up the pictures, crossed out all the words
Don't be fooled by all my tears 'cause everything is fine
You can pick up all the pieces that you left behind

CHORUS:
Cause I never think about you I'm better off with out you
I don't miss you at all, I don't miss you at all
You don't spin around in my head it's like you never existed
And I hope you don't call
I don't miss you at all
And I'm not trying to fight it, no I'm not trying to fight it
So you can cross my name right off the wall
I don't miss you at all

I go out seven nights a week
Doing crazy things you wish you tried with me
And I party like I never did before
I wonder what was I waiting for
Everything is perfect now without you in my life
You can pick up all the pieces that you left behind

CHORUS

I'll just tell myself girl forget the past
No time for regrets no more looking back
I'll forget you more every single day
Every step that I take is getting better

CHORUS

I HATE YOU

I've never been in love before
And I don't really know for sure
What this is, what is this
I wish this feeling went away
I wish I didn't have to say
That there's nothing I want more than to be with you
But I do

CHORUS:
I hate you
It's in the way you say my name
Come up with the sweetest things
Every time I'm really mad at you
I hate you
How you always know what's right
And end up winning every fight
No matter what I say
I wouldn't want it any other way
Any other way

I've never let anyone so close
Every thought I think you know
And I'm not sure if this feels good, it feels so good
I don't think that this is fair
Why do I have to care
Wish I didn't go crazy while I'm waiting for your call
But I do

CHORUS

There's not a thing I wouldn't do
Just to see me with you forever baby

CHORUS

I LIKE THAT GIRL

Tell me what should I do, what should I say.
I'm lost for words so I'm coming to you, sister, will you help me
See I don't know, where to start
To find the keys to win over a woman's heart

Well first things to remember when your game comes into play
(Watch what you say)
Gain your composure, show respect and you'll be okay
(Because the ladies really like it when)
(One) When you don't succeed, don't get offended.
(Two) Listen when she speaks and don't pretend.
(Three) Be more than a lover when she needs a friend
So many things about a girl a guy can't comprehend

CHORUS:
Ooh, ooh, ooh, I like that girl
Ooh, ooh, ooh, I like that girl
Yeah she says that she like you, too
But she's too shy come and talk to you, so
Boy, you have to make that move
If you want her to be yours

Show me a man that will bring me love
Love me for me I'm not asking much
See true love don't come easily
And if it's meant to be, it happens naturally
If you don't look for love, it might actually
Find you

Now tell me what you want, what you need
Cause I be thinking ya'll be bout diamonds and rings
Pretty necklaces nice car, bling bling
I thought ya'll made it clear, love don't' cost a thing
Tell me if I'm wrong or right

I don't want to make the same mistake I made before
She walked out the door cause her love I ignored
I just want to take my time and explore her world
Cause, truth be told, I really like this girl

CHORUS

Now it don't matter the size of your bankroll
Cause I'm an independent women, I can take care of my own
I don't care bout your Escalade or your sprees sitting on chrome
Cause when it comes to a woman, you need a girl that you can take home

CHORUS

You know, mami, you're the best thing
I ever seen come round my way and I
Want you to be down with me like I'm with you, yes, you
Girl you know you drive me crazy, ooh, etc.
You got me saying, ooh, etc.
You got me going, ooh, etc.
You got me singing, ooh, etc.

I'm feeling everything ya'll been talkin' bout
And for her it's time for me to kick the player out
With no doubt it's been running through my mind
Settling down, true love I have found
My world she's forever my sunshine
My pot of gold at the end of the rainbow
See, love is not about the sex or material
But it's mental, heartfelt and spiritual

I like that girl yeah, etc.

I LOVE YOU

Don't be scared
If you really love me
If you really care
If you wanna go there
Baby don't be scared
If you really love me
Just strip down and bear
What's underneath those layers
Behind that smile you wear

CHORUS 1:
Cause you don't have to
    impress my baby
Just a shirt and jeans will do
You've already won me over
Don't try to act like someone else
I love you
I love you

If you really love me
Tell it like it is
Wrap your arms around me
Let me taste your kiss
If you really love me
Love is all you need
You've already got me
Baby can't you see

CHORUS 2:
Cause you don't have to
    impress my baby
Just a simple you will do
Nobody's perfect and it's
    not worth it

Don't try to act like someone else
I love you
I love you

It's not the words you say
It's not the things you do
It's not who you are
It's what in your heart
It's not the car you drive
Or stuff you buy I love you for you
Who you are inside
Don't change
Don't change

CHORUS 1

CHORUS 2

Don't change

I LOVE YOU

Don't keep me waiting
Just pick up your phone
Ring, ring just say hello

Can't say your leaving me
   in the unknown
Let me know
Tell me you love me
   tell me you care
Put me to sleep with a lullaby
Stay with me all night
Hold me tight
Treat me right

CHORUS:
I love, I love, I love you
I trust, I trust, I trust you
My love is burning deep
I got to know are you thinkin'
   of me, baby
I love, I love, I love you (Baby)
I trust, I trust, I trust you (Baby)
My love is burning deep (Tell me)
I got to know

Dreaming about you day and night
Though you aren't here when
   I turn off the light
I'm going crazy when
   your not around
Please don't leave me,
   leave me in doubt

CHORUS

Can't you read my mind
Can't you see the sign
If it's real and it's true
Then you'll know what to do

CHORUS

Tell me you love me
   tell me you care
Put me to sleep with a lullaby

I Miss You

I miss you, etc.
So much

I miss you, etc.
So much

Gotta be strong
Gotta believe
You still belong
Belong to me
When you come back
Back to me
I will be
I will be here

Gotta be strong
Gotta believe
You still belong
Belong to me
When you come back
Back to me
I will be
I will be here
Waiting for you

I (...Still Love You)

Someone's got your hands tied up
You're feeling like you're not enough
Your mind can't seem to make this all make sense, yeah
You walk around with eyes wide shut
Left hand cigarette, right arm slut
You can't seem to find your picket fence
Said there's bound to be a better me
Somewhere inside
A second chance, a faithful man
He's living a lie

CHORUS:
I still love you
No matter where you've been
I still want you
For everything within
Your heart of gold
Your precious soul
My lover and friend, I

A sting of pleasure, band of fame
Luscious treasures, fear of shame
I guess it'd be precise to say you're lost
To ratify or lose your path
Is something that you can't get back
But something you can learn from while you walk

CHORUS

I know you've made a mistake or two
That doesn't change what I feel for you
I pray every day that this will last
I would lose everything, baby you're my better half, I

CHORUS

I TOUCH MYSELF

Turn the lights down low I can't stop the flow
I'm all alone and the mood is right I put the Barry White on
Got 10 little soldiers, can call them GI Joes
Keep a lonely girl satisfied if I can't get you on the phone

I touch myself, etc.

Not a big toy girl, it really doesn't take much
Make up little stories to titillate me when I miss your touch
I'm pretty good at this but it's better with you
But if you're not around, and I wanna get down, what am I to do

I touch myself, etc.

I miss my baby
When I feel the heat
Electricity
It's ringing my bells, bells

I miss my baby
Never there when I need
Someone to play with me
So I do it myself, self

I touch myself, etc.

I WONDER

I was off by a nose, off by a hair
All the things you said didn't
   get me anywhere
All I had was cake when
   you wanted bread
Such simple taste, it's off with
   my head again
Maybe I can't be all the things
   you need

If you can sit in the dirt for just
   a little while
Find the things I hid and buried
   over time
I made a slip, an impasse oh
   me oh my
Pardon my mistakes again
'Cause maybe I can't be everything

CHORUS:
I wonder if I never complain
And promise you that someday
   I will change
If I do everything you say will you
   love me more
I'd give up my dreams to make you
   feel stronger
Never doubting you and
   never wonder
If a good girl should wonder at all
What's behind those doors

The hedges were tall over my head
Running through this maze,
   the devil hasn't got me yet

Shrubs in the garden hiding
   little bugs
Standing in the courtyard, won't you
   please show yourself
'Cause maybe you can't be anything

CHORUS

This grey wall of clay slowly
   washing away
I look up and down spinning
   round and round
These common stones won't hold
   me back no more

I wonder why I never complained
Why it took so long for
   me to escape
I gave my soul to you
Just so you could love me more
I'm still alive and you're
   getting older
Maybe one day you'll wake up
   and wonder
If it's so wrong to wonder at all
What's behind those doors, etc.

IF I CHANGED (...MY WAY)

CHORUS:
If I changed for you would you like me, like me more
If I came to you would it be different than before

Don't wanna let go but you've got to know
    what you're asking of me is impossible
It's up to you if you wanna see this through and take me as I am

Do it, do it, do it my way
Take me as I am
Do it, do it, do it my way

CHORUS

If I did it your way let's just say I would
It wouldn't be me and you'd see me unhappy
So maybe I should stay the way I am and try it my way

Do it, do it, do it my way, etc.

So if I changed for you it wouldn't be good
So I guess I should change you
I'm gonna replace you baby

I can't hate you any longer baby
This mess won't make us stronger no no
I gotta move on with or without you

CHORUS

Do it, do it, do it my way, etc.

IF I WERE A BOY

If I were a boy
Even just for a day
I'd roll out of bed in the morning
And throw on what I wanted and go
Drink beer with the guys
And chase after girls
I'd kick it with who I wanted
And I'd never get confronted for it
'Cause they'd stick up for me

CHORUS:
If I were a boy
I think that I'd understand
How it feels to love a girl
I swear I'd be a better man
I'd listen to her
'Cause I know how it hurts
When you lose the one you wanted
'Cause he's taking you for granted
And everything you had
    got destroyed

If I were a boy
I would turn off my phone
Tell everyone it's broken
So they'd think that I was
    sleeping alone
I'd put myself first
And make the rules as I go
'Cause I know that she'd be faithful
Waiting for me to come home

CHORUS

It's a little too late
For you to come back
Say it's just a mistake
Think I'd forgive you like that
If you thought I would wait for you
You thought wrong

But you're just a boy
You don't understand
How it feels to love a girl
Someday you wish you were
    a better man
You don't listen to her
You don't care how it hurts
Until you lose the one you wanted
'Cause you've taken her for granted
And everything you had
    got destroyed
But you're just a boy

IF I'M CRAZY

I'm a blue flower on a cherry tree
In a white flock I'm a black sheep
Blue jeans, t-shirt, no southern belle
No explanation that binds myself
I'm an uptown girl living downtown
You're a little reserved,
    I'm a little loud
Laugh with me 'cause I stand out
But it doesn't make
    you the in-crowd

CHORUS:
But if I'm crazy, does it
    make you sane
And if I hit the fan, do you feel
    like a man
Am I dangerous, 'cause
    I can't be tamed
If I'm crazy, does it make you sane
If I'm crazy, does it make you sane

Do you feel safe in my insecurities
Are my little mistakes
    the air you breathe
My weakness, your strength
Is that why you insist that I fit into
    your normal scene
But I'm glad there's not a girl
    quite like me

CHORUS

Go and swim against the tide
Unafraid to wonder why
Push the limit cross the line
Live your life as a real dream

Just as crazy as it seems
Got to let you have a star
One that never shined before
No discovering without mistakes
And no envision if you're
    playing it safe
Go and swim against the tide
Push the limit cross the line
Never be afraid to fly
You don't know what you will find
Go and swim against the tide
Push the limit cross the line
Never be afraid to fly
You don't know what you will find
Never be afraid to fly
You don't know what you will find

Should you play a role in society
Never mind about personality
And prefer to like what
    they say is right
Avoid confrontations 'cause
    somebody might just call
    you a weirdo
If you play yourself they'll just let go
Of restrictions, rules, and your
    suits and ties
Well life is a contradiction
    and so am I

CHORUS

CHORUS

IF IT'S WITH A GIRL

You said you always
    wanted someone
With the same appetite as you
But lately you don't have
    time for me
So what am I supposed to do
I know a few sexy neighbor boys
Who'd be glad to entertain me
But every time I want to talk about it
You just go crazy

What about me when I feel lonely
What about me when I get horny
What about me when I need
    some body heat
If you won't get me what I need
Would you be mad at me

CHORUS:
If it's with a girl
If it's with a girl
A little bit of fun never hurt no one
And you won't be competing
If it's with a girl
It's not cheating

If you really want to know
    the truth boy
You still kinda turn me on
But there are other items
    on the menu
I wanna taste them all while
    you're gone
We're living in the 21st century
Don't you want me to be happy

And if you promise you're really
    good boy
Maybe we'll let you join the party

I wanna be good but I'm
    feelin' lonely
I wanna be good but sometimes
    I get horny
I wanna be real good but I need
    some body heat, yeah
If you won't get me what I need
Would you be mad at me

CHORUS

If you haven't tried you might
    wanna give it a shot
See for yourself if it's exciting
    whether people like it or not
'Cause you know we smell good,
    we're sexy and hot
We do it for hours got more
    stamina we never stop
If you haven't tried you might
    wanna give it a shot
See for yourself if it's exciting
    whether people like it or not
'Cause you know we smell good,
    we're sexy and hot
We do it for hours got more
    stamina we never stop

CHORUS

CHORUS

I'm Here To Stay

Don't be scared yeah I know
   you're scared
But you don't have to fear anything
'Cause baby I hear you, I feel you
I know the girl used to
   let you down, let you down
You were hurt when you
   came around
You think that I'm like her, but I'm
   not like her
Now you believe every girl's gonna
   leave you
In a deserted room
But I'm not every girl

CHORUS:
I'll be here for you
When everybody's gone
I'll be here for you
'Cause people come and people go
And break away
We have good days and bad days
But I'm here to stay

I can wait, we can wait, I can
   give you time
Just take it slow 'cause I know
You've been disappointed,
   taken for granted
I've been hurt I've been down
   I've been there before
I got used to someone 'til he started
To use me, finally lose me
You crave and you cry and
   you run and

You finally get up again
But I'm okay now

CHORUS

Yesterday was yesterday
Today will be a better day
And tomorrow's what we
   want it to be
The future's written in the stars
Faith in me is all I ask
I'm everything you see in me

CHORUS

I'm In Love with You

The way you look at me
With that longing in your eyes
Even a blind man could see
Your excuses are just lies
Whenever I'm with you
You give me all the signs
That you want to tell me something
You've been keeping on your mind

I feel it's gonna happen any minute
Saying all the right things
   at the right time
What's taking you so long

CHORUS:
Why can't you simply say
   you love me
Do you know what that can do
'Cause nothing's worse than
   something when it's gone
And it's everything you want
And it's obvious, but you don't
   have a clue
That I'm in love with you
I'm in love with you

You tell me I'm so beautiful
And there's no one you want more
Is there nothing you can say
That I haven't heard before
I'm really getting bored
With your blah-blah attitude
Did I over-underestimate the thing
   between us two

I feel it's gonna happen any minute
Saying all the right things
   at the right time
Don't wait until it's gone

CHORUS

I'm such a mess inside
But I was fine before
All the wishful thinking only makes
   me ask for more
Whenever I back off you make
   believe that you're in love
But you won't let me go
Why won't you let me know

CHORUS

CHORUS

I'm Not a Quitter

Sitting here so frustrated
It's like everybody's hating on me
I don't know what's going on,
  feel I'm losing grip
I'm trying to hold my destiny
  in my hands
But it's slippery and I can't stand
When people don't say what they
  mean, that life is such a trip

PRECHORUS:
I tell myself I'm gonna be okay, that
  all I need is a little faith
Keep your head up, Girl, you're
  on your way
When it gets hard all I say is

CHORUS:
I ain't no quitter, baby (no, no)
No no no no no
I ain't gonna give up easy
No no no no no no
Hate it or love it I won't stop for
  nothing till I'm there
I will keep on fighting
What, you think that I am scared
  (I ain't a quitter)
Say what you want but it won't
  change me (I ain't gon' give up)
I know who I am (I ain't a quitter)
With or without you I'm gonna
  do my thing

Can't hold me down

Nobody said it would be easy
But damn I didn't know it's this
hard
And when it rains it pours, I wonder
why I'm here at all
Oh Lord, tell me what to do (Oh
Lord)
All your dreams are right in front of
you
Yet they feel so far away (so far)
Can't break through that wall

PRECHORUS

CHORUS

Oh, oh, never give up, etc.
Someone trying to hold you down
Can't hold me down, no no

CHORUS

I'M NOT PERFECT

You say you want me back again
You say you thought about it
Tell me you can't live without me
And you were gonna change
Boy do you remember how
You were never satisfied
I was never good enough
It was me you'd always blame
You said I was ugly
You said I was stupid
And I believed you for a moment
But without you I realize

CHORUS:
I'm not perfect, forget it
And I ain't gonna change for you
It took losing me for you to see
This girl is really beautiful
It's too late for apologies
In fact I'm glad you set me free
I'm not perfect, no
But I'm perfectly cool with me

Thanks for all the lonely nights without you
Thanks for making everything all about you
You made my heart bleed,
But you just made me stronger
Now I'm back on my feet
Don't need you any longer

You used to always make me feel
Like I was so unworthy
And saying I look nothing
Like that girl on TV
You looked at me like I was dumb

But now I know that you're the one
Who would have to put me down
So that you could stand your ground
You said I was useless, you said I was worthless
And I believed you for a moment
But without you I realize

CHORUS

But lemme break it down for you
I ain't got no regrets
'Cause a girl like me was as good as it gets
Save the drama for your momma
I ain't coming back manana
Papi keep on dreaming
Keep on feeling
You're the one with insecurities
You ain't gonna put that all on me
All the flowers gifts and cards
Ain't gonna win you back my heart
So quit blowing up my Sidekick
And go back to your model chicks
Hate to break it to you straight

CHORUS

Thanks for all the lonely nights without you
Thanks for making everything all about you
You made my heart bleed,
But you just made me stronger
Now I'm back on my feet
Don't need you any longer

IN ANOTHER LIFE

I have known you my whole life
When you were ten you said you'd make me your wife
And eight years later you won me over
Just as I took the world on my shoulders

I got used to livin' without you
Endless phone calls and dreaming about you
Always said that you were my man to be
But I guess I was in love with your memory

CHORUS:
You know I love you I really do
But I can't fight anymore for you
And I don't know maybe we'll be together again
Sometime
In another life, etc.

I know I said that I would keep my word
I wish that I could save you from the herd
Things will never go back to how we were
I'm sorry I can't be your world

CHORUS

The way you're holding on to me
Makes me feel like I can't breathe
Just let me go, etc.
It just won't feel right inside
God knows I've tried

CHORUS

INEVITABLE

"It's not the right time"
That's what you say, but you're wrong
I'm impatient 'cause I know what I want
I can't wait around 'til you're done
I know she's tall and blonde but I know I'm the one

CHORUS:
You're in love with me, you just don't know it yet
Everyone sees it but you won't admit that you're already in too deep
There's no going back, no
How much longer are you going to hide
Make up your mind or you'll run out of time
I know that she's beautiful but our love's inevitable

You say "don't ask me, about her", that's the rule
It drives me crazy
Just the thought of her under you
Why don't you tell her about me and tell her the truth
It would make things a whole lot easier for me and you

CHORUS

Like the night turns to day, like the storm brings the rain
Oh baby, it's inevitable
It's just a matter of time until you and I will be together

You're in love with me you just don't know it yet
Everyone sees it but you won't admit that you're already in too deep
There's no going back

CHORUS

INEVITABLE

Tell me what ya see
Your eyes follow me
One look at you
That's called chemistry
Can't fool me now
Every time I turn around
You know I'm the kind of girl who
    knows what's goin' down

I know it's obvious what you
    need and I got it
You play your game but I get it
    when I want it
Try to resist it but you know you
    can't stop it
You're just a pawn in my game
    and I run it

CHORUS:
It's inevitable - I'm the kinda
    girl that you like
Irresistible smile in a little while
I'ma cast my spell on you tonight
It's inevitable - I know what
    you wanna do
You don't know what you're
    getting yourself into
Everything I touch is gonna
    turn you on

Show me your claws
Can't hide your flaws
Get your ass off the freezer
Cuz I'ma make it thaw
Don't jump the gun

Cuz you got me here
Everything you want is everything
    you fear (in me)
Boy it's obvious you're intrigued
    come and check it
Gotta keep it on the low,
    we can take it
Any place, any time that you want to
Before it's getting too hot
    for your crew

CHORUS

Everything I say is sexy
Everything I touch is sexy
The taste, the sweat, the
    breath so sexy
Everything I feel is sexy
Everything I do is sexy
The room, the lights the vibe,
    so sexy
Everything I touch is sexy
The taste, the sweat, the
    breath so sexy

CHORUS

CHORUS

Insomnia (Can't Sleep)

I can't sleep most of the time
Try to cancel you from my mind
Never liked you that much anyway
But you try to sleep through till Saturday
Can't seem to keep my eyes shut
Can't start to think about what
You said you said to me when
 I must have lost you again

CHORUS:
Can't make the beat go away
Gotta get me out I can't stay
Gotta feel the rush in my veins
I'm lonely
Gotta look for a party and dance with somebody tonight
'Cause I'm lonely
I feel empty inside cant you make me feel alive
I-N-S-O-M-N-I-A can't sleep, etc.

Don't look at me like that
What you think I'm some kind of manic
Who was asking your opinion anyway
It's my life and you don't have a say
Gotta get, get out of this place
Can't stand to look at your face
I'm gonna get lost in the underground
I'll kill you if you follow me around

CHORUS

Can't sleep, can't sleep, etc.

I-N-S-O-M-N-I-A can't sleep, etc.

INSTIGATOR

Dark mascara on my eyes and I got
My black shirt and my jeans fittin' just right
Val and I gonna kick it tonight like
Dum dum dum - dum dum dum
Leave the house in the car goin' to the club
Slide through the doors give my girl a good luck
Gonna scan the floor to find myself my first stud
Dum dum dum - dum dum dum

CHORUS:
I'm an in- I'm an instigator
Is that your boy? Girl we'll see you later
I'm a tro- I'm a trouble maker
One boy - two boys - three boys - and I...
I'm an in- I'm an instigator
And if he's cute then I'll take the waiter
I'm a bum, I'm a bum bum shaker
One boy - two boys - three boys - and I... etc.

All the girls here seem to have an attitude
But there ain't no stoppin' me - I'm in a party mood
2 AM and the bass still kicks like
Dum dum dum - dum dum dum
My girl Val's hittin' it with the bad boys
And I'm shake - shakin' it with the shy boys
And we won't leave till we've had all the hot boys
Dum dum dum - dum dum dum

CHORUS

RAP

CHORUS

INVINCIBLE

I'm miles away from home
And I begin to hate this phone but
It's the only way that I can get to you
The days turn into weeks
The weeks turn into endless
    months with
Nothing but a promise to hold onto
You and I we've come too far
To let this distance break us apart

CHORUS:
I don't mind the waiting
If you keep believing
And I don't mind the craving
If you swear you won't deceive me
It's so hard when I have to leave
But as long as you're holding
    on to me
We're invincible

Baby, you're worth it

It's like part of me is missing
Thought I couldn't be existing
Without you every day in my life
I'm afraid of getting used to living
In my world without you
Hoping that our love will survive
You and I we've come too far
To let this distance tear us apart

CHORUS

Baby
If we can make it through this time
There will be nothing in my life
That will stand between you and I

'Cause I don't mind the waiting
If we keep believing
And I don't mind the craving
If you swear you won't
    deceive me, oh

CHORUS

Baby, you're worth it, yeah
I think we're worth it
'Cause baby we're worth it, oh yeah

IS IT LOVE

Papa was a rollin' stone but he was smart
Always told me to look out for them chicks who have no heart
Only dealin' with a nigga cuz he got a lotta cars
And the bank account is high

Mama always told me I should never fall for no man
Cuz a nigga's only there to break your heart
They say a bunch of shit to get you outta them draws
Waitin' for you to give it up

PRE-CHORUS:
Now here you are boy, and you ain't what I heard about
Can't help the feeling, won't somebody come and help me out

CHORUS:
Is it love – cuz I don't wanna be in love
But you're the one I'm thinkin' of
So I'll just close my eyes and dance the night away
Is it love – tell me that I'm not in love (I don't wanna be in love)
Ooh, I can't get enough (Go away)
I've been yearning for you're touch
Go, go, go away, etc.
Come closer – look at what you do to me

The only girl I ever trusted hurt me bad
And I never let another in because of that
Told myself it won't ever happen again
That's why I don't believe in love

I had a brother tell me I was his queen
And one day he'd get down on his knees with a ring
And like a fool I believed everything he said
Until I caught him with a bitch in my bed (Damn)

PRE-CHORUS

CHORUS

You got me feelin' a mess
The world is spinnin' so fast
When you touch my hand
Oh, you got me feelin' insane
Is this some type of game
I don't understand
I don't wanna be wrong
But the feeling is strong
And I can't back down
Baby I don't wanna admit
But I can't deny this love I found
Ooh, the way you're touchin' my body
Ooh, I'm feelin like we here alone
And when you back it up on me
I can tell that you want me to take you home
Ooh, when I look in your eyes
I just wanna smile I can't say no
And maybe if we stop resistin'
Love can finally take control

CHORUS

I don't wanna be in love, etc.

Is It Love

If I told you
I'm in love with you
Would you shy away
Would I cry in shame
If I kiss you
Out of the blue
Would it be the beginning of the end
Or the end of the beginning
I don't know what I'm doing
It's all or nothin' now
I've been struggling with myself
I really need to know

CHORUS:
Is it love
Don't want to lose you as a friend
It's getting harder to pretend
Is it love
I can't do this anymore
My heart needs to be sure

Feels like I've known you
Forever and a day
The way you look at me
I'm almost sure you feel
    the same, yeah
Whenever we're together
It's like everyone disappears
We're so drawn to each other,
    oh yeah
It's just us, it's just us, it's
    just us here
We've been in and out of other loves

No one seems good enough
My mind always seems
To lead me back to you, oh yeah

CHORUS

I don't have a choice
I can't fight my inner
    voice any longer
I can't wait another day
It's driving me insane
I got to tell you right now

CHORUS

Is it love
I got to know

IS U IS OR IS U AIN'T

Love is a dance, life is the rhythm
And like woman to man
You're Adam, I am Eve
Put on the music, then choose your shorty
But make sure you don't get stuck with no bad seeds

PRECHORUS:
Before you know it you're entangled
Caught in Charlotte's web
And all you want to know is

CHORUS:
Is u is or is u ain't my baby, etc.

Now, second step is my favorite and best
Put your hip into it, let your body do the rest (your hips)
The hips, give it all you got
It's now or never
But your beauty is like wine
With time it just gets better

PRECHORUS

CHORUS

Oh, you've got to rock your body like a wave
Don't stop, it's working shake it baby
I know you wanna get laid
She wants to know when you get paid
You flash the bling bling
Show her all your ice
So she'll believe you
Jump into your ride
Hope she'll forgive you in the morn'
When she wakes up to mama calling

CHORUS

ISSUES

Nothing, nothing, nothing
It's always nothing when I ask you
    why you're so angry
It's none of you business
I'll tell you when I'm ready
But you'll never be ready
See that drives me crazy
I know there's something
    on your mind
You never want to talk about it
But it hurts me to see you cry
I'm only here to help you
I won't judge you, 'cause we all got

CHORUS:
Issues
You're not alone
Issues
Won't you let me know
Whatever it is it can't be that bad
Issues
We'll figure out a way
Issues
There's got to be something
    we can do
Before the issue becomes you

Happy, happy
You're never happy
Blame your problems on
    everybody else
Hate it if someone knows
    you too well
You make it impossible for
    anyone to help

You're always aggravated
Always have an attitude
Rebel against the enemy that's really
    inside of you
Ain't nobody's perfect and we all
    make our mistakes
You don't have to be ashamed

CHORUS

And no one wants to help
    you anymore
You fight against the world
Not knowing what you're fighting for
Who's gonna love you when you
    don't love yourself
It's all up to you
Only you can make that change

CHORUS

IT AIN'T THE MONEY

CHORUS:
It ain't the money
'Cause money can't buy you love
It ain't the ride
That you took from your dad
   to show off
It ain't the bling, the Tims
   or anything
The boys buy to look fly
'Cause I like them unpretentious
Cute and just a little shy

I see you in school like a fool
Tryin' to look cool with an attitude
Rockin' fake chains and
   the dollar rings
What you tryin' to prove
Thinkin' you're the main man
Who you think you're playin' man
   tryin' to hold my hand
What's gotten into you
You're ain't the same dude I
   used to talk to

I remember when we were friends
We used to kick it with no pretense
But now you're into me
Actin' like a big shot when you
   know you're not

CHORUS

We used to rope skip, skate
   everywhere and it seemed cool
Like ice cream, but you
   changed around

You know I want you back
   tight like that
Like Jill and Jack
But you flip the script when your
   boys called you shit
Tryin' to impress his chick
When all you gotta do is be you

I remember when we were friends
We used to kick it with no pretense
But now you're into me
Actin' like a big shot when you
   know you're not

CHORUS

On a wing and a prayer for all
   the money I don't care
How could I want to be with you
If you yourself ain't true
To who you really are inside
I'll be bidding you farewell
I would hate to say goodbye
If we ain't seein' eye to eye

I remember when we were friends
We used to kick it with no pretense
But now you're into me
Actin' like a big shot when you
   know you're not

CHORUS

CHORUS

IT WAS YOU

Lying sleepless, can't forgive myself
For giving in to temptation
In the darkness when I prayed for help
Everything was spinning in my mind

CHORUS:
I saw a crack in the ceiling
A ray of light came through
I had an overwhelming feeling
Inside I knew it was you
Reaching out to give me faith
Even when I make mistakes
You're the hand that guides me through
It was you

You remind me I should accept myself
Look beyond my imperfections
I keep on trying, in the times I fail
You pick up the broken pieces
Giving me a sign

CHORUS

Your love works in mysterious ways
As the seasons change
I'm growing up every day in your love
When my world fades to gray

CHORUS

It was you

It's Going Down Tonight

Take a shower, dry my toes
Lose the towel, grab my clothes
Spray perfume, paint my lips
Check the mirror, looking fit

Grab my keys, close the gate
Check the clock, ten to eight
Speed through traffic, at your place
Heart is pounding, can't wait

You be the daddy
And I'll be the momma
The neighbors will say
When we make love it sounds like
La-la-la-la-la-la-la-la-la like
It's going down tonight

CHORUS:
C'mon, C'mon, C'mon
I've got what you want
It's on, it's on, it's on
I'll lick you like a chocolate ice cream cone
I know, I know, I know
I know what you like
C'mon, C'mon, C'mon
It's going down tonight

Turn off the news, deal with me
And it feels like a dream
I need to know more of you
Your body tells me what to do

Satin sheets in your room
Isley B's set the mood
Feel your breath on my skin
Touch my legs, we begin

You be the daddy
And I'll be the momma
The neighbors will say
When we make love it sounds like
La-la-la-la-la-la-la-la-la like
It's going down tonight

CHORUS

Let's whisper
Work that spot, etc.

CHORUS

Let's whisper
C'mon, c'mon, c'mon
I've got what you want
Work that spot
It's on, it's on, it's on
I'll lick you like a chocolate ice cream cone
Let's whisper
I know, I know, I know
I know what you like
Work that spot
C'mon, c'mon, c'mon
It's going down tonight, etc.

It's Gonna Be OK

I raid my closet, find
   nothing to wear
My shoes don't match I
   stop to swear
Cause it's that time of the month
When nothing fits
You got to hate it
Just when I thought the worst
   had passed
I got into my car, was out of gas
And I was really mad
But now I'm pissed

I hold my breath and close my eyes
I tell myself just forget it'll be alright

CHORUS:
Just turn the radio up, roll
   the windows down
It's out of your hands it doesn't
   matter now
It will all work out somehow
Life dishes out some crazy things
But in the end it will be ok
I'm gonna be ok
It's just one of those days

I catch him waiting at
   the coffee stand
With what's-her-name they're
   holding hands
And he lets her kiss him
Just like that
Well I bite my tongue and go on by

Thinking darn I'm done with that
   dag gum guy
Why did I waste my time with that
   cheap piece of crap

I hold my breath and close my eyes
I tell myself just forget it'll be alright

CHORUS

It will all work out somehow

CHORUS

JUKE JOINT

Somebody put the juke joint on
Listen to the words of the song
Let me prove what I say is true
That I'm really, really feelin' you
(x2)

Hey, hey, hey shorty
Why you here standing alone
Do you need a little company
Can I help you find your way home

Do you wanna talk to me
I don't need no lines boy
What you got to say to me I'm sure
I've heard a million times before

You got that sparkle in your eyes that a guy just can't miss
Oh, your cinnamon tone, girl, I can't resist

I hear you, baby, listen to this
You got to win all my affection
If you want to sample my kiss

CHORUS:
Somebody put the juke joint on
Listen to the words of the song
Let me prove what I say is true
That I'm really, really feelin' you (I'm sure you do)
Wanna get to know me better
I want to hold you all night long
You can play whatever
Somebody put the juke joint on
Somebody put the juke joint on

Suddenly I find myself, slowly falling
Something about you makes me wanna give your love a try
Come and hang with me, girl
Maybe I could stay here for a while
Closer, baby dance with me
Wanna feel you next to me, I

I put a quarter in the jukebox, the music's not a issue
She really digging your style it's official
And I've been tryin to tell you, man, she want your attention
But ain't tryna hear me now, now she playing hard to get
Your ex-girl friend still be calling your phone
Tell me what's it gonna take for her to realize this
This is love at first sight, kid, open ya eyes
Remember one thing in life true love won't lie

CHORUS

Cosa loca, con sabor
Vamo arriba bilador
Siente el aire esta caliente
Es el juego del amor
De caricias y passion
Este fuego esta ardiente
Sienta la musica

CHORUS

JUNKIE

Mary Magdalene
What did you do with all your dreams
I see you husslin' on the block every night tryin' to get the rock
With all the other fiends
Laughin,' jokin' while you're smokin'
Crumblin,' fallin' when you're cravin's callin'

CHORUS:
First time you tried
What was it like
You told yourself it'd be just for one high
Second time Ray said you'd fly
Third time fourth time fifth time went by
Now you don't give a damn

When they call you a junkie

Mary Magdalene
Life can be so so mean
But if I care for you and you don't care for yourself
You're gonna take advantage of me
So why should I care
Oh ain't it your own mess to clean

CHORUS

So safe in the cradle of your oblivion
Enslaved by the tentacles of your addiction
So far from that little girl and her big dreams
Who never thought she'd grow up to be like this

CHORUS

When they call you a junkie

Just Because You're Beautiful

It's five after eight
You're two hours late
You don't even call, you just let me wait
I'm grinding my teeth
I just can't believe
How stupid I am to let you fool me again
I've made up my mind at least a hundred times
That this time we're done
But then you walk in

CHORUS:
And I forgive you
'Cause your face is beautiful
And I fall for you
'Cause your touch is sensual
You're so emotional
And I hate that I'm in love with you that way
I can't stand that I'm craving you
Just because you're beautiful
Just because you're beautiful

The perfect excuse
I am confused
You just know how to use what you got
To get what you've got to have
I just feel like clay in the palm of your hands
I'm losing myself
But you don't give a damn

CHORUS

I let you get away with getting in my way
When I was just about to say get lost

CHORUS

JUST BREATHE

City lights were flashing by
Rain pounding on the windshield
I was worn by an endless
    working day
As we were passing by that
    moonlit field
By the soft swaying evergreens
I had a flashback staring
    at this place

My mom said Baby what is
    wrong with you
As I suddenly burst out in tears
Remembering when I was fourteen

CHORUS:
Kisses in the playground with
    the cutest boy in the world
And all that I could think of is boy
    I wanna be your girl
Everything was quiet alone
    and in Liverpool
This one precious moment will
    never come again
I can't turn back the time
And here I am chasing dreams
Trying to catch my breath
When all I wanna do
Is just breathe
Just breathe

It'll never be how it used to be
When all there was was you and me
And the sun was beating down
    on my face

I remember the first time
    you said hi
I almost choked I got so shy
All that I could do was smile
And every time I tried to speak
It always was my time to leave
I never got the chance to say
    I love you

CHORUS

All I had was worries on my mind
But from now on I want to
    live every day
Like it's the first day of the rest
    of my life

CHORUS

JUST IMAGINE

The cracks in the street seem to
    follow me wherever I go
They get bigger and bigger always
    threatening to swallow me whole
But I'm getting by always
    one step ahead
Never lettin' go of my dreams
    when I get out of bed

I swam through the rivers
And I made it to the other side
If they say a man can
    move a mountain
Just with his mind

CHORUS:
Imagine what we could do together
Imagine how much it
    could be better
I would hold your hand
We could fight an army of demons
Hey, wouldn't that be cool
Just me and you

Imagine

I been holding out on the front lines
    for too long
Solved a million problems and I
    learned how this girl
    can be strong
But what about the days when I
    can't help feelin' weak
Wouldn't it be sweet having
    someone like you holding me
Whoa

And I walked through
    the wastelands
And came out, came out alive
And if it's true what they say that
    a man can move mountains
Just with his mind

CHORUS

And on the day when the sky
    falls around us
I'll help you hold it up
We'll grow wings and ruffle
    our feathers
Sit it out 'til the rain stops
We make a perfect team
You'll be the captain and I'll
    be the queen
Taming all the stormy seas
Just imagine

I swam through the rivers
And I made it to the other side
If they say a man can
    move a mountain
Just with his mind

CHORUS

Imagine, me and you

KISS ME FOOL

It's in your eyes, it's in your smile
You couldn't hide it if you tried
You can't deny it's all in your mind
And I won't lie to you
I feel it too

CHORUS:
Just close your eyes and
Kiss me, you fool
What are you waiting for
It's just me and you
This moment is yours
You know what to do
Just pull me close to you
You fool

Without words, without a sound
I can still hear you speak
Don't be afraid, there's no doubt
There's something between us to believe in

CHORUS

It's all in your hands
So hold me while you can
Don't let this go
You fool, you fool

What are you waiting for
Kiss me
You know what to do
Just pull me close to you
You fool
Kiss me

KISS MY

I wanna bang my head against the wall
Just to see what it feels like to lose control
It's just the state of mind I'm in
You're just waiting for the minute
That I tell you that you can
Kiss my, you can kiss my

CHORUS:
Run away
Don't run away
You have to be so cold
Are you afraid I might
Hurt your pride
Come on baby, just shut up
And kiss my

Wanna burn your clothes to keep me warm
Tie it to a metal rod in the middle of a storm
Oh you're driving me insane
I wanna hear your sexy voice
Oh baby screaming out my name
Kiss my
You can kiss my

CHORUS

If you just give in to me baby
Stop being such a chicken shit
I'll take good care of you and maybe
I will let you, I will let you

CHORUS

CHORUS

KISSES

I still remember
When I first discovered
The feeling I would get just to
    taste another

Ramon was sweet
But he kiss too sloppy
The way he move his tongue I
    thought he swallow me

Then there was Brian
He acted so mature
But when he kissed he kiss just
    like a little boy

Ronny was sexy
But he had a rougher touch
Had to let him go because he bite
    my lip too much

CHORUS:
Kisses
He's hot, hot
He's not, not
Kisses
He's hot, hot
He's not, not
Baby show me how you kiss

Jay's lips was soft
Just like cotton candy
But I caught him with his eyes open,
    staring at me

Unlike Damien
Who smoked way too much cheeba
His breath was stinking so bad
    I caught a fever

Dante was funny
But I had to cut him loose
He sweat so much I had to kiss him
    in my bathing suit

Nick gave me goosebumps
We could kiss for years
When I touch his lips the world just
    seems to disappear

CHORUS

I like 'em soft
Not too wet
It's how you get me going
Kind of sweet
On the cheek
Baby when you showing
You sensitive but don't get me
    wrong I like it rough
'Cause it's the kiss that's gonna
    wanna make me fall in love
Fall in love

CHORUS

LEFT WAITING

Counting down the seconds
   'til your gone
I'm running out of reasons how
   to make you stay
Don't walk away
I'm trying to be the one
   who understands
I can't pretend to the think that you
   are right, you're wrong
I am torn

CHORUS:
Now I'm left waiting, I fall behind
And something's changing in our
   worlds tonight
And in this place I close my eyes
I never want to leave your sight
It's killing me to say goodbye
Don't let go

I hear your voice playing
   through my head
Think about every word you
   said to me
I can't speak
I can't help feeling insecure
You say it's love but time has got
   me doubting you
Am I losing you

CHORUS

I look in your eyes
You whisper my name
Don't ever let go of me

Don't tell me the time
I know it's too late
I feel your hands
You touch my face
Just keep holding on to me
Save me baby
Please don't walk away

CHORUS

CHORUS

Lemme Feel the Sun

Morning falls I can't open my eyes
Ain't no point looking up at the sky
It's like the sun went on holiday and left me behind

Faces in my face with such misery
It's not my problem still they yell at me
Pull up my hood plug my earphones in
And I leave, I leave

CHORUS:
I imagine the ocean spray
I imagine the clouds give way
I imagine the wind blow these troubles away
Lemme, lemme, lemme, lemme, lemme feel the sun, feel the sun, etc.

On the train, I ride a jubilee
Twenty stops 'til I reach the city
I'm so sick of this system and the same routine

Someone trips, it's me, odd in my ways
Me walk slow, me not know what they haze
I tune out, plug my earphones in, and I escape, escape

CHORUS

Whoa, lemme feel the sun
Lemme, lemme, lemme, lemme, lemme feel the sun, feel the sun, etc.

CHORUS

LET IT RAIN

Shout it out
I can't hold back no more
I let it out
All these feelings that were
    trapped inside
I was frozen there when I looked
    in your eyes

Cleared my head from all the clutter
Things I should have said
It wasn't me, no I can't live like that
I'm waking up and there's no
    one looking back

CHORUS:
Every little tear I'm scared to cry
Every thing I fear that I kept inside
I don't wanna hold it back
    one more day
Oh, wash it away
Every dark thought clouding
    up my head
Every single word that I never said
I refuse to feel ashamed

Clear the sky
Start to breathe again
Nothing too high
Led you through to
I am inside
Every layer 'till you get
    underneath my skin
Let you in, let you in

CHORUS

Let it rain
Let it rain

All the hurt that's been stuck
    inside of me
Make it pour, make it bleed
Let the rain wash me clean

Wash me clean

CHORUS

Let it rain
Let it rain
I don't care
I don't care

LET ME ROCK YOU

I'm the one they call the trendsetter
What I got it won't get much better
My photograph's your screen saver
Heavy rotation on your music player

I'm the real Hannah last
    name Montana
Everybody want to sing it like me
This is my song this is your song
This is our song love it or hate it
Are you ready

CHORUS:
I know you hear me on the radio
You see me on my TV show
On the cover of a magazine
Everybody wants to be like me
Lights, cameras, actions, screams
Tell me who runs the scene
I'm that girl, who's that girl
I'm that girl, who's that girl
Fabulicious girl, on top of the world
Fabulicious, luxurious girl
Let me rock you, rock you, etc.

It's not a party till I get it started
It won't rock unless I'm here
    to run it
When I move everybody's with me
It's cool to get a little crazy

I'm the real Hannah last
    name Montana
Everybody want to sing it like me

This is my song this is your song
This is our song love it or hate it
Are you ready

CHORUS

Sign of the times
You name it, it's already mine
A roller coaster ride
Is nothing compared to a day
    in my life
Irresistible, I'm a natural
I got the world around my fingers

CHORUS

LIFE GOES ON

Look in the mirror in the morning
And an ugly face stares at me
I swear my hips are getting bigger
And oh my god can you believe
One eye is bigger than the other
And my boobs are way too small
Everyone says I look exactly like my mother
And like a duck when I walk

CHORUS:
Life goes on, life goes on, life goes on
Said life goes on, no matter what goes wrong
Life goes on, life goes on

None of my jeans seem to fit me like they used to
And my boyfriend says I'm fat
I try to lose it in the gym, I eat one freakin' thing
And I've gained it back (it shrunk my pants)
I'm spending an hour in the shower
And still I smell myself all day (did I say before I wear men's deodorant?)
All the makeup in the world couldn't cover
All these zits on my face

CHORUS

I'm running around in my towel to make
My morning coffee and I trip and skin my knee
The toaster's burning and the devil's cursing
But my angel she smiles and sings

CHORUS

LIKE 'EM LIKE THAT

Boys, all these boys, any boys
Got nothing but boys on my mind
Asian, Hispanic, Caucasian, and black
So many I just can't decide
They lick their lips, blow me a kiss
Whenever they see me walk by
Some cute, some nice, and sweet sexy bodies
I just can't resist 'em cause I

CHORUS:
I like, I like, I like 'em like that
I like 'em good, but I love 'em bad, etc.

Wow, is it love, I'm in love
When a boy gets that look in his eyes
They never quit coming, they've all got their something
They've all got that je ne sais quoi
Instant attraction, sweet satisfaction
It's almost too easy for me
To get into trouble, cause boys are like bubbles
Their promises don't mean a thing

CHORUS

Give me a man that would give me the world
Though I could never be his girl
But show me a man that has nothing I need
He'll mean the world to me

CHORUS

LIKE THAT BUTTERFLYY

There were times when loneliness
Was the only friend I had
I was sure love was nothing
    but trouble
But I wish I had a little of that
I didn't choose to be alone
But I got used to living on my own
Whenever I tried to go out
It was all about sex and hooking up
I got home frustrated and I hated
That nobody was talking 'bout love
Night after night in my room
Felt unsafe in my cocoon
Frozen

CHORUS:
Just when the caterpillar thought
    that life was over
It woke up and it was a butterfly
Just when I stopped believing you
    came out of nowhere
And with your loving you made
    me come alive
Just like that butterfly

Just like a dream, too good
    to be true
Still I see you when I open my eyes
Forever it seemed till I found
    what I needed
You completed every part of my life
What is a lifetime of waiting
Compared to the memories
    we're making

CHORUS

And if I fly into the flames
If the wall will fall again
It was worth every second
    that we spent
And if your touch will
    break my wings
And I would crash into the ground
Your love is still the greatest thing
    I've found

CHORUS

Just like that butterfly

LISTEN

Every now and then
I get a little turned around
What you say and what you mean
   (It gets a little confusing)
Maybe it's what I wanted to hear
And what you did not say
That got us started on
   the wrong foot today
   (I ain't makin' excuses)

But I wanna tell ya
That I really love ya
I hope it's not too late
I know I should have just

CHORUS:
Just listen
To the words between the lines
To the quiet little signs
Before we almost break your heart
Before somebody's world falls apart
To the rustle in the wind
Before the storm begins
To the voice you hear within
Just listen

Every now and again we start to
   shout at each other
Saying things we sure don't mean
   (But you're words cut so deep)
I might be spoiled and you can be
   a little rough
And things feel worse than
   they really are

And it's killing me

If we trust in each other
And His plan for our lives
And hold onto one another
It'll be alright

CHORUS

If I find my time next time
Before things get out of hand
Think twice before I say a word
I know you'll misunderstand
We could save a lot of time,
   stress and aggravation
Sometimes we gotta just tell
   each other to
Stop, relax and listen, listen, etc.

CHORUS

A LITTLE CRAZINESS

You've had a busy week, I know just how you feel don't let it get you down
Pull out that funky dress from the back of your closet put the music on
Come on and let your hair down, who really cares now it's the weekend

PRE-CHORUS:
A little craziness will do you good
Do whatever it is you wanna do
A little craziness will do you good
Don't worry about it just do you

CHORUS:
Yesterday is history, tomorrow is a mystery
Today is all we got, so we gotta live it up
Yesterday is history, tomorrow is a mystery
Today is all we got, so we gotta live it up

Don't you wait around, come and get on down and ask somebody
To get up and dance, who said you can't dance you know you've got it
Everything goes it's not about who you know and if you're really livin'

PRE-CHORUS

Let the music take control

CHORUS

Live it up, live it up

Don't hold back just let it go now
Let the music take control now, etc.

PRE-CHORUS

CHORUS

Live it up, live it up

LIVE THE LIFE (SHIMMY WITH IT)

You peek at your reflection
You're trying to look your best when
You grab somebody on the floor
And tell them clubs was made for dancing
The music's taking over
You're far from being sober
You're feeling kind of loose right now
It's time to call somebody over

CHORUS:
Hola bonita como estas
Mon cherie je t'aime my belle
I know you want to do it, don't be shy
Kimi kawa ey ee neh
I feel you my pretty thing
It's worth it if you see something you like
Live the life you love
Love the life you live
Do what you want to do right now
Dance like no one's judging
Keep the loving coming
Anything goes right now

You'll get her where you want her
If you do what you're supposed to
Shower her with your cool and she'll want to get to know you
You spent so much at the bar
Tonight just be who you are
If you're feeling kind of wild inside don't be afraid to show it

CHORUS

Let's have fun

LOOKING FOR LOVE

I was just a little girl
One of many who came from broken homes and empty families
Trying to find a way to fill the void
Echo inside a wounded heart so I ran the streets
Here and there searching for a man to love me
Replenish all my heart and self-esteem
But when your eyes start to cry
And you're much too hurt to even realize what is going on

CHORUS:
I was looking for a friend
I got a lover
I was searching for love
I got rejection
Every heartbreak left its scars and traces
I was looking for love in all the wrong places

I gained a name for myself (I gained)
A reputation that I'm ashamed to tell
I tried to disguise
As the promises quickly turned into lies
Days took time passing by
Loneliness became my best friend
I tried to repress all the pain I had from within
I had no answers to my questions
No guidelines for my life
But deep down I knew this can't be right

CHORUS

So many years went by thinking about who I am
And where I want to be in this world, where I stand
But I realize what God gave me
It's not a broken heart, but a room for love and poetry
An inspiration to keep going and believe, oh yeah

CHORUS, etc.

LOVE IS MY DISEASE

CHORUS:
When you're gone it feels like my whole world's gone with you
I thought love would be my cure but now it's my disease
I try to act mature, but I'm a baby when you leave
How can I ever get used to being without you

Don't say you got to break away
That look in your eyes is making me nervous
You slide like silk through my arms
I'm trying hard not to feel helpless
When you first put it on me I was hooked undeniably
But if you take that away from me
I won't know how to breathe

CHORUS

Every time I lose myself in your head
I close my eyes, don't wanna be found ever again
And now you got to leave me here
When I just got so addicted to that sweet feeling

CHORUS

Here's what I'm going through when you're gone
Showin' serious symptoms of withdrawal
Talkin' all night to my stupid pillow
Curlin' in my bed like an armadillo
Waitin' for that call only makes me crave for your voice
But when I get you on the phone I only want you boy
The longer we talk the more I feel incomplete
'Cause I just can't get what I need

CHORUS

LOVED AND LOST

Brother I know it ain't
  your business
(but you just lost another good one
Didn't know what you had till
  she was gone)
She wanted to love you
But like the moon
(you kept her at a safe distance with
  a lot of ache and resistance)
You were super jaded, love's
  overrated, felt suffocated
Too much too soon, but you're
  missing out on what life's about
If you're scared that she'll play
  you for a fool

CHORUS:
It's better to have loved and lost
  than to have never loved at all
'Cause even if she breaks your heart
  it'll be well worth the fall
You tell her to stay if that's
  what you want
Before it's too late, did she
  read you wrong
Life is too short to play it safe
You don't even see the time that
  you waste if you're just in
  it for the chase
It's better to have loved and lost
  than to not have loved at all

You walk you stumble, you fall,
  you run

(You take a chance every
  step you take
You only learn when you
  make mistakes)
You trust and give your heart away
So hold on and stuff will change
(We've all been on both sides
Nobody's wrong, nobody's right)
You were super jaded and so afraid
It gets complicated
So you let it go (yeah baby)
No one said that love wouldn't hurt
And if you don't go there you'll
  never know

CHORUS

Lock up your heart
  (Don't let nobody in)
Got nothing to lose
  (But ain't got nothing to win)
Don't know that much
  (But this world is crazy)
And when somebody loves you
  don't let them get away

CHORUS

Life's too short to play it safe boy
Life's too short to play it safe, etc.
At all, etc.

LUCKY

What If I left one minute sooner
Would everything turn out the same
Change my direction down the street
Would I ever know your name
Destiny might have walked
    right by me
While my head was up in the sky

CHORUS:
Sometimes you get lucky
And you make the right mistake
A little accident of grace
And everything falls into place
Sometimes you get lucky
And the right one comes along
You're defying gravity
And come down on the upside
Sometimes

Was I the one who made
    this happen
Or was it just a smile from God
Was it I wanted you so badly
I'd have found you no matter what
Tonight I could be drowning
    in shallow waters
Instead of rolling up in your arms

CHORUS
Sometimes you get lucky
And you make the right mistake
A little accident of grace
And everything falls into place
Sometimes you get lucky
And you can't believe your eyes

You're defying gravity
And fall down on the upside
Sometimes

Sometimes you get lucky, yeah

CHORUS

(sometimes you make the
    right mistake
and everything falls into place) etc.

LUST

When I look into your eyes

Something about the way you look at me
Keeps me wonderin', could this be my destiny
Maybe take a chance at love again
Claim you as my man, and spend eternity
With you as my king
Sharing every dream,
With love and everything
Hold onto me
Don't ever leave me, now
Keep me in your arms
Don't let go

(They say)

CHORUS:
When you find love
Then hold and treasure it
Don't let it slip away
Could this be love (Could this be real love)
Cause it feels right but I'm afraid it might
Just be lust

Could this be lust or love that I feel for ya
Cause if it's not love tell you now what's up
I don't wanna lead you on but it's too late
My intentions were to love you, let's conversate
On the real I feel lust got the best of me
And I ain't mean to break ya heart, girl, seriously
I'm not sure of this love but I'll stop frontin'
It was a one night stand now we feelin' something
And if love take ova it'll be alright
It'll open up our eyes and give us insight
I wasn't plannin' to raise no family with you

But understand this is real I just met you
Plus we just left the club and you tipsy
You wanna come to my hotel and freak me
When you look into my eyes tell me what you see
You see a playa from the love and you want me

CHORUS

There's an old sayin', "If you can't get the one you love,
   love the one you're with"
But I'm not positive that this will be one hundred percent
I thought that you loved me, you made my heart believe
I believed it, too, but you expect more than I can do
But what about the plans we made, why you gotta be this way
I'm not sayin' I'm not in love with you, but I'm not ready to commit so soon
But it wasn't too soon, to take what you need
Don't drown in fantasies, check reality, I gotta be a man for me

CHORUS

MAKE ME OVER

I stare at this face and I can't find
A sign or a trace of my soul tonight
I try to erase but I can't hide
My past and I laugh at what
    lives inside
I've taken over me
It's getting hard to see
What I will, what I am, what I
    used to be
I always do the things that aren't
    good for me
When I breathe when I see that
    I'm self destructing

CHORUS:
Make me over
Mend and fix me
Make me pretty don't give up
Save and teach me
I promise I'll be nice and easy
Till I'm done now
Make me over
Make me over
Take me over

Don't trust and don't lust for
    these brown eyes
Cause they cheat and they speak
    only sweet lies
I yell and I scream just to get by
I love how you run when
    I sit and cry
Don't think I like to be
    so controlling

I'll change my thing, this personality
But time and time again
I seem to give in to my
    sins to the end
I'm self destructing

CHORUS

Dress me, undress me
I'm messy I'll be your anything
Don't leave me
Believe me
I could be everything

CHORUS

MAKE YOU LOVE ME

Can't walk down the street, can't sit in my room
Can't close my eyes without thinking of you
Can't smell a rose, can't look at the moon
Can't take a breath without missing you
Such a beautiful fate, but it doesn't make sense
Without you, babe

CHORUS:
If I could I would make you love me
If I could I would leave this place
I'm the one who could make you happy
Tried so hard, but I can't walk away

Why can't you be here, why did you leave
Is it my fault you don't love me
Why do I cry, why don't you call
Why does it seem you don't care at all
You don't feel a thing, I don't understand
Why I need you there

CHORUS

Get away etc.

If I could I would make you love me
If I could I'd forget your face
I know I could make you happy
I try so hard, but I can't get away
Get away from you
Don't go away

MAYBE I'M WRONG

Where do I begin
How do I start
To tell you about this crazy feeling
Taking over my heart
I hear it in your voice
I see it in your eyes
It's that something I've been
    searching for
All of my life

CHORUS:
Maybe I am wrong but I got
    this feeling
You could be the one but it's
    too soon to tell
I'm a little shy, damn I wish that I
Could find the words to tell you
    how I feel

Maybe I'm wrong

Maybe you don't care
It's all in my head
Maybe it's better for me
To move on and forget
Better play it safe
So I don't get hurt
Even though everything inside of me
Wants it to work

CHORUS

I was okay till you came along
Invaded my mind now you're all
    that I want

This isn't like me
I thought I was strong but you
    make me weak

Maybe I am wrong but I got
    this feeling
You could be the one but it's
    too soon to tell

CHORUS

But maybe I'm wrong
What if I'm wrong

MAYBE MANIANA

One day
Some day
If you're

Do I wanna? Don't mind if I do
Gonna have a little piece of you
Let you have a little taste of me
Oh oh oh, taste me

I wanna be here 'cause I want to be
Not because you have a leash on me
Boy you don't know what you're
    getting into
Oh oh oh oh

CHORUS:
One day, I'm gonna be your baby
Some day, I'll be your pretty lady
If you're lucky maybe
La la la la la la la
Maybe mañana, etc.
Ah ah ah ah ah, etc.

I can see my future in your eyes
I can sit and talk to you all night
I'm gonna love you for the rest
    of my life
Lies lies lies lies

You gotta flip the game and
    play to win
All my ladies don't you dare give in
You're full of when it comes to love

CHORUS

One day
Some day
If your
Maybe mañana

CHORUS

MAYBE TONIGHT

Shouldn't do this but I'm struggling
With this feeling I can't ignore
I don't want to complicate things
But I can't hold it back no more so we go

CHORUS:
Slow, grind
Feel it, take your time
I'm not hypnotized, hit me there
Breathe in and out
Bodies bare, up and down
What, what's my name
Maybe tonight
Tonight is gonna change your mind
And baby tonight
Tonight I'm gonna change your mind

It feels right but we know it's wrong
Go back to where you belong
I should go home I should leave you alone
But one look at you and we're back doing so

CHORUS

CHORUS

Slow, grind
Feel it, take your time
I'm not hypnotized, hit me there
Breathe in and out
Bodies bare, up and down
What, What's my name

ME AND MY SHADOW

I tried to escape from you for the longest time in my mind
But I can't seem to get away from this place
Cause every time I see your face I break

I know everything, everything I've got to say to you babe
But I give in so easily, yeah you weaken me
It's so frustrating 'cause I know you're not good for me

CHORUS:
Never felt so unloved by someone who said he loves me
So disrespected by the one who's supposed to protect me
My worst enemy, my best friend, I hate myself for letting you in
Wherever I look I see you wherever I go I feel you
But it's just me and my shadow

My friends say I've changed and they don't know me anymore
Say I'm different now and I don't even know myself
Or what's left of me without you

I dropped all I am just to make you happier
It's never good enough
All that time I put you first while you put me last
I can't get away from the demons that you cast

CHORUS, etc.

Meet Me in the Bathroom

Just stepped up in the club for free
About to grab me a booth
Be all up in the VIP
Get some vodka and some orange juice
Lookin' for a man who can grab my hips and shake em' from right to left
Don't give a damn what he look like
    just don't come with that funky ass breath

PRE-CHORUS:
We can get high
We can get low
We can get dro
Just meet me in the bathroom
We can get high
We can get low
We can get dro (ya'll ready to party)

CHORUS:
Cuz if you kick it to me, baby I can kick it to you baby
    we can kick it to each other all night
And if you're hollerin at me baby, I'll holla back at you
    and we can holla to each other all right
Cuz if you checkin for me baby, I've been checkin for you shorty
    we been checkin for each other tee-hee
Cuz if you rub all up on me baby, I'll rub all up on you
    cuz in the end its all about you and me
You got me sayin (oooweeee…)
Boy, you got me feeling (oooweee…)
You got me thinkin (oooweee)

Why the hell everybody in the club watchin everybody else
Don't nobody even dance no more sittin still can be bad for your health
I got me on a tight little dress showin off my little legs and shit
I aint got no titties but I got a big bootie that's it

PRE-CHORUS

CHORUS
You got me dreamin

Strangers become lovers when spirits run free
Let's talk less and grind more when you are with me
You're talking my ear off just shut up don't think
I'll pass on the blah blah just give me another drink

You got me feelin'
You got me thinkin'
You got me dreamin'

CHORUS

CHORUS

(I'll kick it you first, I don't have a problem with that)
(Yeah, you lookin' cute, shit)

MORE THAN YOU WILL EVER KNOW

Every time I see you I wanna talk to you
And tell you how I feel about you
But I just can't get up the nerve and say the words
Every time you walkin' past me after school
Wanna come up to you and let you know the truth
But I just can't even express myself
'Cause I'm so caught up and on you

I ain't even sayin' I got a chance
And I ain't even sayin' it makes sense
But I just can't deny that feeling inside
Every time I hear your voice
And I'm dreaming of you at night
Though I know that it just ain't right
But I can't seem to fight that feeling inside
That someday you'll see

CHORUS:
I love you more than you will ever
More than you will ever
More than you will ever know
I can't explain what I'm trying to say
And you don't even understand
I love you more than you will ever
More than you will ever
More than you will ever know
I wish you could see what I see in you
Every time I see your face

All my friends say I'm trippin'
Cause I'm spending all my time day dreamin' bout you, yeah
But they don't see you the way I do
They think I'm playing myself for you
Cause I've never even talked to you

And you don't even know my name
Boy I'm going insane

I ain't even sayin' I got a chance
And I ain't even sayin' it makes sense
But I just can't deny that feeling inside
Every time I hear your voice
And I'm dreaming of you at night
Though I know that it just ain't right
But I can't seem to fight that feeling inside
That someday you will see

CHORUS

Tic tock time goes through my head
I'm waiting, procrastinating wishing you were here with me baby
I wanna be around you 24/7 you got me open like a 7-11, get that paid
I'm writing our names in the shape of little hearts
Everywhere even on the bottom of my flip flops
Can't you see you got the key to my heart

I ain't even sayin' I got a chance
And I ain't even thinkin' it makes sense
But I just can't deny that feeling inside
Every time I hear your voice
And I'm dreaming of you at night
Though I know that it just ain't right
But I can't seem to fight that feeling inside
That someday you'll see

CHORUS

MOTEL

You don't even know my name
Sexy, but it don't make no difference tonight
You'll be so glad you came
Daddy, I'll make you forget the world outside
No need to hide your stares any longer when I walk by
I know you want it
And I'm gonna give it to you (I know you want this)
Boy, ain't no reason to be shy
Ain't nobody gotta know what we do

CHORUS:
I'll take you to the motel, I promise that I won't tell
It's over when I get you under my spell
Oh yeah, what's up what's up, etc.
I'll take you to the motel, my game is unparalleled
Come see me when your girl don't do you well
Oh yeah, what's up what's up, etc.
If you see what you like and you're feeling my vibe
I can get in your ride, take I-95, we can spend the night
'Cause if you ask around I'm world renowned
Ain't a bitch in town that can put it down
For the ride of mine

Nothing that I wouldn't do with you
I know there's a fantasy on your mind
What you wanna do
Ask no questions, no taboos, trust me
If you've got the cash I've got the time
Something in your eyes tells me you feel this is wrong
And you don't know why wrong feels so right
Rule number one is just don't fall in love
'Cause you gotta know, I'm in love till the night

CHORUS

I'll make you feel like ooh, oh, yeah, etc.

If you see what you like and you're feeling the vibe
I can get in your ride take I-95, we can spend the night
Cause if you ask around I'm world renowned
Ain't a bitch in town that can put it down
For the ride of mine

I'll take you to the motel I promise that I won't tell
It's over when I get you under my spell
Oh yeah, what's up what's up, etc.
I'll take you to the motel my game is unparalleled
Come see me when your girl don't do you well
Oh yeah, what's up what's up, etc.

MOUTH SHUT

I kept my mouth shut from the start
I guess I left you in the dark
You thought you knew me
    but you don't
You say you'll love me but you wont
When you find out who I am

I kept my mouth shut for too long
All this time you got me wrong
Now we're in this way too far
I'm about to break your heart
Tear everything we had apart

CHORUS:
'Cause I'm feeling lost
When I'm in your arms
The reasons are gone
For why I was holding on to you
I tried so hard
To be the one
I don't like who I've become

Won't keep my mouth shut anymore
I've had my share of closing doors
Now I know I'm not afraid
I know exactly what you'll say
But I'm sorry it's too late

CHORUS

(I kept inside of me for
    all this time)
(Thought that I could make it
    work if I tried)

(But I'm sorry to admit that I
    have lived a lie)

CHORUS

I kept my mouth shut for too long
Now I know that it was wrong
I wish I told you from the start
That this was never meant to last
We should've never gone this far
Won't keep my mouth shut anymore

MOVE ON

This is it you know I had enough
I'm tired of you pushin' luck
It's all the stupid things that you do
That makes me so fed up with you (here we go)

Here you go talk, talk, talking again
Need to cut the act out cause its just pretend
What you say is not fair (no that ain't fair)
And if you know me better than you'll realize that I don't care

But when you don't think (I don't care)
You do flawless things I'm just giving you fair warning
About the hurt and pain
I'm fine without caring don't try to scare me
Your words don't mean shit to me so I wont let it get to me, no
But who will be your friend that day when you fall
And when you need someone to talk to who can you call
No I don't need nobody else but me and myself
Don't mean to seem selfish but I can't help it

CHORUS:
What it all boils down to
Through all the hate she still loves you
Wait a minute the bottom line
It doesn't matter who's wrong or right
By the end of the damn day
It's not about what you had to say
She's your sister why can't you make up
Let the past be gone
So you can move on (Move on)

Stop listen up, no I ain't tryin' to hear it now
So why am I wastin time if you being childish
We're just two women conversing so why are you so upset
You're not a women yet (Silly me how could I forget)

So what's the deal with you and your man friend (you wanna know)
When are you going to break it off with him (it's over)
Whatever, go mind your own
I think it's best that I leave you (me) alone

CHORUS

Can't stand the things you say (don't you ever shut up)
Choices that you make
(Why do)
Why do you keep hating on me
Girl you're so clueless, you're foolish you don't understand
Oh you could never be me
When will you understand,
I cant change who I am
You're too damn stubborn to receive hate
So what
That's your problem
Oh well
Can I help you
Please

CHORUS

MR. SMITH

Dear Mr. Smith, how have you been
I hope the life you've chosen
   was worth runnin' from
   your three kids
I ain't bitter, but when I look
   in the mirror
I see you, and I don't like myself

I wished you'd called when my first
   boyfriend broke my heart
Do you care at all, I finished school
   and made it so far
Do you ever wonder how your baby
   girl's all grown up now
And if she's got your smile

CHORUS:
Why didn't you fight for me
Man I was only three
I was still new to this world
Wanting to be Daddy's girl
Wanting you to hold my hand
And teach my brother how
   to be a man
I just need you to show me love

So Mr. Smith do you wanna know
   how I've been
The void you left's been fillin'
Up with strangers unwilling to clean
   up the mess you left behind
And it's the same old shit every time
Every guy I mess with just always
   seems to fail

'Cause of some old issue I got
   with you I keep making
   the same mistakes
If your own Daddy can leave
   you just like that
How can I make the man I love stay

CHORUS

And that I could be valuable
   and beautiful
Should respect myself a little more
Show me how to deal when
   I feel insecure
Even though Mama did the best
   she could
To raise me like two parents would
She couldn't give me what you can

Dear Mr. Smith I hope this letter
   finds you well
And that you'll take to heart what
   I had no chance to tell
I don't wanna hold nothing
   against you
I'm a big girl now
But you let me down

MR. WATTSON

Oh boy I just can't wait for history class
It's my favorite hour of the day
Up on the chalkboard I just love your ass
When you write notes it shake, shake, shakes
So when you get back my pop quiz
What will you think when you read this

CHORUS:
Mr. Wattson I want to get with you
I won't tell a soul what we're gonna do
Wanna get my hands in your khaki pants
Teacher teacher, what you gonna do
'Cause I am coming on to you

I can't put my finger on what's so sexy
And why I want you in my bed or on your desk
Is it your power, your authority
Or for the thrill of being so so bad
Can I please see you after class
There's something that I have to ask

CHORUS

Now you know it's a fantasy of yours
You know it's a fantasy of mine
So why waste time
Let's do this thing tonight

CHORUS

CHORUS

Come and get it

MY BABY

Lights are turned down, way down low
Get on the floor now here we go
Move a little closer, rock my body
Feelin' kinda hot, but don't get naughty

CHORUS:
My, baby's turnin' me on (my baby) etc.
Give me what I want, only what I want
You know what I want, I want it baby
Give me what I want, only what I want
You know what I want, dance with me baby
My, my baby's turnin' me on

Crank the noise up, way up high
I could dance to this all night
Don't stop baby, don't you leave
Cause I can feel you feelin' me

CHORUS

CHORUS

My Company

I just returned from a fantasy
How can I cope with reality
Where's everyone when you need them the most
I'll just sit in the dark give myself a toast

CHORUS:
I always need company
I always need someone to love me
Couldn't you be, be that for me
Couldn't you be, be that for me
My company

I looked at the waves and they drew me in
If I swim for too long can I come back again
Why don't you lay your weary head down
The monsters are asleep you're safe with me now

CHORUS

It's okay if it's not okay
Is this normal? A masquerade
There is nothing you have to say
There are other ways

CHORUS

Couldn't you be, be that for me
My company

MY HEART'S FOR YOU

I called you like a hundred times in the same damn night
Boy you say you care but you're never there
So this is what I do: act a fool for you

I know I'm about 1000 miles from me to you
But I'm working hard just to get us through
So you know you can't be mad at me
I'm the one you need

You already said that yesterday
So I'm sitting here wasting my time away
You've never been this cold before
I don't even know you anymore

Just hold on I'll hold you soon
Don't worry girl I miss you too

I'm worried now you don't love me at all
It's not that hard to call

CHORUS:
Just 'cause I didn't call you
Don't mean that I don't think of you
Just cause I don't have time for you
Don't mean that I don't care for you
Sometimes days get so crazy
That I don't know what to do
But believe me 'cause my heart's for you

Can't you see it's breaking my heart
I try to hold on tight but we're falling apart
I really can't stand being alone
So baby won't you just come home

Baby girl don't you understand
Cause I'm here and you know it
With the ring in your hand

But baby boy it's not the ring that I need
It's you to be here with me

CHORUS

Baby be strong girl don't give up
You gotta hold on to our love
Gotta believe, gotta believe in us
That nothing came between us

Boy I love ya, boy I need ya, boy I want ya
Baby come back home, just come back home, etc.

CHORUS

Baby be strong girl don't give up
You gotta hold on to our love
Gotta believe, Gotta believe in us
That nothing came between us

CHORUS

I'll call you my own

MY REFLECTIONS

I felt the moon smile on us
Your words gave me comfort then
We walked down that empty road
And drew our hearts in the sand
You spoke of how you could
    touch the stars
You said our destinies were
    aligned with Mars

CHORUS:
You gave me wings to fly
You gave me dreams and they
    never came alive
And I wish that they were real
I wish that you were here
I look at my reflection

I turn away from your gaze
Never to see you again
In these ruins of my heart
Shattered pieces is all that remains
I'm afraid to be alone
In this deserted place called home
In the corners of my soul

CHORUS

It took some time for my
    feathers to grow
It took some tears for me to know
It's you I blame forever to never see
    the sky the same
I'm finished mourning you,
    I'm breaking through

My new life I found and I am
    ready to let go

You gave me wings to fly
You gave me dreams but I'm
    leaving you tonight
I've got to make these
    demons disappear
And overcome my fears
I look at my reflection

THE NATURE OF A GIRL

The first time I caught your eyes
   looking at me
I couldn't help but think what
   a stupid girl
Totally over dressed and
   shallow underneath
Flashing fingernails and
   artificial curls
I'd never make a move in
   a thousand years
But you didn't care came
   over anyway
Your piercing voice was ringing
   in my ears
And I couldn't wait for you
   to walk away
You were convinced I'd be into you
And I had to prove you wrong
But the more I tried the more I lose

CHORUS:
First I was mad at you
Now I'm mad about you
Couldn't be with you
Now I can't be without you
All your endings and imperfections
Became the heart of your attraction
Turned everything around
   in my world
Is that the nature of a girl
The nature of a girl

Girly girl talk hand and hand
   on the boardwalk

And watching chick flicks was all
   I thought you did
Silly smiles, butterflies and
   matching cell phones
Shouldn't be a thing that
   guys should dig
You were convinced I'd be into you
And I had to prove you wrong
But the more I tried the more I lose

CHORUS

All the little things you did
That I simply couldn't stand
   about you
Turned into everything
That made me fall in love with you
It's everything you do, etc.

NEIGHBORS

I think it's safe to say
You and me don't get along
If you had it your way
This wouldn't be my home
But I'm not moving
I'm not the type to run
Just keep complaining
I'm still gonna have my fun

PRE-CHORUS:
What you want
Bangin' on my front door
What you want
Didn't I make it clear before
Don't you know
Don't you know I pay rent too
You act as if this place belongs to
you

CHORUS:
If you always thought that my
    music was loud
Then you gonna hate me now
Wake up the neighbors, neighbors
I'll turn up the stereo extra bass
Imma let you feel my 808
Wake up the neighbors,
    yeah, neighbors
Wake 'em up

It's three in the morning
Now look who I've woken up
I'm really sorry
I don't think you've had enough
If it's you screaming

I can't hear a word you say
You've got a problem
Come back another day

PRE-CHORUS

CHORUS

You don't wanna test me
Things could get nasty
I've got the records and
    the speakers
That will shake your pictures
    off the wall
Don't be offended
That you're not invited
You're only hatin' cuz you wanna
    get into my party
But your misery is really
    not gonna go

CHORUS

CHORUS

No No No

No no no no no
I want to but I gotta not let it show

Ouch there you go again
Knock knock knock hello and
    there you are
Running through my mind
I wish I could just change
    the channel
Switch you off and rewind
Would it be a crime if I just
    called you now
To tell you what I feel for you

CHORUS:
No no no no no
I want to but I gotta not let it show
Let you have a blueprint of my heart
I want to but I better not start
Cause if I tell you what I'm feeling
You just might get scared
Better yet take away
I'm never gonna go
And anyways you already know

Ouch how it hurts to pretend
That we're just friends even
    though we are
But the chances are
That we'll never admit what
    we both feel
And there it goes
We will never know
Unless I find a way to say
What I gotta communicate
Can't wait another day

CHORUS

I'm hanging around everyday
    after school
What will it take to break on
    through to you
Baby, can't you make a move

CHORUS

No Strings

It's the first thing on my mind
    when I wake
It's the last thing on my mind when
    night defeats the day
I need it so bad
It makes me feel like a woman
And it's so good
Let me make you feel like a man

CHORUS:
Baby let's have sex
No strings attached
Real good sex
Baby I need to relax
I don't even know you
And I don't care
Cause you've got what I want
And I want all you've got
Baby come on let's do it right here

I need what I need when I need it
I'm just a woman child
I'm not gonna lie about it
I'm untamed and wild
It makes me stronger
I can't help it
Make it last longer
As long as you can take it

CHORUS

And now strip
Strip for me baby
Do it nice and slow
Take off your shirt

Take off your shoes
Take off your belt
Take it off baby
And do what I need you to do

I need to relax
I don't even know you
And I don't care
Cause you've got what I want
And I want what you've got
Baby come on let's do it right here

Let's have…
I need it baby

234

NOBODY LIKE YOUR BODY

Breathless - when I look at you
Sleepless - when I think of you
Pointless - to deny its true
I'm addicted to your touch
Endless - time without you
Flawless - everything about you
Focused - my thoughts revolve
    around you
I'm addicted to your touch

CHORUS:
Ain't nobody like your body
Got us talkin' body language
Got me feelin' kinda naughty
Don't like it but I do, can't stay
    away from you
Ain't nobody like your body
Ah, ah, ah, am I dreamin'
Got me feelin' kinda naughty
Follow me, follow me, etc.
I got the secret, you got the key
Follow me, follow me, etc.
If you can keep it, then you got me

Three seconds is all it took
Three seconds you had me hooked
Three words I wanna hear
I'm addicted to your touch

Two hearts
It won't be long before
Two hearts beat as one
One look

It won't take much cuz
I'm addicted to your touch

CHORUS

I got the secret, you got the key
If you can keep it, then you
    got me, etc.

CHORUS

NOT AN INNOCENT GIRL

I can see what you perceived
Don't be too quick to assume
That I'm clueless and subdued
'Cause I don't play by the rules
Yes I've had my share of naughty
Now I'm not squeaky clean
I'm nothing like what you thought
If you know what I mean

CHORUS:
You're looking for a centerfold,
    looking for a saint
You can see a sweetheart,
    humble and afraid
You're looking at the oyster,
    what about the pearl
I am not an innocent, I am
    not an innocent
Girl (Go on) girl (Go on)
(Go on, keep on looking), etc.

Don't judge by the surface
There's much more to be found
Sometimes all the treasure's hidden
Underneath the ground
You may take advantage 'cause
    you think I'm naïve
When I sting you, you'll be running
Shuttin' down your beliefs

CHORUS

You don't know one thing about me
I'm innocent until proven guilty
Now take a little time and get ready

'Cause I will have you calling
    for your mommy
Let me shake it up, let me
    cause a stir
Maybe, I'm gonna show you
    all my dirt
You better stop now I'll make
    you check twice
I can be naughty but not so nice
You gotta take a peek into my world
To understand that I am not at all
    like what you heard
I get up to mischief
Watch what you say to me
'Cause I might be tricky
And I'm very sneaky

You better be concerned, oh
I am not an innocent
Girl, etc.
Hey
Go on, etc.
Keep on looking, etc.

CHORUS, etc.

OH WHAT A WOMAN

CHORUS:
Whoa, there she goes
Look at her
Oh what a woman
She's beautiful, magical
Got it all
Oh what a woman

She's the single reason why man falls in love
Simply irresistible, she's second to none
A picture of perfection from her head down to her feet
She's the one that every girl would love to be

Whoa, there she goes
Look at her
Oh what a woman

Guys want to spell out her name
She's got beauty and brains
And a heart of gold
Like an eclipse of the sun
If you stare too long
You'll go blind, don't you know

She's sophisticated
She's celebrated
She's underrated
Love it or hate it

CHORUS

She's the single reason why man falls in love
Simply irresistible, she's second to none
A picture of perfection from her head down to her feet
She's the one that every girl would love to be

Whoa, there she goes
Look at her
Oh what a woman

It's like she fell from the stars
Somewhere from Venus or Mars
She's one of a kind
And she's got marvelous curves
She shines like diamonds and pearls
The boys wait in line

She's sophisticated
She's celebrated
She's underrated
Love it or hate it

CHORUS

She's the single reason why man falls in love
Simply irresistible, she's second to none
A picture of perfection from her head down to her feet
She's the one that every girl would love to be

She's the definition of grace
There's just something about that look on her face

CHORUS

She's the single reason why man falls in love
Simply irresistible, she's second to none
A picture of perfection from her head down to her feet
She's the one that every girl would love to be

Whoa, there she goes
Look at her
Oh what a woman

THE ONE

I can be the one…

Boy I'm so into you
It's just the way you do that
    thing you do
I'm feeling you
It's an emotion running deeper than
    I ever knew
How you make me feel so good
I try to play it cool
Start acting stupid when
    you know me
You should get a clue
It's like my heart is taking over
Can't deny it's true
Though I don't want to feel this way
I got a crush on you
When you come up on the scenes
Start putting your moves on me
You know that you're making me
    wanna be bad
I wish I could say what I mean
I'm s-s-s-stuttering

CHORUS:
I can be anything you want
I'll give you everything
I'm not trying to bribe
Will you be good to me
When the time has come
'Cause I can be the one

You been holding back so long
So many ways I've been imagining
    you might respond

Cannot restrain myself whenever
    you are coming on to me
It feels so good
It's like this all the time
The different things that I would
    do to you
If you were mine
Thoughts of crazy sex and dough be
Going through my mind
I'm a good girl but not this time
I can't understand the part that
    you're giving me
Baby it's killing me
Why can't you see I want you bad
Got to have you baby

CHORUS

ONE STEP BACK

CHORUS:
Oh oh, etc.
One step forward
Oh oh, etc.
Two steps back

One step forward, two steps back
Girl how can you get with that
He only calls when he's got it bad
I can't believe you believe all
    the lies and deceit
And everybody knows cause it's
    out there in the street

One step forward, two steps back
Don't you get it sister, what's next
You'll wake up when there's
    nothing left
Girl how low will you go
    'til you know
That you'll never hold a man when
    he's already over you

CHORUS

One step forward, two steps back
You got to move on up out
    of this mess
If you really think about it, girl
    you're blessed
Cause if you see the good in the bad
You'll figure out what you
    had wasn't worth one
    single tear you shed

Like you call him 95 times a day
You still believe it should be you
    in her place
Every week you drive by his new
    girlfriend's house
Making a scene like that's gonna
    turn things around
If you try to solve the problem by
    ignoring the facts
Every step forward you take will
    just put you two steps back

CHORUS

One step forward, two steps back
Sorry I got all upset
It's only cause I still got your back
Girl it hurts me to see how he
    treats you so mean
You got to leave him
Cause you deserve better than that

THE ONE THAT GOT AWAY

I saw him at the corner store
He gave me candy
I came back for more
Asked him for his name
He said, "Call me Jesse James"

He was 6'2", lots of style
Had the recipe to make me smile but he got
Too popular with the girls
So I erased him from my world

The next boy was cute and shy
But he never really looked me in the eye
Secretive, I was intrigued
He was sweet
His name was Pete
Sweet Pete

The first time that he took me out
He didn't know what to talk about
So I took the initiative and told Pete he had to leave

CHORUS:
So I'm back to square one with Mr. Good-For-Nothing John
Ever since he brought me down
I can't get off the ground
It's not like I don't try
And I'm pretty easy on the eye
But the one I really crave
Is the one that got away
With each boy it gets worse
I'm still stuck on the first
I really hate to say
I want the one that got away

He's the star of the football team
Could be found in every girl's dream
We'd been talking for a while
You could say that he's on trial

But whenever we're alone
He jolts like a gramophone, 'cause
When he goes off with it
With him goes his appeal

CHORUS

Here she goes again
With another boy on her hand
What goes around comes fast in this small town

All these rumors that gotta start
I just want someone to give my heart
No love with James being on the football squad
None of 'em can compare
None of 'em can compare
To my John

It's not like I don't try
And I'm pretty easy on the eye
But the one I really crave
Is the one that got away
With each boy it gets worse
I'm still stuck on the first
I really hate to say
I want the one that got away

I want the one that got away

OPEN YOUR EYES

I try to get through to you
But you're not there
I try to open your mind
But you don't care
I wish that you could see the other side
Why are you so blind

CHORUS:
Open your eyes
Open your eyes
Don't judge me by the outside
If you don't even know the inside
Open your eyes

You turn your head away when I get too close
You try to shut me out and fit me in your mold
I wish it could be you on the other side
Why are you so blind

CHORUS

CHORUS

PAPA DON'T NEED TO KNOW

How bad, how bad do you want me
Sitting on the stoop drinking 22's
Trying to hold back but I
    feel the booze
Arms crawling up and down
    my body
It's gonna be a problem
'Cause you're so sweet like candy
And oh, how you stare at me
Anyway you know my body
You're gonna be a problem
I know you really wanna turn me on
And you wanna get to know,
    just meet alone
I say you got your feelings and
    that's kinda hot
But you better slow your role before
    you get caught up

CHORUS:
I can't take you home to papa
'Cause papa, he don't play, oh no
He'd go get his gun if he ever
    knew what we do
But papa don't need to know
How bad, how bad do you want me
Take you home
Etc.

We're at the movies in the back row
You've got me feeling high with
    the lights turned low
Only you know where my
    hands is at

But you can't make a noise if
    you're feeling that
It's like we're in here alone
The way your body feel, ooh,
    it got me in a zone
Don't know what you're doing to me
Got me out here in public
    feeling nasty
You said you really got plans for me
More than just the sex you wanna
    care for me
And that you really are a nice guy
And that you don't know why you
    can't come inside

CHORUS, etc.

PAPER PLANES

Eight years old
And pretty I was told
I wanted to know
Everything there was to know
About boys

I was confused
But I had a wild imagination
And I thought

CHORUS:
If I write a letter every day
And fold it into a paper plane
Open the window, look outside
And let it fly
Just let the wind take it away
From my hand
I'll see where my heart lands

Years went by
And I thought I wouldn't survive
When my first crush said goodbye
Locked away
My secrets and wishes in a book
Thought no one understood

CHORUS

And tore out the pages everyday
I turned them into paper planes
Looked out the window,
    watched them fly
Just let the wind take it away
From my hand
And see where my heart lands

I've taken needle and thread
Stitched up my heart time
    and time again
But I have angel wings
They're magical things
And I still believe
I will find you

CHORUS

So I write a letter every day
And fold it into a paper plane
Open the window, look outside
And let it fly
Just let the wind take it away
From my hand (watched it fly)
I'll see where my heart lands, etc.

PERCULATOR

Had to bribe the bouncer to get in tonight
He was makin' a scene, I'm not a V.I.P. I'm not on the guest list
Had a really rough week workin' 9 to 5
Tryin' to please everyone but me but now they can kiss my

PRE-CHORUS:
When I get on the dance floor
Do what I came for
I let the music take control of me
And when I get my moves on
Get in the groove zone
Then there's no stoppin' me

CHORUS:
I'm a perculator
Imma work this place up
All my girls ya'll ready
I'm a perculator
Imma stir this place up
All my boys ya'll ready

I'm like a slave to the bass drum
It's in my veins and it's in my brain now it's running my system
I'm taking the lead, and I'm turning this space around
Blame the beat takin' over my feet and I ain't done until the night is done

PRE-CHORUS

CHORUS

PRE-CHORUS

CHORUS

PLAIN OL' LOVE

Now you should be here with me
And where you're at puzzles me
And I'm sittin' home all aggravated
That's just plain ol' love
And you don't say where
    you've been
You just walk right on in
And I'm supposed to act like
    nothing is wrong
But I'm still mad just because

I should let you go
But I can't say no 'cause I
    love you so
Much more than you know
And sometimes it makes me cry
Hurts deep inside
But still I wanna stay right
    here 'cause

CHORUS:
When it's good it's so good
When it's bad it's real bad
And what used to make us happy
    now makes us crazy
But that's just plain ol' love baby
When it's there it's all there
When it's gone it's all gone
'Cause what used to make us happy
    now makes us crazy
Now that's just plain ol' love baby

Had our dinner by candlelight
'Cause you tried to make it right
But I wanna fuss and fight

Baby that's just plain old love
How we went to bed on it
'Til you turned and rubbed my back
Made love to me 'til I had to give up
Now that's just damn good love

I should let you go but I can't say
    no 'cause I love you so
Much more than you know
And sometimes it makes me cry
Hurts deep inside
But still I wanna stay right
    here 'cause

CHORUS

CHORUS

PLAY IT SAFE

People try to tell me
What they think that I should do
Oh but I'm not listening
To the voices, I refuse
Losing my direction
Wearing someone else's shoes
What's the satisfaction
If everything has to be approved

Always gotta be spontaneous
Never wanna stop bein' curious
I don't ever wanna do
    what's obvious
No there ain't

CHORUS:
No limit to my loving
Living every day like it's my last
I don't want to go on wasting time
Living in the past
Rules are made for breaking
Get out of the box and have
    some fun
Don't let nobody tell me
    how it's done
What it comes down to is this
Life is made for living
I cannot imagine
Letting another day go by
Let my dream slip away
As long as I'm breathing
I won't stop believing
That I've gotta make my
    own mistakes
I will not play it safe

I can't tame my spirit
I like it just the way it is
Living to the fullest
Sometimes you gotta take a risk

Always gotta be spontaneous
Never wanna stop bein' curious
I don't ever wanna do
    what's obvious
No there ain't

CHORUS

Sin limites
Si me fascina
Vivir cada dia como si fuera
    mi ultimo
Las reglas estan hechas
Para poder romperse
Salir de lo normal y gozar
La vida esta hecha para vivir

CHORUS

POP THE CHERRY

I was just fifteen, a woman, child, a tender thing
My only care was kissin' boys and rockin' tight designer jeans
And I liked a guy that had an older brother Todd
Who told him what he should do when he'd have a girl up in his house

This boy I dug so much told me that I would feel a rush
I did not know what I should think 'cause I had never felt a touch
From the body part that only boys know all about
I was so scared that he would sit there, smile and just whip it out

CHORUS:
Look at the girl just acting grown
She got him all in the zone
He just can't wait to get her alone
And pop the cherry, pop the cherry
Look at that boy lookin' like a man
Feelin' all on her can
She just can't tell it's in his plans
To pop the cherry, pop the cherry
Pop the cherry, pop the cherry, etc.

First he told me to get on the bed and just relax
He started to get close to see exactly how I would react
And I couldn't disappoint him I had come too far
To say no now would be like teasin' a baby with a cookie jar

My skirt was up so far I felt his hands they were so soft
My mind was racin' kinda like it never had before thus far
No time to think right now, I'm feelin' something overwhelming
My body it's excited but it's too much for this little girl

CHORUS

CHORUS

POPULAR

I hate to say it but they play this
damn song in every club
But it's me so I'll show love
But it's me so show me love
When I walk into the room people
    stop and stare
It's like nobody else is there
You know it's me not you
Who said anything about you

CHORUS:
Boys and girls pretend to know me
    they try so hard
And I get what I want my name is
    my credit card
Don't try to hate me because I
    am so popular
Pop, pop, popular (etc.)

Most guys I dated got intimidated
So now I date up
If you know what it means so they
    shut up
If you know what it means so just
    shut up 'cause I don't wanna
    give half away
On the day we don't make out
If you know what I mean when we
    wake up
If you know what I mean when we
    break up

CHORUS

You always wanna be 'round me
So you know what it's like
When the world is at your feet
And you're VIP tonight
You've either got it or you don't
And I'm sorry you won't
Get there by using me
Just go on do your own thing

CHORUS

CHORUS

PORN

Is that your boyfriend
I think I know his face
He's kind of handsome
Don't you guys live around my place
My name is Lola
I work at the video store
Around your corner
Yeah I definitely seen this guy before
Why don't you ask him what he was
    doing last night
I wonder what he's gonna tell you
'Cause he told me to be quiet…

CHORUS:
'Cause every guy is into porn and if
    he's not then he's a liar
And if you make him feel it's wrong
    he's gonna do it in the quiet
You know it's natural so why don't
    you just try it out together
Don't get me wrong, don't
    shoot the messenger
I'm just a girl that's on your side,
    but your man's got
    something to hide

Now you're disgusted
Hello! Welcome to the real world
Think your baby's busted
Well maybe it's just you that
    got burned
Nobody's perfect
You only see what you wanna see
So he keeps it secret

But don't you go blaming it
    all on me
And don't you wonder what he does
    every other night
And why he didn't tell you?
But he told me to be quiet

CHORUS

I've seen literally every guy
    on the street
You'd never think I'd catch my
    roommate's grandma in the store
I bet you didn't know she's
    into hardcore
Everybody's got that little
    dirty fantasy
The teacher from your second
    grade, the preacher man
    for heaven's sake
And even you and me

CHORUS

Yeah man I've seen every guy in
    our neighborhood
I know what they all like, it's not
    too pretty

PRINCESS IN DISGUISE

Like a perfect ten in a magazine
Were the girls that caught my eyes
Sophisticated queen with the
    sex appeal
Beauty no less than a dime
But the girl that really caught
    my heart
Wasn't anything like that
At first glance you wouldn't see it
But she was really bad

Papasito, ven conmigo
Dejame demostrar a ti
Que tu no puedes ver
La mujer (marya-dentro) de mi

CHORUS:
She's just an average girl
Ain't got no mink and pearls
Still she's like royalty
She's a princess in disguise
She's got a heart of gold
Within a tale untold
That's where her beauty lies
She's a princess in disguise

Her smile is like a twinkle in the sky
A diamond in the rough with the
    heart of a child
Her true beauty is more then
    skin deep
Because the essence of a woman is
    hidden underneath

CHORUS

Tomame al castillo que estan en
    los nubes
Hasme princesa de tu corazon,
    mi serviente de amor
Desde alli, viajar a otros lugares
Para vivir momentos inolvidables

You stole my heart and sealed it
    with a kiss
No matter where I look, it get
    no better than this
My princess, my goddess, you came
    from up above
I'll treat you like royalty, with
    all my love
Your heart is pure, together
    we explore
We build on honesty, one solid core
You caught my eye, I can't deny
You're in my heart, you
    are my pride

CHORUS

CHORUS

PROVE ME WRONG

Am I overanalyzing you
Am I digging too deep
Are my expectations of this
   relationship out of reach
You see a match made in heaven
I see a dark cloud above your head
And it won't take a lot now
For you to push me over the edge
Yes I do feel love for you
But I know how love can feel
I'm unsure what this will be
You say feelings need to grow
I should try to give us a chance
But I see the beginning of the end

CHORUS:
Prove me wrong
Baby, I'm falling
Reaching for something worth
   holding on to
Prove me wrong
I am afraid this is not where
   I belong
Baby please prove me wrong

Wish I could close my eyes
To the merciless truth
Let go of every doubt I ever had
And surrender to you
Is it just physical
Is that all we share
And is loving somebody with only
   half a heart really fair
And I don't wanna make a promise

A promise I can't keep
And deprive you from the one
   you really need
Baby someone who would miss you
Every time you leave
And I fear it might not be me

CHORUS

Maybe I should be a little more
   patient with you
And not jump to conclusions every
   time I'm unsure
'Cause sometimes there is magic
And I get lost in your eyes
That's when my heart cries
Cries out for you

CHORUS

Pucker Up

Momma said, "Love yourself the way
    that you are
If you're well-behaved and classy it
    will take you far"
But somehow I was born with a
    mind of my own

PRE-CHORUS:
Denim on denim with polka-dots
    mixed with stripes
Army boots and leather shoes, neon
    signs, leopard print tights
What's the fad? Checkered? Plaid? I
    don't care – who really knows
'Cause anything, anything, anything,
    anything goes

CHORUS:
I'm just a girl with the really
    big dreams
Always trying hard to be me
My hairs all messed up, on my nails
Jingles, jangles, rings and things
I'm a really, really good tease
I'll be a prom dress, I know
    what I want
So you better pucker up,
    pucker up, etc.

I'm a brat yes I know
But I got sugar lips
Sour sweet vixen queen
Come on baby give me a kiss
Super rad, a little bad

I'm the one who rocks the boat
'Cause anything, anything, anything,
    anything goes

CHORUS:
I'm just a girl with the really
    big dreams
Always trying hard to be me
I've got highs I've got lows
From my head to my toes
Yeah you get what you see
I'll be a prom dress, I know
    what I want
So you better pucker up,
    pucker up, etc.

PRE-CHORUS

CHORUS

Give me a kiss
Pucker up, baby

PURE

Naked cowboy in a snowstorm
  posing for a buck
A homeless person faking
  a broken leg
Only the tourists give a fuck
Ninety-foot billboard says you won't
  get laid without a push-up bra
I push my way through the crowd
Trying to make it home before dark
There's a message on my phone
You say you want to spend the night
But before I let you into my life
It's gotta be, etc.

CHORUS:
Hot as the sunshine
Clear as a mountain spring
Deep as the deep blue waters
True as the voice within
And if you ask me if I'll be with you
Tomorrow baby I'm not sure
Only if your heart is pure

Everything is disposable and if it's
  old it gets replaced
Plastic toys, plastic hearts beating
  behind plastic breasts
I wanna feel the pulse in your veins
Hold onto something real, cry
  tears of joy
And when I'm in pain I'm not
  afraid to bleed
Show me a perfect imperfection
You don't have to play it cool

And I'll show mine to you
It's got to be

CHORUS

We don't have time for
  time anymore
What makes you think you'll have
  time for me
It takes more than a night of
  beautiful sex
For you to make me believe
That you're really sure
And what you're gonna give is pure
It's gotta be

CHORUS, etc.
Sure, etc.
Only if your heart is pure, etc.

QUARTER PAST FOREVER

Hush, don't say a thing
Sweetheart, just listen to me
Close your eyes and I'll meet you in your dreams tonight
'Cause I know you're missing me
And it's obvious to see
That we can't get enough of the happiness we bring each other

CHORUS:
I'll meet you there a quarter past forever
I know a little place where we can finally be together
Just close your eyes and I'll be with you tonight
Etc.

And I promise I'll be there
Once I figure out what to wear
And I'll meet you outside
And then I'll hear you say "Baby, you look so fine"
We'll take a walk around the city
We know those lights can be so pretty
I just want this night to be
A time to forget all our worries

CHORUS

Hush, don't say a thing
Sweetheart, just listen to me
Close your eyes and I'll meet you in your dreams

CHORUS

QUE SERA

I get the bed you get the couch here's your keys
Let's forget we ever met don't you worry bout me
So sick to my stomach when I think about the wasted time we spent together
Planning on forever, oh whatever
Cheat me once shame on you, cheat me twice shame on me
I'm an idiot that I couldn't see what's underneath that beautiful face
Thought these were my worst days but surprise, surprise I'm doing just fine

CHORUS:
Oh, que sera, sera, etc.
Whatever comes I'll be okay
Whatever life throws my way
You wish I'd hurt but I'm free as a bird
I'm happier now
Que sera

PRECHORUS:
I could never go back to a thing that didn't last
And I'm sorry to say that you're living in the past
If you really believe I would kiss your sorry ass
Took you long to get in but now you're out so fast
The way you played your cards should have told me who you are
Always going all in and then you hated when I'd win
This time you went too far I should have known from the start
That you'd gamble with my heart

CHORUS

I feel it in the air
There's something better out there
Hello to the new me
So goodbye baby

PRECHORUS

CHORUS

Rainbow

We were so close, like two swords in one heart
But you're giving me this feeling that we're drifting apart
You don't come to me like you use to, and I don't cry on your shoulder
I'm trying to understand this before darkness takes over

PRE-CHORUS:
Did we lose touch cause I didn't show you love
Did I say too much, or didn't I say enough
Did I let you down last time you came around
I hate to see you pull away

CHORUS:
It's like our rainbow's fading to black and white
And I just don't know why we have to fight
Do we have a problem, can we resolve it,
Is it something that we gotta talk about, can we figure it out
Cause if we can't work it out, make it right our rainbow's gonna turn to
black and white

The distance between us is growing everyday
Filling up with words we had no chance to say
What we had was like magic, we always thought the same thing
I'm afraid we might lose that
The colors are always changing

PRE-CHORUS

CHORUS

Our rainbow
The shades have turned to black and white
Every color disappears when you're not here
Our rainbow turns to black and white
Can we resolve it, we gotta get over it
Can we resolve it, we gotta get over it

(spoken)
I just wish we could be back the way we were before – as friends
I mean right now, it just seems like something's wrong

No more fights, no more arguments
I wanna be best friends

(spoken)
It just doesn't make sense, I mean I know how it can be
Wrong at times, but I just wish it wouldn't come to this

Can we get over this
We got to get over it

RECIPROCITY

If you only knew, if you knew
   the truth
How I really feel about me and you
You've been on my mind for
   the longest time
Got me so confused got to
   talk to you

There are days I feel I'm
   your everything
You put the colors in my world and
   I spread my wings
But then there are those days you
   won't even return my calls
And I get so unsure if you care at all

CHORUS:
So I ask you now
Do you feel the same way
Do you see a future in my eyes
Or is this just foreplay
So I ask you now
Is it really mutual, is it
   just chemistry
Is it meant to be or is it really
   like they say (I give give,
     you take take, etc.)
Reciprocity

Feels like we've been we've been
   here before
And I can't pretend I don't want
   you anymore

See I fell for you and I hurt myself
Now I've got to protect this little girl
   that still believes in love

CHORUS

You give me your words but talk
   is cheap
You give me your body but ain't
   what I need
You know I'll do anything to
   be with you
But I'm not so sure
If you would do that for me too

So I ask you now
Do you see a future in my eyes
When you see me baby

CHORUS

RED FLAGS

I never thought that this could
   happen to me
He was everything I wanted
We seemed perfectly happy
One day I woke up, he was gone
Just like an unsolved mystery
Still don't know what went wrong
I found you on his MySpace
Right where I used to see my face
You looked so wide-eyed and
   cute there
It was my everyday nightmare

CHORUS:
Maybe I should try to save you
   from the misery
Tell you about his history but I'm
   not that nice
Maybe I should put the red flags up
Try to warn you about your love
But I'd love to see you cry
When you go down this show is
   getting too good
Can't stop it now and if I told
   you the truth
I'd be a fool

Somebody pass me the popcorn
I feel so entertained
Its like you're the sequel to my
   previous reality
He wasn't even the best
I got in over my head
I can't believe he picked
   you over me

What makes you think he's
   gonna last
How quick a minute can go past
Watch out cause when he goes
He'll go really fast
Once he turns and sees
   a better piece of

CHORUS

Some guys aren't really meant to
   be dated
Some shows are simply overrated
Such promising previews and
   so little content
So little content, etc.

CHORUS

RED LOLLIPOP

It all feels so surreal, baby
When we were all alone
Almost died the very first time
That I heard you on the phone
Funny feelings in my stomach
When it comes I cannot breathe
You got me feelin' like a different
   kind of girl cuz this ain't me

CHORUS:
Somethin' about you
Is crazy, you're the (Shh)
Somethin' about you
I don't know what it is
Turn me on, turn me on, etc.
You're the one, you're the one, etc.
You're like a red lollipop, etc.
Like a lolli- lolli- lolli- lollipop,
   pop, pop

Life with you is so beautiful
No matter what we do
Could be twisted, high,
   or sober, man
I'm always feelin' you
Your flavor when it's spicy
When it's sweet, it's always right
I'm ready to dig into you
Please let me have a bite

CHORUS

To all my ladies
Who recognize a good brother

When he's standin' right in
   front of ya
Fellas
Holdin' it down for your girl
Cuz you know she is down for ya
Playas
Who neva know what they're missin'
Cuz they never follow through

Cuz I'll never know true joy
The kinda love that I'm gettin'
   with you, boy
Cuz I'll never know true joy
The kinda love that I'm gettin'
   with you, boy

CHORUS

You're like a red lollipop, etc.

Cuz I'll never know true joy
The kinda love that I'm getting'
   with you, boy

Rescue Me

I get this feeling like this place is closing in on me
Sleazy guys, cheesy minds trying to flirt with me
Moving closer, rubbing up against my silky skin
I can't breathe

CHORUS:
Come rescue me
Take me away from this crazy place
Come dance with me
Let's have some fun just one on one
After hours when they close
Take me for a ride
I can feel it, something special's in the air tonight
If you're a really good boy, show me you can wait
Then maybe later we can play

Maybe later we can play, play

I think I like you, haven't felt this way in quite a while
I put the ass into class and I feel your style
The floor is packed and all the guys are dancing way too close
But now you're with me, let 'em know

CHORUS

Come on
Won't you rescue me
Oh come and rescue me, etc.
Won't you, won't you, won't you rescue me
Come and rescue me

CHORUS

Then maybe later we can play

REVENGE IS SWEETER (THAN YOU EVER WERE)

I saw it in the news
You told me they were wrong
And I stood up for you
'Cause I believed you were the one
You had all the chances in the world
To let me know the truth
What the hell's wrong with you

PRE-CHORUS:
Are you even listening when I
   talk to you
Do you even care what I'm
   going through
Your eyes stare and they're staring
   right through me
You're right there but its like you
   never knew me

CHORUS:
Do you even know how much it hurt
That you gave up on me to
   be with her
Revenge is sweeter than you
   ever were

I'm so mad at you right now
And I can't even find the words
And you're on the way down
I can't wait to see you burn
You try to make me hate that girl
When I should be hating you
What the hell's wrong with you

PRE-CHORUS

CHORUS

Nothing can save you now
   that it's over
I guess that you'll find out when
   you're no one
Don't say you're sorry now 'cause I
   just don't care

Nothing can save you now,
   nothing etc.

PRE-CHORUS

CHORUS

Rock Me Slow

Rock me slow
Don't let go
Baby, hush don't tell me, I don't want to know
Sing a song just for me
Let me melt into your heart while I dream
'Cause I want to get lost somewhere in some sweet part of you
I wanna fall in so deep that all I see is you

CHORUS:
Tonight
I want you
I need you baby
I wanna be with you
No matter what you do
And lose myself in you

Rock me slow
Don't let go
Trace my body with your fingers hold me close
Close your eyes, make a wish
Hold my hands, touch my face, fill my lips
'Cause I want to get lost somewhere in some sweet part of you
I wanna fall in so deep that all I see is you

CHORUS

Hold me, kiss my tears away, and make me feel like yesterday
It's nothing but a dream, wake me up
And even if it isn't true just love me like you used to do
Help me find a place where I belong
'Cause I want to get lost somewhere in some sweet part of you
I wanna fall in so deep that all I see is you

CHORUS

Rock me slow
Don't let go

Run with It

Imagine
You're standing there, twenty years from now
Staring yourself in the mirror
Alone
All is gone
Thinking you lost the one you love the most
And it's
Hard to find
Peace of mind
When you know you could have had it all
Say it
Right here, right now
You've got to make your decision count

PRE-CHORUS:
You can sit it out
And wait until you see your chance
You can try your luck and dare to dance
Dream away your life and never live your dream
Or breathe every breath you get

CHORUS:
And run with it
Every breath you get
Run with it
This is your time
This is your life
Run with it
Don't walk the line
Make up your mind
Run with it

You decide
What will be
Don't complain and look for sympathy

'Cause it's
Time to wise
Open your eyes
You're the author in the story of your own life
Love is
Painful, shameful
Love will
Always save you
So don't you let it go

PRE-CHORUS

CHORUS

An empty life
Open the sky
Hear your voice like a thousand cries
Don't turn away
Love will say, "I'm coming after you"

So if you breathe, breathe, breathe deep
If you just breathe deep, breathe deep
You gotta say
Every breath you get
Run with it

PRE-CHORUS

CHORUS

SAFE WITH YOU

Don't have much to give you but I'll give you all I got and baby
Sometimes people never love at all
'Cause nothing's for certain, that is for sure
But we got each other and we don't need nothing no more

CHORUS:
Whatever may be happening out there
I don't care
'Cause I'm here
Safe with you
And even if the sun forgets to shine
I don't mind
I'll be fine
Safe with you
Where I belong

If the sky is crying far away
And you and I just have today
We better move and hold on tight
'Cause all my faith begins and ends with you
All my hope begins and ends with you

CHORUS

And I know I'll be safe with you, etc.

Safe with you

SAFETY

It's been a long road
A journey worth the struggle
I overcome the obstacles in my way
I'm on a quest for safety
Questioning the path that I
    should take

Oh and I beheld the beauty
    of the light
That shined from sea to shining sea
Oh one thing that I know is love is
    taking over me
I believe

CHORUS:
In the spirit of your love
With open arms you lift me up
Above the clouds 'cause I believe
In the spirit of your love
With open arms you lift me up
Above the clouds 'cause I believe
I find safety in your arms
I find safety in your arms

I'm smiling everyday
When men sigh, my body's
    crying away
Oh I've been thinking to myself
How we can be so happy then
Let it slip away

So consumed by the gray in my sky
With the sun shining bright, right
    in my eyes

I realize that there's so much more
    to my life
I didn't see
I believe

CHORUS

Oh and I beheld the beauty
    of the light
That shined from sea to shining sea
Oh one thing that I know is love is
    taking over me
I believe

CHORUS

SAND ON MY FEET

Wakin' up this morning
Saw the sun come through
   my blinds
And I looked up on the porch
And found an owl shrieking by
But never could I have imagined
Such a place like this
And you're lyin' next to me
I wanna wake you with a kiss
And all the crazy things about you
That I so adore
Are the little things that keep me
Coming back for more

CHORUS:
And it feels like love
And it feels so good
And it feels like love
(I wanna feel like the
   roarin' thunder)
(Wanna be the heaven that your
   sky is under)
Oh, I say, you say, oh (It's like love)
All that I need, baby it's true
The sand on my feet and you

I will go wherever you go
Take me where you lead
Lead me where you want
My heart doesn't know
Anything but what you say
You're the one for me
You make me feel complete
I can silent read your whisper
And my lips still feel your touch

And I'm oh so glad to be here
Oh so glad to be here (the summer
   wind blows)

CHORUS

But you and I have walked
   the oceans
Miles along the shore
And a thousand seagulls
   called on me
So we came right back for more
And I love to feel the water
It makes me feel so free
Underneath the purple sky
Every time you look at me
I reach up to forever
With the promises you keep
They fill me with such happiness
It makes my heart believe

CHORUS

How many lovers
Have walked along the shore before
Before you and I
How many said goodbye

SAVE YOUR LOVE

Hey you, I barely know you
It's all so new but it feels
Like we've always been together
I know it may sound crazy
Do you believe in love at first sight
'Cause I didn't 'til you
   caught my eye
It's too soon to say goodbye, too
   soon for me to cry
But you have your life and
   I have mine

CHORUS:
It's out of our hands now
I'm hoping somehow
We'll make it through this
I know we can do this
Tell me you love me
Say you'd let nothing
Come in between us
And whatever's gonna
   happen tomorrow
Save your love for me
Save your love for me

Hey you, you got to stay strong now
Please don't make this any harder
Than it really has to be
Ooh babe, promise you'll call me
Day and night any time you like
And when you miss me
Just look up at the moon imagine
   I see it too
And no matter how far apart we are
I'll be thinking of you

CHORUS

Save your love for me
Save your love for me
Hey you, I barely know you

CHORUS

Save your love for me

Science of Love

You called me up
My heart is pounding
Can't barely breathe
I just got over you
What do you want
You're like a broken record
Spinnin' in my head
Why can't you let me be?
I don't understand
What it is about you
The more you reject me
The more I want from you

PRE-CHORUS:
You're always on my mind
Always have been, always will be
I think about you all the time
I don't want to, you're a habit
And I'm running and running
   and running and running
   away from you
Every time when you come
I come undone can't
   escape from you

CHORUS:
It's the science of love etc.

I'm thinking to fight it
To get away from you
Something always pulled me
Right back to you
I don't understand

What it is about you
The more you reject me
The more I want from you

PRE-CHORUS

CHORUS

PRE-CHORUS

CHORUS

SCREAM

One paycheck away from poverty
Tryin' to keep it together but God
    it ain't easy
It's not like the news offers
    anything better
Just talk of the rich but tell me how
    do you get there
Got the keys in my hand
Can't go anywhere can't
    afford the gas

CHORUS:
Don't tell me ok 'cause I
    need a solution
Don't tell me it's alright 'cause I'm
    hurtin' now
Don't hold me stay calm preaching
    it'll get better
'Cause I need an answer, etc.
The walls are closing in real
    fast on me
I got tears in my eyes, I can
    hardly see
I can't breathe, breathe, breathe
I wanna scream, scream
Wanna scream

But that won't fix a thing
Words caught in my throat, I can
    hardly speak
Bourbon's now the only friend
    to comfort me
Even my boss' jobs just expired
Cutting jobs faster than
    they can hire

Got one ticket in my hand
    to fly away
But walls got me scared

CHORUS

Promises won't move my
    feet anymore
Actions speak louder than words
I don't believe you anymore
Don't care what you say
I gotta survive
And do it my way

I will, etc.

CHORUS

Wanna scream for me
Why don't we scream together
    and make a change
Scream, etc.
You need a change

SECRET

You're a little obsessed with me
And I'm a little bit scared of you
The way you look and stare at me
Maybe it's time I let you know

CHORUS:
You could call me six times but still I won't pick up the phone
You could spend all your money on me
but still I'll say no
You could write a million letters everyday confessing to me
That I am the girl of your dreams
But nobody ever asked me
I never looked at you that way
'Cause I always thought you were gay

Every time you come around
You just look me up and down
And then you try to hold my hand
I'm confused now I don't understand

CHORUS

You told me lies
You made me believe
It would be fine
If there was nothing to see
I'd be undressing in front of you
I told you secrets that no one else knew

CHORUS

See You When I Will

I can't believe how fast all these years have gone by
So much loved and so much lost, these are the moments in life
When the only things you have are yourself and today
And tomorrow seems so far away

PRECHORUS:
It takes courage to go on at the end of the road
When you're on your own, I'll see you when I will

CHORUS:
We're moving on from here
We're going on our separate ways and I don't know if we'll meet again
I'll see you when I will
We've had our good and bad and I don't know what to feel
You're all I've ever known, but now we're on our own

Try not to look back, it's easier if we don't
So much lies ahead, so much more to know

PRECHORUS

CHORUS, etc.

SELFISH

Why you calling me this late
I was just about to fall asleep
Do you even know what time it is
What do you want now
If you just need someone to talk
   about your day
Babe I'm sorry I got to get up early
Why you always worried
You're gonna drag us down

And we fight and we cry and we
   don't say goodbye
We forgive and forget why do
   we do this

CHORUS:
If you really love me let me breathe
How can I be happy if I don't
   feel free
You got to give me a chance to miss
   you again
Build a little mystery, let love in
Don't you understand I don't want it
   to end like this
But I got to be selfish

You want to hear what's going on
   in my life
But just as long as I am weak and
   you can save me
But when I'm strong that's when
   you hate me
Are you even listening to me
Hey, I'm talking to you

Anything you say is just to
   spoil my mood
Are you gonna hang up on me again

And we fight and we cry and we
   don't say goodbye
We forgive and forget baby
   it's pointless

CHORUS

This isn't adding up no more
With you I'm less than I was before
The more you ask the less you
   get from me
I got to do what's best for me
So I can save what's left of me
And be selfish
And be selfish

If you really love me let me breathe
How can I be happy

SERENADE

Hush - I've heard it all before
Roses are red and I know I'm adored, baby
Hush - don't play another song
Don't waste your time in the rain all night long
Losing sleep, serenading me

CHORUS:
Saying la, la la la, la la la, la la la, etc.

Your voice sends chills down my spine
Something inside me wants you to be mine
Hands like a painter from the past
And lips that mold words into songs that will last
In my heart you'll be serenading me

CHORUS

CHORUS

Sexiest Man Alive

Hey Mr. Sexy
Could you please spare me some time
I'd love to get to know you
Baby I will make you mine
Way your body's moving
Boy you're driving me insane
Come here a little closer would you whisper me your name

CHORUS:
You're the sexiest man alive
You send me chills and get me high
I'm gonna take you home tonight
So there's a chance you'll blow my mind
Sexy baby, etc.

Take me to the ladies
Let me powder up my face
Get me a little tipsy
Put your hands up on my waist
You ain't gotta worry about any other guy
Everything about you boy's like heaven to my eyes

CHORUS

Feeling kind of sexy yeah I think you know
Give me one call get you on the floor
Yeah I'll tell you everything that you want to know
Look real sexy I'm about to blow
Don't stop girl drop it like it's hot
Yeah real smooth don't grind through the spot
We're getting down like this
Down like that
Yeah down like that

CHORUS

SHAKE

Shake, I'm in here now
See some shorties there
   gettin' down
Some soul sistas, the boriquas
Look at all them hot señoritas

Everybody's lookin' so hot
Sexy, papi, baby you got it
Come to me, siente mi si
Cerca de mi

Oh, I'm up on you
Baby let me know what
   you wanna do
I'm gettin' high off the vibe you're
   sendin' me
Girl, you got my heart stopped
   in a daze

Feel the rhythm, sexy, exotic
Wanna feel ya next to my body
Era un arte todo la noche
Para chulo y mueve tu culo

CHORUS:
Shake - I'm feelin' the vibe
Shake - Are you feelin' the vibe
Shake it, ooh, I'm feelin' the vibe
We're just dancin'
Shake - So you're feelin' my vibe
Shake - Yeah I'm feelin' the vibe
Hang low to the floor 'til ya
   touch ya toes
Hang low to the floor 'til ya
   touch ya toes

Girl we don't want one bottle of
Cris, we want it all
VIP baby, we buyin' the bar
Check out all the functions
   in my car
You got it right, you with
   some superstars
We got the party makin' like
   it's fiesta
Ooh la la, singin' whateva

Hanging low all night, hanging low
   all night
Hanging low all night,
   c'mon shake it!

CHORUS

Get low! (get low)
Na na na na whoa
Na na na na whoa
(Mueve ese culo)
Na na na na whoa
(Y vibra con migo)
Na na na na whoa

I'm lovin' the way mami is
   look real good
Sexy exotic model with
   high-heeled shoes
Dressed in lingerie, shakin'
   the Fatty Koo
Body so tight making me
   wanna say ooh
You a bad girl, but I would be a fool

Not to get your name and number
   and see what you can do
But I don't really care right now
Just long as you shake your
   body for me

Shake, shake, shake
Shake, rattle and rollin', etc.
Shake, (your body) shake,
   (she's movin') shake
   (she's groovin')
Shake, rattle and rollin', etc.

Now I know you cant deny I already
   turned you on
And I love the way you shake and I
   wanna take you home

So don't stop, twerk it all night long
Cause the party keep going on 'til 6
   in the morn

Shake – touch ya toes

Shake - So you're feelin' my vibe
Shake - Yeah I'm feelin' the vibe
Hang low to the floor 'til ya
   touch ya toes

Siente la vibtacion, vamos acercate,
   mueve ese
Culo y vibra con migo, sientete
   al igual de mi
Cuerpo con tu cuerpo

SHAMELESS

Why should I be soft spoken
When you spoke out for me
Why would I keep you hidden
When you crossed the sky so I could see
How you gave your life
So we could be
Sealed for eternity

CHORUS:
I'm shameless when it comes to you
I'll say this cause your word is true
It has the power to change all we choose to believe
And I do
I'm shameless, I'm shameless

Why would I be uncertain
When you made a place for me
Why would I stand unmoving
When you've asked me to run
And you set me free
And I'll testify with my life
What you have done for me

CHORUS

I'll shout it from the rooftops
I've never been the same
Since I first called out your name

CHORUS

CHORUS

I'm shameless for you
Oh Lord, I'm shameless

SHE'S A DANCER

Knew just how to get it poppin
Once she started wasn't stoppin'
She so she so
Way she movin' in this party
With her oh so sexy body
She so she so

CHORUS:
She's a dancer she's a dancer
And she's dancing for the dollar
Looking hip about to holla
She's a dancer she's a dancer
Dang she know she's fine
So she's gonna dance all night

Now the bass is droppin' harder
Speakers thumpin' in the corner
Sound like alright let's get back to shorty
Oh she shakin' like some jello
How she do it in them stilettos
She so she so

CHORUS

CHORUS

CHORUS

SHUSH OFF THE RECORD

All I really wanna do
Is spend a little time with you
I don't really care who knows
Or if on my face it shows
You got that kind of swagger I like
Cool sexy damn you're fine
You got it written all over your face
And baby I can't wait

CHORUS:
We can have
Sex in the living room, sex in
    the cab home
Sex in the closet, sex when
    we're all alone
Sex in the kitchen, sex in the Jacuzzi
Sex when it's itchin' you gotta
    seduce me
Sex in the shower, sex for
    three hours
Sex in the attic just like
    we're rabbits
Sex in my room, sex in the pool
I'll give it to you but you gotta
    promise me baby that it's
Off the record it's off the record
    baby it's shush, shush, etc.
Don't tell nobody

I just wanna sport a thug
Somebody I can hold and love
I won't be scared if you're
    not scared
Take my hand and say the word

Nobody's gotta know what we do
A little thing between me and you
If your imagination's running wild
You can come home anytime

CHORUS

Oh boy what you do to me baby
Won't stop till we run out of places
Oh boy I've been going crazy
Shush, shush, shush, shush

CHORUS

CHORUS

THE SIGN

He disappeared without a chance to say goodbye
Didn't stop to tell you why it went wrong
You still hang on but there's nothing you can do
He's already over you
Now he's gone

CHORUS:
Who said life was always gonna be fair
Who said honesty would get you somewhere
Maybe your stars were not aligned
Or fate had a change of mind
Or maybe it's a sign

You really tried, you tried so hard to read his mind
You gave your all to make it right for him
So he lied to afraid to let you know
Couldn't wait to let it go and run

CHORUS

It's a sign to move on
It's your time to rise
And break the chains
That hold you down

CHORUS

It's a sign

SILENCE IS GOLDEN

One more time around this carousel
I'm leaving behind this old carnival
I know too well
That everything I want to say will come out wrong
And you'll be gone before too long
And I'll be strumming some old song
Trying to cover up what I've done

CHORUS:
I never told you something
I've been holding this in
I make a point to try avoiding disappointment when I can
Would you listen to me
If I admit I'm guilty
Of letting you believe
That silence is golden
When silence has stolen
All my words from me

I don't shed no light on anything dead
And I don't put my pride in jeopardy
I know I'm only lying to myself if I
Keep hiding behind this old disguise of mine
But I wouldn't know how to go about
Revealing my heart's whereabouts

CHORUS

Wish I could take away everything that holds me back today
Why am I so afraid to make a mistake

CHORUS

SILVER BULLET

I can feel it coming
I answer my shadow
And welcome its embrace
My blood is getting thicker
My vision starts to blur
My love turns to rage
Our time is running out
You've got to save yourself
I can't control me anymore

CHORUS:
Set me free
We don't have a choice
You've got to destroy
What I've become
I beg for you to kill it
Shoot the silver bullet

The moonlight is blinding
It steals my will away
Please help me
I don't know who you are
But I still know your face
I can't remember anymore

CHORUS

CHORUS

My breath is getting shallow
The pain grows in my chest
But I'm chained in no more
I feel you in my arms
I hold you one last time

SIMPLE THINGS

How do you explain this funny
   feeling deep inside
Makes me smile when I'm lonely
Comforts me when I'm sad
How do you explain this sweet,
   sweet smile on my face
It just keeps getting better
With each passing day

CHORUS:
For so long
I did not know
I was searching in all the
   wrong places
Thinking if I spent more money
   than I could
If I worked harder than I should
Always havin' friends to feel good
I'd be happier
Losin' my breath in the hustle
Just stressin' over nothin'
Forgetting the real joys that lie in
   the simple things

How do you explain when there's
   more month at the end
   of the money
Your situation tells you to worry
But you see the flowers in bloom
How do you explain the soft caress
   on your face
That tells you its getting better
   with each passing day

CHORUS

For so long (Long)
I did not know (Know)
I was looking in all the
   wrong places
Thinking if I played more games
   than I could
If I worried more than I should
Spinnin' my wheels with a lover
That meant me no good
Losin' my breath in the hustle
Just stressin' over nothin'
Forgettin' the real pleasures that lie
   in the simple things

Sun shinin' on my face, his
   strong embrace
Mama called him, Daddy called him
To see if I'm okay
The fresh air I breathe
Enough food to eat
A warm place to sleep at night
Ah, the simple things

CHORUS

I spent more money than I could
Harder than I should
Friends to feel good (Thought this
   was gonna make me feel happier)
Losin' my breath in the hustle
Stressin' over nothin'
Forgettin' the real pleasures that lie
In the simple things
Hey, hey look at 'em, simple things

SINGLE, SEXY AND SEARCHING

Lately I've been going through a lot of changes
Finally I got the courage to break the chains
That made me a prisoner in my own home
Held me back for so long
But now I'm free and I hate waiting

CHORUS:
Single, sexy and searching
Could it be that you're my type
Single, sexy and searching
I just don't want to waste my time
Something about you makes me feel like
Maybe I should give you a try
Show me that you're worth it
'cause I'm single, sexy and still searching

Now's the time to work up the courage boy get busy
Maybe I will let you get close, get to know me
Make it quick or I move on
Leave those hands where they belong
'Cause I want class
And I ain't settling for less

CHORUS

For the one who makes me happy
For the one who keeps me safe
For the one who understands me
When I've had a crazy day
For the one who satisfies me
When I wanna misbehave

CHORUS

We get busy 'cause I'm single, sexy, and still searching

SKIN DEEP

What you starin' in the mirror for
Tellin' yourself you're ugly
What you wearing those high heels for
When they're torturing your feet (you know they're killing you)
Why you puttin' all that make-up on
Hiding your pretty face
Blowin' all your money in that salon
Tryin' to find ya place

PRE-CHORUS:
In this world you fit in or you're out
And you're made to believe that this is what it's all about

CHORUS:
And don't you know

Real beauty shines from within
It's what you're wearing under your skin
Your perfect imperfections
Led you in the wrong direction
And made you think
That you are incomplete

But looks are only skin deep

Why you flippin through the magazine
Trying to be those girls (well stop it)
Gettin' all frustrated
But it's not the end of the world (its superficial)
So what if you can't get into a size three
You're beautiful to me (beautiful to me)
Stop trying to be Tyra's top model
Girl go and find your own way to follow

PRE-CHORUS

CHORUS

From the side walk
To the boardwalk
To the cat walk
Don't talk
About the way you walk
But it's not your fault
So if the girls talk,
Watch you like a hawk
They love to hate
And they can't wait
To get inside
And make you cry
Cry, cry, cry
Just let 'em know
That you made ya own
Now being you is not all wrong
Do ya thang
Let your light shine
They'll come around
In God's time

And if they don't
Just let it be
When they stop being shallow
Then they'll see
Girl, I'm tellin' you (Come on!)

Just be yourself!

PRE-CHORUS

CHORUS

SLEEP WITH ME

We've been circling around this
   issue for a week
I think about it all the time I'm
   losing sleep now
I think we both know it's as far
   as we can go
Without crossing the line
I might as well be twelve years old
   cause when we touch
It's like I never ever liked a boy
   that much
Except we're both grown, your face
   just turns me on
Come on, come on, come on,
   come on

CHORUS:
Do you wanna
Do you wanna sleep with me, etc.
So be a good boy cause I'm
   a good girl
And if you make me feel good
I will give you the world
Do you wanna
Do you wanna

There is nothing like the very
   first time
You don't know what you're
   gonna get
But you don't mind
Uncharted territory
It could be hell or glory
Let's just go for a ride

Go wash yourself and you can touch
   my secret places
Kneel to my altar cause this body
   here is sacred
I like you sexual, spiritual
Come on, come on, come on,
   come on

CHORUS

Are you a good boy? Tell me, 'cause
I'm a good girl
So be a good boy cause I'm
   a good girl
And if you make me feel good
I will give you the world

CHORUS

SLEEPLESS

Red neon sign casts shadows
In my cheap motel room
Smells like sex and vinyl
Again you came and left too soon
And I grow stronger every time you come around
Yes I grow stronger every time you let me down

CHORUS:
I've been sleepless since you left me
To go back where you belong
These secrets drive me crazy
I want to tell her what's going on
But I know what you would answer
If I asked you to stay
And I can't keep on living this way

I hear someone at the door
How could I've doubted you
But it's the cleaning lady asking
When I'll be checking out of our room
I hold on tighter just to smell you on the pillow
I hold on tighter when I should be letting go

CHORUS

When you crawl back into her bed
Without making a sound
Shower off my perfume
So you won't smell like me
When she's going down on you

CHORUS

Don't ask me to do it
Can't do it

SLIDE

INTERLUDE:
Get crunk
Status, put them hands up
Get right
'Cause we 'bout to party all night
Shot down
You know we gonna shut this down
We got this whole night
Now we gonna party like young jive

Slide
Slide (Get slick), etc.

All the girls wanna know where the boys at
All the boys wanna know where the girls at
Boys looking at the girls saying, "Uh uh."
Girls looking at the boys saying, "Uh huh!"
All the players wanna go where the chicks at
All the chicks wanna know where the players at
Players looking at the chicks going, "Aight."
Chicks looking at the players going, "Get slick."

CHORUS:
We got the style
We looking fly (Get slick)
We got the looks
You got the books (Checkbooks)
We got the rhythm (We got the soul)
We got the fire (It's out of control)
We got the beat (This beat's sick)
Turn up the heat (Get slick)

Slide
Slide (Get slick), etc.

The boys trying to go home with some numbers
Chicks up in here dressed like it's summer
Boys holla at a chick like, "Ay shorty."
Girls holla back saying, "We just wanna party."

Its getting late but we just getting started
Black Eyed Peas said, "Let's get retarded"
The girls talking like Luda saying "Get back"
Boys up in here looking like, "Forget that"

CHORUS

Everybody get your booty on the floor
Come on over and let's get this party on
Get your back up off the wall
What you waiting for
Keep these hot joints bouncing off the wall
All night long

INTERLUDE

Slide
Slide (Get slick), etc.

CHORUS

Everybody get your booty on the floor
Come on over and let's get this party on
Get your back up off the wall
What you waiting for
Keep these hot joints bouncing off the wall
All night long

SNAP

Girl why you acting so timid and shy
Hoping a boy would pick
   you up tonight
It's a misconception 'bout who's
   in control
There's only one thing girl you
   got to know

PRE-CHORUS:
It's not that complicated
Don't be hesitating
You know the guys are waiting
Don't miss out on the fun
Let them know what you want
I promise you they'll respond

CHORUS:
If you want a guy to come to you
You don't have to make a move
All the girls, all the girls
All the girls gotta do is snap
1-2-3 like that
You know he won't fight back
So all the girls around the world
All you gotta do is snap

Can't let the boys do what they
   want to do
They'll end up walking all over you
You gotta stand up and
   demand respect
Just snap your fingers and they'll
   do the rest

PRE-CHORUS

CHORUS

And if the boy you with won't
   turn you on
Don't be afraid to switch him with
   another one
Hands up you feel my hands, he
   looks and smiles
Because what really counts is what
   he's got inside

And if the boy you with won't
   turn you on
Don't be afraid to switch him with
   another one
Hands up you feel my hands, he
   looks and smiles
Because what really counts is what
   he's got inside

CHORUS

CHORUS

CHORUS

All you gotta do is snap

So Damn Beautiful

Excuse me could you say that
    one more time
I didn't understand a word you said
I'm sorry I got distracted when you
    looked into my eyes
They got all blurry in my head
If only I could get it straight
If you just let me concentrate
I'm trying not to lose myself
But I'm not doing very well

CHORUS:
I wish you weren't so
    damn beautiful
Make me lose all my principles
I want to resist but I can't let go
Don't want to say yes but I
    can't say no
It's pathetic I feel stupid
But it's out of my control
I wish you weren't so
    damn beautiful

No I don't mean what I just said
I mean I said it but believe me
    I didn't mean
Just how like I was liking you
Although I really want to say I do
I hope you didn't get me wrong
I didn't mean to lead you on
Thinking I come on to you
When honestly I do

CHORUS

Don't think that I came all this way
    to see you
I am here to see a friend of mine
But since it seems you don't
    have plans
We might as well just spend
    a little time
Ok that's a lie

I wish you weren't so
    damn beautiful
Why you make me feel so insecure
I want to resist but I can't let go
Don't want to say yes but I
    can't say no
It's pathetic I feel stupid
But it's out of my control
I wish you weren't so
    damn beautiful

So Damn Happy Right Now

Woke up, rain falls
I guess I won't get to see the sun
But I don't care
Downtown, white hall
I look at my watch and start around
Too late, but it's okay
I missed the train and I tried to hitch a ride
Time just isn't on my side

CHORUS:
But I'm so damn happy right now
Nothing can bring me down
'Cause I got a message from you
Now I know that it's true
That you love me
I'm so damn happy right now

Strangers passing
Can't help but make them smile
Must be contagious
My problems, my worries
Gonna put them all aside
Couldn't care less
Every minute, every second that goes by
All I think about is you

CHORUS

CHORUS

CHORUS

So Good

Passion, love, exciting and fire (so good)
(Let's go)

On the side walking pass me by
I couldn't help but notice that look in your eye
Both had the same thing in mind
But before I knew you were gone and I didn't think twice
Who would've thought that we'd meet again
Hanging out at a party with some mutual friends
I was happy I must admit
Till I saw the nasty girl that you came here with

If you only knew I was feeling you
Would you come with me (would you come with me)
If you only knew what I was thinking
Boy wouldn't you agree

CHORUS:
You would look so good, so good on me
You would look so good, so good on me (you lookin' good baby)
Got the body type that fits just right
You got that something that I like
It's in the style, the way you smile it drives me wild
You would look so good, so good, so good on me
(So good, you feelin' that)

At the club checkin' out a band
I was having fun hanging out with my new man
Then you stepped out of the crowd
And you gave me the feelin' that I'm missin' out
Can't believe the chemistry
Now you're really showin' how you're into me
You always want what you can't have
But the truth is baby

CHORUS

(I'm feelin'hypnotized)
You would look so good on me, etc.
(Sing to 'em ma)
So good, etc.

I'm having déjà vu seein' you boo, do what you do
I don't think you got a clue just give me the cue
I remember small things like the size of your shoe
That you hit up Saks 5th introduce you to Wu
Players be hatin' don't want to see Razor and Jaydn
I'm sittin' here thinking wow 'cause we're both taken
As long as there's patience I'm be faithfully waitin'
Keep my heart circulating with this money we're makin'

CHORUS

(It's your secret admirer)

So Simple

I know you know that I feel you
   feeling me
So baby why you act so cold
I'm sure you think that you
   can fight it
If you only look away 'til it's gone

But if it's love, you can't escape it
I see through you like you're naked
And you wish you could hide
You're saying no but I don't buy it
'Cause it's obvious you deny it
When I look in your eyes

CHORUS:
It could be so simple
If only you try
It could be so beautiful, so magical
So natural for us
It could be so simple
But you're making it hard
If you don't mean what you say
And keep fronting away
It's impossible for me to love you

You always figure there's
   a million reasons
Why you should prepare for failure
When all you need is just a feeling
That will tell you what is
   right for you

Cause when it's love you
   can't escape it
I see through you like you're naked

And you wish you could hide
You're saying no but I don't buy it
'Cause it's obvious you deny it
When I look in your eyes

CHORUS

You got me going round and
   round in circles
Confusing matters 'til I can't think
   straight anymore
One day you can't wait to
   be with me
And then you don't call
What is it you're still waiting for

CHORUS
So beautiful, so magical
So natural for us
We could be so beautiful,
   so magical
So natural for us, etc.

SOLITARY SOUL

I was still picking up the pieces
Of what I thought would be the love of my life
When you walked in and put my toothbrush on my sink
And decided that I would be your wife
I'd been burned before so many times
I didn't give you more than two nights and a day
You wanted to convince me you were different from the other guys
The more you tried the more it made me want to say

CHORUS:
I'm a solitary soul
I won't give up control
I've fought too hard for my freedom to let go
I'm a solitary soul
What you're asking I can't do
I can't open up and let my feelings show
Even for you

The third day came and the sun rose on your face
I didn't even mind your clothes all over my floor
I couldn't deny that in your arms I felt safe
You said do you like the ocean
I guess it struck a chord

CHORUS

How did you know that I had so much more to give?
I was so frustrated but you saw it's just a phase
And every time I was about to turn around
You said "I love you" and "I am here to stay"

CHORUS

Only you could take me by the hand

SOMEBODY

Ever since you first opened
    your eyes
Something happened that
    changed my life
A bond grows stronger everyday
It's the love that words
    cannot explain

CHORUS:
To the world you might just
    be somebody
To the world you might just
    be nobody
But to me, to me you
    mean the world

The sun rises when you smile
The rain falls when you cry
I come runnin' when you call
You're my heart
You're my soul

Everything you are was made in love
Your tiny hands, wiggly toes, cute
    giggles and your sweet little nose
I want you to be the best that
    you can be
Afraid of nothing, wise, and carefree

CHORUS

The sun rises when you smile
The rain falls when you cry
I come runnin' when you call

You're my heart
You're my soul

CHORUS

The sun rises when you smile
The rain falls when you cry
I come runnin' when you call
You're my heart
You're my soul

CHORUS

S.O.S

Staring at the phone all day won't make you call me
Sitting here playing it off won't change a thing
Writing love letters that I'd never dare to send you won't tell you
How far deep I've gone since I met you

CHORUS:
I feel I'm stranded on an island
And you're miles away from here
I try to make waves but the ocean's quiet
Can anybody hear my S.O.S, my S.O.S.?

Closing my eyes to the truth won't persuade you
And letting you hold my heart will only cause more pain
Westerly Persian wind cannot save me
'Cause I'm still holding on to what's been gone.

CHORUS

CHORUS

SOUL SEARCHING

What the hell you fighting for
You ran out to slam the door
Took your things and you deserve better
Girl, get yourself together
What you think you crying for
You cannot ring a bell
Put him through so much hell
Cause when you love somebody
You gotta treat him right, just know that

PRE-CHORUS:
Love and hate
Are sometimes way too close to one another
And pride and hurt
Get mixed up in your feelings now it's all become a blur

CHORUS:
You ought to do some soul searching
Gotta do some soul searching
Be careful what you say
Be careful what you do
Before you get possessive, obsessive, passive-aggressive
And don't care for the truth anymore
You ought to do some soul searching (think about it)

What the hell you calling for
Three nights alone and you can't stand it anymore
Let it ring he picks up
You hang up again, knows it's you
But won't play your game because

PRE-CHORUS

CHORUS

304

Sometimes when you sleep over it
You look back and you laugh about it
Next morning you can't remember how
You could ever get so caught up in it (ain't it like that)
When you step back, look on together
You see that you're pride got in the way
It's so much easier to walk away
Than to listen to what he has to say

Doesn't matter what you've been through
You love him, he loves you
Be careful whatever you do
Doesn't matter what he's said or done
You win some, you lose some
Trust the love you first felt inside

CHORUS

SPEECHLESS

Feels like I have always known you
And I swear I dreamt about you
All those endless nights I was alone
It's like I've spent forever searching
Now I know that it was worth it
With you it feels like I am
   finally home

PRECHORUS:
Falling head over heels
Thought I knew how it feels
But with you it's like the first day
   of my life

CHORUS:
'Cause you leave me speechless
When you talk to me
You leave me breathless
The way you look at me
You manage to disarm me
My soul is shining through
Can't help but surrender
My everything to you

I thought I could resist you
I thought that I was strong
Somehow you are different from
   what I've known
I didn't see you coming
You took me by surprise and
You stole my heart before I
   could say no

PRECHORUS

CHORUS

You leave me speechless
(the way you smile, the way you
   touch my face)
You leave me breathless
(it's something that you do
   I can't explain)
I run a million miles just to hear
   you say my name
Baby

CHORUS

Spring Cleaning

It's a brand new day
Sunshine's on my face
I open up the window and breathe
Say goodbye to all the mess
That's crowding up this place
It's time to get this weight off of me

Got to do some spring-cleaning
Kick out the boys and
    stop dreaming
Starting out fresh with
    a new beginning
Out with the old, in with the new
Delete those numbers
    from my phone
Tell them to leave this girl alone
It's way too dusty inside so
I've got to mop the boys out
    of my life

CHORUS:
Bluebirds started singing,
    daffodils are springing
Temperature is changing, so am I
I guess that's the reason you are
    out of season
Hail to a new day, baby, bye-bye

I got 20 new messages on my phone
Like I've got nothing better to do
It's like every single time I tell
    them no, no no
They find another way to
    get through

Got to do some spring-cleaning
Kick out the boys and
    stop dreaming
Starting out fresh with a
    new beginning
Out with the old, in with the new
Delete those numbers from
    my phone
Tell them to leave this girl alone
It's way too dusty inside so
I've got to mop the boys out
    of my life

CHORUS

You're like a fly that won't go away
I'll be foolish to let you stay
I'll take out my spray and
    wash you away

CHORUS

CHORUS

STAND UP FOR YOUR WOMAN

She lights up the room without
   even tryin'
With every move every eye wants
   to find her
Is it what she said or how she acts
That constantly makes the men react

The man that she loves just
   thinks of himself
He's always too busy with
   everything else
Every time he calls she's
   always there
But when she needs him
He doesn't care

CHORUS:
She rises with the sun
And won't stop till after dawn
Keeps a smile on her face
Overworked and unpaid
But she does it with style and
   so much grace
She's a trendsetter, a go-getter,
   a sister, a friend
Glamorous she's loyal to the end
Listen up boy it wasn't me
Stand up for your woman
Stand up, etc.

When the man comes home
And the kids cry mommy
Not a day to rest from Monday to
Sunday (is the game on)

Rushes to school to get kids on time
Cooks his dinner while he
   spills his wine

He laughs with the fellas
Calls plays in the game
Cheers his team on while
   she's in pain
She turns her back
And hopes it gets better
While her friends say get it together

CHORUS

If you appreciate the work
   she's done
Let your woman know she's
   second to none
Show her she's your gift from above
Your source of love, show her
   she's the one
'Cause a woman's work is
   never done

CHORUS

STARLIGHT

For every person in the world
There's one star in the sky
So they say
And when you miss somebody
Somewhere up there there's the one
Never far away

And I'm looking up at the stars
And I'm wondering where you are

CHORUS:
Starlight, I'm alone tonight
But when I look at the sky
I see your love shining bright
And I imagine you're by my side
'Cause when I'm with you everything feels right
So I'm wishing on that star tonight

Don't want to take for granted
The love you give to me unselfishly
So many times I've wanted
To thank you from my heart
You've always believed

That there's nothing that I can't do
You gave me something to hold on to

CHORUS

So many places
So distant, yet so close
As the night turns to day
Yours is the one I miss the most

CHORUS

STARSTRUCK

(Hello everyone, it's me)

How did I get so lucky
It's like the world revolves around
me
I'm not so different
But everybody wants to be my friend
Other girls are super pretty
But the boys still line up for me
I don't know why
But I guess must be doing some-
thing right

CHORUS:
I must be doing something right
'Cause everybody gets starstruck
when they see me
Always tell me I'm a hot shot
I say easy 'cause I know just what I
got
And right now it looks like I'm larg-
er than life
On every billboard on the side of
the Times
Blown out of proportion what a
crazy ride
But I feel like just another star in
the sky
With a little bit of luck
So don't get starstruck

On every page of the tabloid
Don't people get annoyed
Reading the same thing about me
Over and over again

Paparazzi instigatin'
Wishing they caught me hatin'
But Hannah Montana's got
Nothing but love for her friends

CHORUS

On every page of the tabloid
Don't people get annoyed
Reading the same thing about me
Over and over again
Paparazzi instigatin'
Wishing they caught me hatin'
But Hannah Montana's got
Nothing but love for her friends

CHORUS

STAY

Ever felt so alone
Lying here in the dark
The room is stone cold
And I'm crying out my heart

Hungry but can't eat
I'm tired
I can't sleep
Look in the mirror
But I don't recognize me

I need you now more than ever
Hold me through the night
I don't wanna be here forever
Promise me you'll

CHORUS:
Stay, stay, stay
When there's no one else around
Say, say, say
That you won't leave me now
Save, save, save
Save me from the dark
Take me in your arms
Promise me you'll stay

Stay, stay
Promise you'll stay
Stay, stay

And today's a stormy rain
I try to run, try to escape
I can't carry on
I let my life go to waste

I gave my everything
To make it this far
And it's killing me
To watch it all fall apart

I need you now
More than ever
Hold me through the night
I don't wanna be here forever
Promise me you'll

CHORUS

Stay, stay
Promise you'll stay
Stay, stay

Raindrops like tears
Wash away my fears
Your face appears
I feel you near

Wake up and see
You gave to me
Please don't leave
I need you to stay

CHORUS

Stay, stay
Promise you'll stay
Stay, stay

STEPPIN' OUT

I been spending the past five years
Trying to keep it real with you
I've been wasting all these tears
But you don't give a damn
   how I feel
Now ain't it true

I don't think you'll ever change
You've always been this way
And baby every day I pray
That you will come around
But see the lonely nights
Without you by my side,
   made me strong
Used to love you so
But now I'm letting go

CHORUS:
I'm steppin' out on you
Nothing can hold me back
I'm through with you
I'm steppin' out on you
Nothing can stop me now
I'm getting over you
'Cause I've been doing my best and
   breaking my neck
Just trying to please you
You been letting me down and
   stressin' me out
Now you're over due
Where's the part that says
   it's my problem

I been letting you in my life
Trying to make everything right
   unlike you
Don't you think another man
Can't be getting' me just the same
   as you do

Got a ticket to a brand new day
Pack my bags, I'm on the train
I know you can't stand it boy
I ain't even looking back
Ain't no stopping me, I'm
   breaking free
Still got my dignity and that's
   all I need

CHORUS

If you play with a dog he'll lick you
   in the face
And think it's all part of the game
He'll only go as far as you let him
Got to draw the line
Now I think it's my time

CHORUS

CHORUS

STILL I RISE

(Sometimes things just go down like that)

From the womb sometimes I could hear my mamma cry
Not even born, but I felt how she was hated every night
My first breath already had a bitter taste and I
Thought things in life just go down like that

CHORUS:
It makes me stronger, every time it hurts
It makes me wiser, every lesson I learn
It makes me harder, every time I'm burned
Still I rise every time I fall

Six years old, daddy lost his occupation to cocaine
Mommy's torn, turns to alcohol to numb her from the pain
Told my little sisters, got to hang in there with her
Sometimes in life things go down like this

CHORUS

Fourteen years old, hardly grown
Had a baby girl to call my own
Thought suicide was my only road
But she gave me a reason to carry on
'Cause I could not let it go down like that

CHORUS

CHORUS

Finally, I thought I'd found the better half of me
Had it all, gave me a honeymoon in Egypt overseas
When I started trusting in his promises
He changed his mind
Things go down like that

STOP LET'S GO

We're driving on emotion and the sun is in the ocean
And the night is falling in your eyes
You move a little closer your dress comes off your shoulder
And there's almost nothing left to hide
I'm rolling down the window the hot summer wind blows
Baby I'm getting lost
It's a sin to surrender but the white line down the center
Ain't the only one I wanna cross

CHORUS:
Stop – let's go – before this moment passes by
You lose that look that's in your eyes
Don't let the fire die
Stop – let's go – before we gain control again
And lose the salty taste of sin
And break the spell we're in

In a trail of utter passion
We leave our inhibitions scattered all along the beach
With the moonlight on your body, we run into the sea
Till the tide's pushing you to me
Kisses under water, you gently pull me under
The waves as we stop to breathe
Your body's on the border, you're beautiful torture
And it feels like an eternity

CHORUS

There is no tomorrow, there's no yesterday
There is only here and now, don't let it slip away

CHORUS

Stop – let's go – before this moment passes by
You lose that look that's in your eye
Don't let the fire die

STRIPTEASE

Conversation is really what I want
But I pretend to look
   out the window
Cause I know you are watching
Vibrations are getting even stronger
I turn off the AC cause baby want to
Make you sweat mi amor

CHORUS:
Take that shirt off
Let me see some more
Take that belt off
Let me see some more
Show me what you got
From your abs to your six pack
What's up with that
Take those shoes off
Let me see some more
Take them jeans off
Let me see some more
Show me what you got
From your abs to your six pack
What's up with that

All the boys strip for the girls now

Take my keys boy I'll meet you
   at the pent house
Start the Jacuzzi get juicy baby
You ready for me
Off limits is your ticket
Tonight come inside I know you
   a little shy

CHORUS

You can be my VIP
I'll dance for you
You dance for me, etc.

CHORUS

All the boys strip for the girls now
Take it off

You can be my VIP
I'll dance for you
You dance for me

Striptease for me, yeah
Take 'em off

You can be my VIP
I'll dance for you
You dance for me

It's uncontrollable this feeling within
Tell me where we can begin
Come on and dance for me
Striptease for me baby
It's irresistible the smell
   of your skin
Your eyes say come right on in
And I'm inviting you

CHORUS

STUCK ON YOU

Childish games of hide and seek
Nothing left to hide beneath
I paint my face in black and white
Quiet as a mime

All the things I feel inside
Immobilized in my mind
Without a word you vocalized
Tears in my eyes

CHORUS:
I'm on the edge of breaking down tonight
I can't speak my mind
But I cannot lie
And every day's just another waste of time
If I can't begin to face the truth that I'm
Stuck on you

Tried every remedy for this merciless disease
But all I found is misery
And no one to accommodate me

Building this wall between
Where I am and where I long to be
And everyday I hesitate
Makes it harder to speak

CHORUS

I wish you didn't matter so much to me
Or I could just forget this whole catastrophe
This life is passing by as I waste my time dying
To tell you what you mean to me

CHORUS

STUPID BOY

Stop begging me
Stupid, you're stupid
Stupid boy get out of my mind
Stop bugging me every time I try to
    forget we even met
You're back in my head
Tell me why
Why does everything have to
    be so confusing
Can't you just give me a clue
Is there something there 'cause
    there's something missing
I'd hate to think it's you

CHORUS:
They say if you love somebody
    let them go
And if they come back well then
    you'll know
Oh, sweet destiny I'm waiting
Stupid boy

Stupid boy just admit you're
    in love with me
I'm so impatient
Every day I wonder if there will be
    a sequel to this movie
Same cast different story, with you
    in my life
'Cause everything happens
    for a reason
That's just another sign

CHORUS

How long you going to
    make me wait
Baby, what's it going to take
For you to understand that I'm
    everything you need
I won't be afraid
I'm going to go ahead and say the
    words that we left unsaid

Well I love you baby,
    don't you know
And if you'll come back I won't
    let you go
Oh, sweet destiny I'm waiting

CHORUS

I'm still waiting
Stupid boy

SUBSTITUTE

Everybody knows, everyone but you
It clearly shows you don't get him
    like I do
He's only dating you 'cause plans
    fell through with me
So he settled for number two

My mind, no disrespect
You're cool but you two
    don't connect
Don't be fooled 'cause this
    game's correct
Said he loves you, lie and say
    you're the best

PRE-CHORUS:
Don't be mad at me cause
I got just what your boyfriend
    needs and
He won't do for you what he'll
    do for me
He might not be my type, but I won't
    say no if he says

CHORUS:
Won't you, won't you, oh
Won't you stay with me tonight
Don't you, don't you, oh
Don't you wanna come over
    to me tonight
And I'm not fronting girl
Sometimes we get it on after he
    drives you home
I give him what he wants
And if I'm in the mood

This is how we do
Sorry, damn, face it
You're just a substitute

I know it's wrong but I don't
    feel guilty
Can't help that his minds
    always on me
If you wonder why he's
    slow responding
He's daydreaming about our late
    night bonding
My mind, no disrespect
He plays you like a game I guess
Don't get caught up, he's
    all about sex
This is as real as it gets

PRE-CHORUS

CHORUS

PRE-CHORUS

CHORUS

SUMMER BITCH

I run my fingers through her hair
All I wanna do is hold her hand
And we lie
Our bodies intertwined
Staring at the sky all night
She's my summer love

She looked in my eyes
Told all of her lies
And I didn't know

CHORUS:
She's a summer bitch
She's a summer bitch
Bitch

As we waste all the days away
All I wanna do is stay forever
And pretend this would never end
And we could always be together
She's my summer love

And then she tore out my heart
And ripped it apart
And watched me bleed

CHORUS

What a bitch

SUMMER DAYS

Wearin' nothing but my summer
    dress on my body
I wave goodbye to all that
    emptiness, and I
Feel the sun on my skin
Warmin' up my heart within
Countin' the days

Lyin' in the park
Feelin' the spark
Til it get's dark
Doin' nothin' all day
    (daydreamin' away)
Messin' around
While I drown
Fallin' for somebody

CHORUS:
I can't wait for those summer days
    (seize the day)
Feel the sun shining on my face
Let someone take my breath away
And we'll see, ooh, ooh, and maybe
That someone is you

I've been ridin' on my bike
Rollin' down to the beach
Callin' all my friends
To come swim with me
And no more grades on my mind
And no exams to fail
I'm countin' the days

Endless nights, leopard skin tights,
Water fights, walkin' barefoot

Feelin' so good, if only I wouldn't
    have to wait

CHORUS

Lyin' in the park
Feelin' the spark
Til it get's dark
Doin' nothin' all day
    (daydreamin' away)
Messin' around
While I drown
Fallin' for somebody

Endless nights, leopard skin tights,
Water fights, walkin' barefoot
Feelin' so good, if only I wouldn't
    have to wait

CHORUS

CHORUS

Summer Love

I run my fingers through her hair
All I wanna do is hold her hand
And we lie
Our bodies intertwined
Staring at the sky all night
She's my summer love

She looks in my eyes
And I lose track of time
And I can't believe

CHORUS:
She's my summer love, etc.

As we waste all the days away
All I wanna do is stay forever
And pretend this would never end
And we could always be together
She's my summer love

She looks in my eyes
And I lose track of time
And I can't believe

CHORUS

You're my summer love

SUPERMODELS

(Here we go, single and fabulous)

Kickin' at home in my sweats,
   yo workin' on the tae-bo
Watchin' fitness videos
Gotta go do my hair up, get dressed
   so I look hot and stuff
Take off my glasses, put on
   my lip-gloss
Trippin' on my high heels (got my
   sneaks stashed in my bag)
Rockin' my new jeans (checkin' if
   I took off the tags)
Time to switch it up (be the leader
   of the pack)
And bring some sexy back

CHORUS:
Boys go wild everywhere around us
Dressed in style all the looks
   are on us
Can't hide everybody follow us
Like we supermodels,
   like we supermodels
No excuse, we're eye candy
We pick and choose, whatever
   comes handy
Stoppin' traffic every street
   we crossin'
Like we supermodels,
   like we supermodels

Red carpet got the walk down got
   this place on lock now
Paparazzi snappin' our shots wow

We're reppin' like celebrities
   everybody wants a piece
But we're going ìuh uh, pleaseî
Sexy like some cool cat who gets
   everything she wants
Let's keep it like that, that's where
   we're comin' from
Steppin' up like it's official
   (sassy, uh) collectin' guys
   like collectibles

CHORUS

(Supermodels, single and fabulous)

CHORUS

You can't touch this
You know you want this
Too bad you missed this
No excuse we're eye candy
We pick and choose whatever
   comes handy
Stoppin' traffic every street
   we crossin'
Like we supermodels,
   like we supermodels
I'm eye candy like
   a tootsie pop, etc.

SURPRISE MIX

At first we were the picture of a perfect love
It wasn't long before you started acting up
Leaving phone numbers in your pocket
But that's alright'cause you'll be needing
Them phone numbers after tonight

PRE-CHORUS:
I felt too comfortable
Believed that you were the one
I planned on being with you
Because I fell in love
But tables start to turn and
My patience is running out with you
Thought I was playing
Guess you were fooled

CHORUS:
Surprise
Bet you didn't think that I
Had enough strength inside
To leave this situation built on nothing but your lies
Had about enough of those
You can come and get your stuff
Surprise
Look who's saying goodbye

Did you expect that I'd accept the way you treated me
Don't call to check, what happens next
This wasn't meant to be
It's been confirmed that we are over
Although I tried to make this love thing last forever

PRE-CHORUS

CHORUS

CHORUS

SURRENDER

There are times you love somebody and get nothing in return
Sometimes somebody loves you more than you can bear
There are times when love takes over, you just crash and burn
But once in a lifetime you look up and it's right there

CHORUS:
And you surrender
Loving is so good it can't be real
You surrender
I can't believe how strong you make me feel
No one in this world can love me better
I think I never knew what love can do
I surrender to you

Sometimes love takes you for granted till you almost slip away
There are times you get so jealous love turns to hate
Sometimes your mind begins to wander into the arms of someone else
Just for you to come back crying to the one who stayed

CHORUS

Love's still there when the beauty is gone
Love is the reason why a child is born
It's what keeps us holding on
When we're fighting and everything goes wrong

CHORUS

I surrender

SURVIVE

I don't want to talk about it, it makes me want to cry
   (don't wanna talk about it)
Every time I pour out my emotions I feel emptier inside
I don't know how to play it like I'm not in love with you
But I'll try even though I do still

CHORUS:
Miss you, just like the air that I breathe
I need you with me
I'm not gonna lie
I can't imagine my life without you
But I suppose I will survive

I'm not going to play myself every time my cell rings
Checking for your name
I promise that I'll never tell you how I feel
   when I know that you don't feel the same
Didn't think that you could hurt me so
I just got to let you go
But every time I find myself alone

CHORUS

Don't try to explain why your love's changed
Boy you really broke my heart this time
I won't let it take away my pride or who I am inside
Boy I'm torn between everything
How could I feel nothing
Would've done anything if it'd mean I could make you love me
You're the one that I need
But you still believe we can never be

CHORUS

I'll be fine, don't worry about me
I'll be okay

SWEAT

It's 4 o'clock in the mornin'
Girls keep on comin'
About to reach the end of the list
Celebrities flashin' the bands
   on the wrist
DJ's spinnin' Motown
Inside it's really goin' down
The floor is packed
   the speakers' crankin'
People losin' their clothes,
   they're dancin'

CHORUS:
Sweat is drippin' down your body
You're tryin' to hide it but
   you're feelin' on somebody
   and the party is hot
And you keep on grindin'
Steam is present on the floor, your
   feet are gettin' sore
But you're feelin' the groove and
   you just can't stop
And you keep on movin'

Sweat – shirts are getting' wet
Sweat – your makeup's
   runnin' everywhere
Sweat – your hair is lookin' crazy
   on your head
But I don't care

A long line at the bathroom
Smelling candy and perfume
People passin' numbers and tryin'
   to get hooked up to the VIP room

Prince is in there jammin'
Supermodels hangin'
The new girl Tina, Jamie and Denzel
Hockin' sippin' champagnin'

CHORUS

Sweat – the party's goin' crazy now
Sweat – everybody's gettin' down
Sweat – somebody's rubbin' up
   on you (And you go)

Hips are goin' crazy
Everybody's ready
Faces stumpin'
Hearts are pumpin'
Speakers are bouncin'
Bodies interlockin'
Walls are shakin'
Glasses breakin'
It's jumpin' like a basement
   moonlight party in June

CHORUS

Sweat – shirts are gettin' wet
Sweat – your makeup's
   runnin' everywhere
Sweat – your hair is lookin' crazy
   on your head
But I don't care

Come on, bounce like that
Bounce, bounce

SWEATER

Memories like snowflakes
Falling in my head
Seems I'm always longing for
The one thing I can't get
They say it's sweeter to let the
    feeling grow
So I try to let go

Minutes pass like hours
And I'm drifting alone
Waiting for the rapids
When I get ya on the phone
The more I fall for you
The harder it gets to be alone

CHORUS:
I picture you hugging me like
    my sweater
On a cold winter day
We brave the stormy weather
And wish the clouds away
And we can be together
Hold each other come what may

Seasons are changing
Leaves are turning red
But I don't even notice
I can't seem to forget
Sunshine's on my face
But I won't let it make me smile

CHORUS

Can things ever go back again
To the way they were back when
Our love was innocent
And fear was just a stranger
When a wilted rose won't
    bloom again
And yet I seek a happy end
Knowing if I pick the scab
This wound will never mend

CHORUS

Sweet Sunday Mornings

Pacific coast highway
Waves crashing blue
Winds blowing at me
And I picture you

And sweet Sunday mornings
What love brings to you
Love is like a dream
And it's just me and you

Open my window
Sing me a song
Baby can't you see that this
Is where I belong?

With your hand in my hand
I still feel the love
I really wish that we could
   go back to
The way that it was

CHORUS:
They say if it doesn't kill you
It'll make you stronger
Oh but I can't be without you
   any longer
Every time I let it go baby, it's true
Nothing compares to you
Nothing compares to you

Sweet Sunday morning
All by myself
I'd rather be alone
Than with somebody else

Tears in my coffee
Wondering how
Baby, how did we end up like this?
And where are you now?

CHORUS

I'm running fast
Fast as I can
To get you back
Does it get back you again?
I cannot live, I cannot live
If we can't be
We can't be as we were
I cry at night, I cry at night
I cry for all the words
All words I didn't say
On Sweet Sunday
Sweet Sunday

CHORUS

TABOO

Whatchu say
Who, what, who

Mother says I'm too flirtatious
Ha, it's outrageous
Says I'm going through stages
But I can't help it
Blame it on Cupid

See wherever we going
All the boys wanna get to know me
Keke this, Keke that
Here's my number, won't you
   hit me back

CHORUS:
Boy
You're getting me all confused
I'm gonna get lost in you
But I know it's taboo, taboo,
   taboo, taboo
Boy
When I look into your eyes
There's something I feel inside
But it's taboo, taboo, taboo, taboo
Is it just my imagination
Or is it some kind of infatuation
Every time I say no, no, no
You think I say cool, cool, cool
Gotta keep my self control
Taboo, taboo, taboo, taboo

Now I'm getting older
Boys are getting bolder
I dusted off my shoulder

'Cause I don't want no rich kids
To think I'm playin' you

I try to tone it down but
I'm just like a bullet
What you gonna show in time
You bet I won't miss out
Taboo, taboo, taboo, taboo

CHORUS

I know we're just friends
But we have some feelings
I know you know we do
But it's taboo, taboo, taboo, taboo

Taboo, taboo, taboo, taboo, etc.

CHORUS

Take It Like a Man

You always mind what I say but I say what's on my mind
Always complain about my love but I think you just love to complain

Please don't act apologetic, boy you look so pathetic
Now that everything's falling apart
Should have stopped for just a minute
Before you pushed to the limit
Now it's too late to win back my heart

CHORUS:
I bet you wish you could take it all back
Should have seen this was coming
You never thought that I really had
Power of a woman
Should have loved what you had as much as you said
    instead of trying to change who I am
Now just take it like a man

You never let me be me, so I just went along
You loved me when I was weak, but now that I am strong
I don't care what you think, I don't care what you say
And I'm gonna do things my way
And I'm here to let you know that you've gotta let it go
There ain't no way I'm gonna stay

CHORUS

Seems you have the misconception love's just physical attraction
Never care to know what I'm all about
You've had every chance to show me that you meant the things you told me
And I wonder if anything was true

CHORUS

TAKE ME ON THE FLOOR

The lights are out and I barely know you
We're going up and the place is slowing down
I knew you'd come around
You captivate me, something about you has caught me
I was lonely now you make me feel alive
Will you be mine tonight

CHORUS:
Take me on the floor
I can give you more
I want you I want you I want you to show me love
Just take me on the floor
What are you waiting for
You kill me you kill me you kill me with your touch

My heart is racing as you're moving closer
You take me higher with every breath I take
Would it be wrong to stay
One look at you and I know what you're thinking
Time's a bitch and my heart is sinking down
You turn me inside out

CHORUS

I wanna kiss a girl, etc.
I wanna kiss a boy, etc.

Now everybody kiss

CHORUS

TAKE ME WITH YOU

It's too cold outside for you to go anywhere tonight
If it was 90 degrees I'd still want you right here next to me
Even in a crowded room I still feel alone without you
Please don't leave but if you have to

CHORUS:
Take me with you
Take me with you
Don't make me miss you
If leaving means being without you
Take me with you

If you could only see
Just what you're doing to me
I can't picture me without you
That's just like a star without a moon

CHORUS

I won't get into your way
If you won't leave that smile with me
But make sure when you pack your bags
To leave some room 'cause I'm coming with you

CHORUS

CHORUS

If leaving means being without you
I'm coming with you

TALKING TO SOMEBODY/PROOF

Do you lie
Whatchu gonna do
Whatchu gonna say

I found your password
I was warned it may be wrong, but
   I sure had no bad intentions
I just guessed and the first thing
   I tried was right
There it was – all these love letters
   before my eyes
Sayin' all these beautiful words
   to all these kind of girls
Does any of this sound familiar

CHORUS:
I know you're talking to somebody
Because you write to her like you
   write to me
Do you lie to her like you lie to me
Don't lie, you're talking
   to somebody
Don't explain 'cause I know what
   you're going to say
Don't tell me it's not true, no, no
'Cause baby I got proof

I was always behind you
Back in school, in your job, when
   you needed someone to run to
I thought we had a thing
It was me and you against the world
Had I only known about
   them other girls

I supported you all this time
Made sure that you're all fine
Does any of this sound familiar

CHORUS

You're gonna miss me
   when I'm gone
Don't want you answering my phone
Don't you think those girls
   ain't gonna leave
And when they do you'll come
   running back to me
'Cause I'm so over you
Now I got better things to do
Just to let you know, we're through

CHORUS

I know you're talking to somebody
Don't explain 'cause I know
   whatchu gonna say
Don't deny the truth 'cause baby
   I've seen the proof

THAT BOY

Tell me what should I do
What should I say
I'm lost for words
So I'm coming to you sisters
Will you help me

See I don't know
Where to start
To find the keys to win over
That boy's heart

They say just remember when your game comes into play
Gain your composure show respect and you'll be okay
Because the fellas really like it when
When you don't succeed, don't get offended
Listen when he speaks and don't pretend be
More than enough for when he needs a friend
So many things about a voice you'll really comprehend

CHORUS:
Ooh, ooh, ooh I like that boy
Ooh, ooh, ooh I like that boy
Yeah I know that he likes me too
But he's too shy to come talk to me
And I don't know how to make that move
I want him to be mine

Is he the one who will give me love
Love me for me, I'm not asking much
'Cause true love don't come easily
And if it's meant to be it'll happen naturally
If you don't look for love it might actually find you

CHORUS

Now it don't matter the size of your bankroll
'Cause I am independent, I can take care on my own
I don't care about your escalade or that your sittin' on chrome
'Cause when it comes down to a girl
You need a girl that you can take home

CHORUS

You know baby you're the best thing
I ever seen come 'round my way
And I want you to be down with me like I am with you
Yes you, boy you know you drive me crazy
Ooh yeah, you got me going ooh yeah
You got me going ooh yeah, you got me sayin' ooh yeah

I feelin' everything ya'll been talking 'bout
And for her it's time for me to kick the player out
With no doubt it's been running through my mind
Settlin' down, true love I have found
My world, she's forever my sunshine
My pot of gold at the end of the rainbow
See love is not about the sex or material
But it's meant to be heartfelt and spiritual

Ooh I like that boy yeah

THAT THING

I once met an old man who walked kind of funny
We started talking and he told me his life story
He was raised in Compton, LA and caught a stray bullet on his way home
And as he woke up the doctors told him
He'd never use his legs again

Sure was a sweet young nurse who cared for him
And soon she became the star of all his dreams
He wanted so badly to impress her
And be her man
That for years day after day
He learned how to walk again
All because of

CHORUS:
That thing they talk about
That could make a cripple dance and a blind man see
That thing they talk about
That could make an old woman feel like seventeen
It's stronger than pride
It's bigger than any word describes
And you thought it was a miracle

That very same thing could make you feel like nothing
Like you're so miserably lonely you wish you would die
You could spend a lifetime searching and never find it
But the moment you give up and turn around
It knocks you off your feet

CHORUS

A million dollars couldn't buy it
The FBI couldn't hide it
The strongest army couldn't fight it
And yet, the smallest heart can have it anytime

CHORUS

THAT TINGLE

Ain't never really happen like this
That I met a guy that turn me on
So quick, so slick, so mmm
You knew exactly what I want

When you got in the room,
    I start shaking
Someone's talking to you
My heart starts aching
And you don't even notice
    I am there

CHORUS:
Boy you give me that tingle
Got me laughing when I had
    a bad day
Got me chillin' every time
    that I'm late
Got me stuttering, I don't know
    what to say
And I'm not even single (tingle)
I just don't know what it
    is about you
Feelin' no matter what I do
Stumbling crazy over you, oh
Can't eat all week, can't
    sleep at night
Got me wondering if you're thinking
    about me sometime
Get weak when I hear you speak, oh
You give me that tingle

Got me feeling real silly right now
Writing love letters you'll never see
So hot, so good, so mmm

Whenever you talk to me
Whatever you say, can't
    help laughing
When I go away, feels like nothing
Nothing on my mind but you, etc.

CHORUS

If you've ever felt the way I feel
Let me hear you say oh
Diggin' somebody for real
Let me hear you say oh
Feelin' those chills shift from
    down your spine
Gotta think about somebody
    all the time
Let me hear you say oh

CHORUS

THAT'S THE FEELING

I think I could fly now
There's nothing left to hold me down
I'm high in the sky now
And if I should die
I think I've seen and done it all
I'm ready to try now
'Cause in this life
It's all about giving what you are
It's all about do it or you don't

CHORUS:
Oh it's a feeling you just can't describe
An unlocked treasure buried deep inside
Yeah, it's the feeling that I cannot hide
When I look in your eyes, that's the feeling
Yeah, that's the feeling

On top of the city
All the eyes are onto you
Hold it together, yeah
I made me an angel
Tracing halos in your hair
Keep me from danger
'Cause in this life
It's not about what you take and what you got
It's about what is in it and what's not

CHORUS

It doesn't matter if I'm rich or if I'm poor
If I'm successful and I got what everybody's working for
'Cause I hold it in my arms and I feel it in your kiss
It took a while to recognize it
But now I know just what it is

CHORUS

THIS IS HOW IT FEELS

You keep calling my
    phone non-stop
Don't you know I won't pick it up
You never leave a message
Look how you've changed

You got nothing to say
Getting in the way
You show up at my house
You're getting so obsessive
Like I have time for you

Wasn't it me you didn't want?
Wasn't it me who was hanging on?
No I done that before, let go
I want you to know

CHORUS:
This is how it feels
When you wait for a call that
    never comes
Lie awake at night 'cause you
    miss someone
This is how it feels
When the trust you had is broken
And you're left to burn with your
    heart wide open

You wanted me, not to tell me why,
    why and how
You had the heart to fuck up
    my whole life
That's just so you
Now I've moved on by myself

And maybe I won't forgive I'll just
    forget you lived
And hope it hurts

Wasn't it me you tried to blame?
Wasn't it me you threw away?
But before you go there's something
    you should know

CHORUS

You taught me how to hate you
When I was so in love
And when I tried to save us it
    was not enough
So what the hell is different?
'Cause now that I am gone
You're crawling back to tell me
    I'm the one

This is how it feels!

CHORUS

Do you only want me 'cause you
    can't have me?
Do you only want me 'cause
    I'm gone?, etc.

This Is the That

That is the that, etc.

I'm looking for my sugar
I'm looking for it sweet
He got to have taste that go
Tweet tweet tweet
He could be naughty and he
    could be nice
He better have money that go
Ching ching ching
Ching ching bling
Money that flows

He got to have heart but he need
    to have soul
Got to make up the love and
    lose control
He got to be cool and should
    good on me
So every car going by go
Beep beep beep

CHORUS:
That is the, that is the that, etc.
If you're coming to me hurry, boy
I ain't gonna wait
That is the, that is the that, etc.
Show me what you got boy
You know it better be hot

You got to move it to the east
When I shake it to the west
From the south to the north
Say yeah yeah yeah
Cause when I'm on the floor

I only run with the best
Are you with me now
Are you in or out

If you're feeling what I'm saying
Just let me know
Holler to me now say oh oh oh
Turn the music up turn the lights
    down low
Check up on me sugar
Let's go go go

CHORUS

You act like you can't see
You was examining me like
    I ain't marvelous
Girl I'll scoop you up
    in the quickness
If you trying to figure out if I got
    rocks and bling
I'll make you freeze up like
    a hockey rink
It's a breeze when I'm talking to you
It's an issue if I'm not with you
That is the that is the that
Oh, so what is the what is the what

CHORUS

CHORUS

CHORUS

THIS LOVE

I can see it in your eyes
Taste it in our first kiss
Stranger in this lonely town
Save me from my emptiness

You took my hand
You told me it would be ok
I'm trusting you to hold my heart
Now fate is pulling me away, from you

CHORUS:
Even if I leave you now
And it breaks my heart
Even if I'm not around
I won't give in
I can't give up
On this love

You've become a piece of me
It makes me sick to even think
Of mornings waking up alone
Searching for you in my sheets
Don't fade away

CHORUS

Every night I try to sleep as much as possible
'Cause in my dreams nothing is impossible
I think about your touch when I'm lying next to you
I'm going crazy, do you feel it too?
Every day gone is now another day closer
And missing you, it makes me love you more than ever
Tell me the truth, no matter what we're going through
Will you hold on too, 'cause

CHORUS, etc.

TIGHT

It's Friday night
Hittin' the club with my girls tonight (what)
I'm hanging out with my girls tonight (who)
Tamika, Ranisha, Shaniqua, Alicia
Myesha, Aylisha, Janelle, Shanelle
Danielle, Michelle, Rochelle, Anelle
Leave your troubles at the door
Ya'll know what you came here for

Tell your friends to come along (okay)
My crew, your crew, we can get it on
And wear that little thing I like, you know, a thong
I wanna see you bounce and shake it all night long
Baby, leave your digits on the dresser
I'll call you (sure you will, yeah, whateva)
Okay, I'll have it your way
It's all right with me, so what's it gonna be

PRE-CHORUS:
Ladies, (hey) open up a bottle of Cris, and make your man lose it
You ain't gotta hurt nobody, shake it on the floor
Let him know that you want some more
Fellas, you know your game is tight you'll be leavin' with a lady tonight
Take her home and lay down that pipe
And make this night last forever

CHORUS:
Do what ya gotta do to the music
Take it slow and lose your mind in the music
Let these brothers know you know how to move it
Don't procrastinate, get right to it
Cause if you know what it is then the game's on
Sky's the limit, baby girl, you go on and on
Too hot in here, I wanna take my clothes off
Take my clothes off

Body goin' through convulsions like you on crack
Yeah, baby, you can dance, but your game is whack
The way I work it on the floor, I know you like that
I'm with my crew Fatty Koo, you know where I'm at
And maybe I can take your cell, but I won't hit you back
Come get with me, you feel you won't, but you still wanna
For me the night is goin' just how it's supposed ta
It makes me kinda wanna get a little closer

PRE-CHORUS

CHORUS

You wan come test me
My style's too sweet, he can't touch me
This lady's style spittin' lovely
Are you really ready for this jelly
Ya like it when we do it right there
Tell your man come chill right here
While the models take down their hair
Strike a pose and step right there
Ya wonder how I waltz in these jeans
There's room for two in these jeans
Lookin' so fresh and so clean
I talk slick with my woman's means
You don't have to call, I'ma be okay
Said I'm chillin' with my girls tonight
So it's gonna be all right
I said it's gonna be all right

PRE-CHORUS

CHORUS

Come on dance with me

CHORUS

THE TIME IS NOW

Isn't it funny how things fall into place
When you least expect it
From a distance this girl and her heart looked disconnected
Life's been throwing these signs in my face
But I was distracted
Playing safe instead of turning the wheel
Where my heart directs it

PRE-CHORUS
Go, go, go, go, go
My heart says
Go, go, go, go, go
But my mind says
No, no, no, no, no
No matter what I do I'm somehow
Always getting stuck in-between

CHORUS:
If there ever is a time the time is now
By living life that's not mine
I'm letting myself down
I think I'm forming much too long
I got to let it out
And if there ever is a time the time is now

I took a lifetime getting to this point
And I knew I would regret the rest of my life
If I couldn't run with it when I could
Daddy always said the way is where your fear is
Nothing's holding me back right now
But my own insecurities

PRE-CHORUS

CHORUS

CHORUS

TO BE LOVED

I can see your face
Everywhere I look
Everywhere is nowhere without you
What seemed to be like days
Is just a moment in time
But it meant the world to me
Cuz I knew
What I've been searchin' for all
   of my life
I had it right here in front
   of my eyes
What I've wished for was
   nothing compared
To what I received when you're
   here with me

CHORUS:
And if you never come back
And today was all that we had
And if I wont see tomorrow with you
In my arms it won't matter because
Now I know what its like to be loved

You're so far away
But I feel you so near
Its like you never left me
Never said goodbye
I can hear your voice in the crowd
I can feel you touch me right now
I can see your smile when
   I close my eyes

And I hold onto that every night
To help me understand
When I ask myself why

Of all the people out there
You chose to be with me
To share a love so rare

CHORUS

What a beautiful thing
To feel your love within
Like a child that sees the sunshine
On the first day of spring
Just to know it's true
There is someone like you
Who can make me believe
There is nothing I can't do

CHORUS

Now I know what its like
To be loved

Today's the Day

It's Thursday, a typical Thursday
For everyone else but not for me
I'm tired of the man trying
    to hold me down
And damn it I deserve to be free
Every time I get a second to breathe
My boss is on the loudspeaker
    calling for B (calling
    Brenda Radney)
Well get used to me not
    being around
Peace, I'm out everyone you'll see
This dude's standing in my way
Yelling at me, girl you're late
But I'm laughing in his face
'Cause today's the day

CHORUS:
Today's the day I'm leaving
Take my badge and my keys
I don't work here anymore
I don't care if you still need me
Save your words for another day
Because I'm gone
Erase my information
You can keep my short vacation
I'm done with being patient
Waiting for my raise that never came
Working endless hours
Think you abuse your powers
I'm walking out and
I know you'll remember my name

Now I know I should be kind of
    feeling bad
Just walking out like this
But I don't and I wont you can cope
Cause I ain't putting up
    with your shhh
I'm sorry these final days ain't
    worth my time
It sure ain't worth the crappy pay
Just to let you know all the money
    in the world
Could never make me stay because

CHORUS

It's time for me to get away
From this delusion
And I know you'll remember
    my name
It's time for me to get away
From this illusion
And I know you'll remember
    my name

CHORUS

And I know you'll remember
    my name, etc.

TOO MANY PILLOWS

There are too many pillows
    between us
And too many ways to fall
Too many words to saw through
I can't sleep 'till you've
    heard them all

There are too many pillows
    between us
I'm so anxious to see them gone
Once the sheets are off and
    the covers are lost
What if we realize we were wrong

CHORUS:
They say love is sure
And if you're lucky to find love
Don't let it slip away
But they seem to forget all
    the pain of regret
When you lose the love you made
But that's a chance I'll take
That's a chance I'll take

There are too many pillows
    between us
And time keeps moving on
And I'm scared if I don't tell
    you my heart
Someone else will come along

There are too many pillows
    between us
No I can't even count them all

But one by one we can throw
    them all off
And tear down these walls

CHORUS

I can never forgive myself
    for giving in
To the fear of letting go
Though I may not know what to say
I'm trying anyway
I've gotta let you know
Let you know

CHORUS

TOO SHY

You got me feeling like
I'm feeling like I never felt before
You got that something got me open
Make me want that thing
   some more
Like every time I see that picture
That I want to come and get you
Think about the time I met you
Oh baby baby baby
I think about every time I kiss you
And how I just can't resist you
Do you know how much I miss you

CHORUS:
Just take it one step at a time
'Til you give me all the signs
Wish that I could read your mind
Can't be wrong if it feels right
Is it fate or is it I'm only
   dreaming all this time
I want to let you know but
   I'm too shy to tell you

So many times a perfect moment
   passed me by
Thought I was ready
But I just can't seem
   to find the nerve
To let the words come
   through to you
Like every time when you
   come on over
I really want to go there
I'm afraid it's going nowhere
Oh baby baby baby

And every time I get in closer
You don't do what you're
   supposed to
You only let me hold you

CHORUS

You ain't got to be nervous shorty
I'm shy too
If we have a love accident I
   promise I won't sue
Love is love we give we're
   the perfect strangers
Only God would like it if we could
   share these angels
A kiss is a memory a touch
   is a feeling
But when you're in my arms I feel
   like I'm holding a million
You're living proof that
   dreams come true
I've been sleeping a long time until
   I woke up and found you

If we both keep running away
   from the truth
How am I ever gonna get with you
If you want a woman then act
   like a man
Somebody's got to be the first
   to make a move

CHORUS

TOUCH DOWN

Bass drum hittin' hard kickin' like a needle aid
Floor under my feet is shaking like an earthquake
Strobe lights in my eyes got me seeing stars
And you got to get my body baby whoever you are
Fast forward to the beat of 2024
Future sound hypnotic tearing down the floor
East Coast, West Coast, Asia and Africa
Pumping in the airwaves banging loud in Africa

PRE-CHORUS:
Flippers up
Everybody throw your flippers up
Flippers up flippers up take 'em to the top
Touchdown, touchdown take 'em to the ground
Touchdown all the way down to the ground

PRE-CHORUS

CHORUS:
A 747 is safer when it stays on the ground
But everybody knows that it was meant to fly, etc.
Why you standing in the corner winking around
Come on get up on the floor and rock it
Don't be shy, be shy, etc.

Everybody glistening shining in sweat
Ain't nobody leaving cause we ain't done yet
Red Bull, energy flowing through my veins
Watch me get low on stage
Rewind to the sound of 1999
Prince singing like it was the end of time
Party like tomorrow is judgment day
Armageddon is making my body get up and break

PRE-CHORUS

CHORUS 2

Don't be shy with me
Go through the motion in slow motion
Baby it's time to slow it down
Let me see your hands
Go through the motion in slow motion
Do it a second time around
Take it on down

Touchdown, touchdown take 'em to the ground
Touchdown all the way down to the ground, etc.

CHORUS

Go through the motion in slow motion
Baby it's time to slow it down
Go through the motion in slow motion
Do it a second time around
Let me see you get your hands up

Now baby touchdown, touchdown
Take it to the ground

TOUCHED

Saw you standing in the dark
And I like your energy
I'm feeling you way from afar
Boy you're distracting me
My heart is racing body's aching
And I'm shaking all because of you

Now I'm thinking about
   who you with
'Cause you got me curious
If you don't come closer
   I'ma have a fit
Tell me boy what you thinking too
Got to know if you feel
   the same way I do

CHORUS:
I can be your lady
You can be my baby
So don't keep me waiting
I want to be touched, want
   to be touched, etc.
Cause I got this problem
Only you can solve it
But you got to come to me
I want to be touched, want
   to be touched, etc.

You got to get to know me first
And we can take it further
And I can't help but flirt cause
   I'd be crazy
If I let you leave without
   your number

Boy don't make me wait
   too long for you

Now I'm thinking about who
   you're with
'Cause you got me curious
If you don't come closer
   I'ma have a fit
Tell me boy what you're
   thinking too
Got to know if you feel
   the same way I do

CHORUS

I never believed in love at first sight
But you make me want
   to give it a try
You wont regret boy if you let me in

CHORUS

TROUBLE

Sexy sexy
Sexy sexy
That's right

Ridin', ridin', ridin' pulled up
   at the light
Turn the music up, make sure she
   caught my eye
Shorty where you heading, come
   on up inside
Let's go find a place where we can
   chill all night

Sexy sexy I can't deny it
Sexy sexy and you can't hide it
Sexy sexy don't try to fight it
I like your vibe it's going
   down tonight

CHORUS:
Well it's just me and you so what
   you gonna do
Girl like you with a guy like me
   about to be some trouble
Girl I'm in the mood to do
   something freaky with you
Guy like me with a girl like you,
   about to be some trouble

Riding, riding, riding giving
   it some gas
I can tell you like it when
   I'm going fast
Baby take the wheel, mama
   just lay back

I'm telling you no lie, want it
   just like that

Sexy sexy I can't deny it
Sexy sexy and you can't hide it
Sexy sexy
I like your vibe it's going
   down tonight

CHORUS

Guy like me with a girl like you,
   about to be some trouble

Sexy sexy I can't deny it
Sexy sexy you can't hide it
Sexy sexy don't try to fight it
I like your vibe it's going
   down tonight

CHORUS

CHORUS

TRUE LOVE

CHORUS:
At the end of the day
Go home to the one who loves you
Don't waste your time playing around
You know that true love
Doesn't always come easy
So treasure what you found
Treasure what you found
'Cause true love may never come back around

Baby come home to me now
Don't you know I need cuddles and kisses from you
It feels like forever since you went out late
Are you thinking of me
'Cause I'm thinking of you
And I want you to know that I love you
And miss you more than anything

CHORUS

Patience is one of those things that is hard to achieve
But I want to believe that you're faithful to me
I know you are, babe

I don't doubt that you love me
Or doubt that you're true
Which is worry when I'm waiting for you
And I drive myself crazy

CHORUS

CHORUS

TWO BOYZ

Some girls might think I'm lucky
But I don't know what to do
I got myself in a predicament
And now I don't have a clue
I don't know how to begin
I feel my loving to sin
But I swear I'm innocent
My feelings taking control
And now it's taking its toll
But it just don't make sense

Why is falling in love so easy
But being in love's so damn hard

CHORUS:
'Cause I'm in love with two
    different boys
And it's difficult for me to
    make a choice
One of them has my heart
And the other one I loved
    from the start
I don't know which way to turn
Whatever I do one of them
    will get hurt
How did I get myself in this mess
It's so hard having to confess
I wish I could take both and not
    let either know
But one day it will show

It's tearing me apart
Having to share my heart this way
Don't wanna just go for one
And send the other one away

Why does it have to be like this
I can't win one way or another
I have to make up my mind
But either way it's over

Why is falling in love so easy
But being in love's so damn hard

CHORUS

My head is spinning with all
    these emotions
Trying to keep my options open
Whichever way I go it
    seems so wrong

Why is falling in love so easy
But being in love's so damn hard

CHORUS

Two People

I was just thinking how you're doing
That's when the phone was ringing, sure enough it's you
You read my thoughts before I say them out loud
And when you try to keep me guessing I know what it's all about

CHORUS:
Cause we're two people, one heart
I feel you with me wherever you are
When the days get lonely and times get hard
We're still two people one heart

Your silence comforts when words aren't enough
You show me the meaning of love

CHORUS

Sometimes I wonder why you know me so well
Why it feels so good just to be close to you
No matter if it storms outside and everything goes wrong,
We laugh about it and move on

CHORUS

Two Sides to a Story

It was the month of May I was so happy on this day
It had been so long since I had seen your face
The moment you walked through the door
You smelled like her, I could have sworn
Oh, I didn't say a word but inside I felt so hurt

CHORUS:
You probably never realized
You were the sun in my sky
Every day would set and rise
With only you on my mind
I will wait for you to worry
But looking back you'll be surprised
Oh, there's always two sides to a story
And it's time to tell mine

You always thought we were so tight but your best friend gave me the eye
Just ignoring everything we had he went right behind your back
I can't deny he was my type and you were out that summer night
But the thought of being untrue made me save my love for you

CHORUS

Why do guys take their loved one for granted risking to lose her
Just to find that she is all that they wanted when it's over
And the bridges are burned

CHORUS

UNBELIEVABLE

I wish you didn't love me, I wish you'd make this easy
It was love that caught me, now it's fear that keeps me with you
I want to be by your side, so I can close my eyes
To crawl with emptiness inside that kills me when I am with you

You try to break me, you try to hate me
So you can fall out of love
You want to make me believe that I'm crazy
That I'm nothing without you

CHORUS:
It's unbelievable, but I believed you
It's unforgivable, but I forgave you
Insane what love can do
That keeps me coming back to you
Irreplaceable, but I replaced you
Now I'm standing on my own
Alone

I feel you in my shadow, my heart feels cold and hollow
No matter where I run I see your eyes always follow me

You try to hold me, you try to own me
Keeping something that's not yours
You want to make me believe that I'm crazy
Make me think that you're the cure

CHORUS

You're still haunting me in my sleep
You're all I see, but I can't go back
'Cause I know it's wrong for us to go on
And I'm growing strong to confront my fears

CHORUS

UNBREAKABLE

It's raining in my mind
Words like broken pieces
Shattering between us
I watch the plates fly by
I'm tired of playing Jesus in this dusty circus

We've been there before
And I can't live like this no more
I said I can't live like this no more

CHORUS:
Are you even listening to me
You only hear what you wanna hear
The sound of breaking china
Is ringing in my ear
Did you get a single word I said
Maybe you should be a little more careful
'Cause my love is not unbreakable

Why should I give in
This is getting boring
You're so unforgiving
You think the world revolves around you
But the gravity is changing
You don't even notice
Making me feel guilty
Isn't working anymore
I remember we were lovers
And now we're fighting wars

CHORUS

If you really care handle with care, etc.

CHORUS

'Cause my love is not unbreakable

UNCHARTED TERRITORY

So unlike me
What's going on
I'm usually not the one
To be afraid
Hesitate
Second-guess what I've done
Am I over thinking it
Complicating it
Should I let go and let it be

Never done this before
How am I supposed to know
Where I go from here
No prescription, no rules
No direction, no science
That will make it clear

PRE-CHORUS
Like the first man on the moon
Columbus 1492
Like baby steps
And babies don't worry
So why should I

CHORUS:
Uncharted territory
Uncharted territory
When I'm in uncharted territory
Uncharted territory

Sort of unprepared
Just a little scared
Say "Go get it girl"
Grab a hold of it

Slip inside myself
Find clarity
Patience
Don't give up on me

Am I over thinking it
Complicating it
All I've gotta do is do it

Never done this before
How am I supposed to know
Where I go from here
No prescription, no rules
No direction, no science
That will make it clear

PRE-CHORUS

CHORUS

When I'm in uncharted territory
Uncharted territory
Why should I

We've gotta be brave now
Don't play it safe now
Now why should I
Why should I worry, etc.

PRE-CHORUS

CHORUS

UNCONDITIONAL

No safety net, no parachute to hold on to if you fall
No plan B and no promises, no guarantees at all
When you're ready to love like you've never been hurt before

CHORUS:
That kind of love is unconditional
It's in your heart completely irrational
When you're willing to give though you might lose it all
That kind of love is unconditional

Unscripted, unpredictable, it short-circuits your brain
No price tag, no instructions, and nothing to explain
When you know what to do though you've never done it before

CHORUS

When you're standing naked you got nothing to hide
When you feel accepted you don't criticize
Cause you're already perfect in each other's eyes

CHORUS

UNDERNEATH

You know that East Coast girls
  always say what we mean
And shy Southern boys often
  don't say a thing
But opposites attract and you were
  drawn to me
And something 'bout you sparked
  my curiosity

They say that good guys usually
  don't come in first
Good girls fall for bad guys, but
  with us it's reverse
Not your average love song between
  you and me
The way the story unfolds
  defies gravity

CHORUS:
Don't have to put on my makeup
I can leave out my contacts
Don't have to dress up for you
To think that I'm beautiful
If I have a moody day
I don't have to act like I'm okay
I'm overdramatic and you know
how to handle it
Act natural, be emotional
Show my insecurities
I love the way that you love me
For who I am underneath

They say that guys keep
  conversation short and sweet

And girls can talk for hours 'til they
  put you to sleep
But you're the one who checks up
  on me throughout the day
You stay on the phone even if there's
  nothing to say

Most guys that I know like to go
  out at night
But you leave that to me 'cause
  you're not that type
And we don't need to do anything
  special to be happy
We've got what we need
Make each other complete

CHORUS

Link by link, you unravel me
Sometimes I am rough
  around the edges
But you handle me gently
And layer by layer, I uncover you
Discover a side of you that
  I never knew
Underneath

CHORUS

Who I am underneath
I love you for loving me
For who I am underneath

UNDERNEATH

Underneath, underneath, etc.

You're feelin' lonely
Think nobody loves you
Maybe you just need to love yourself
    a little more
Don't let your insecurities (no, no)
Beat you up inside (no, no)
You're beautiful so go and
    let it shine   .

I see you lookin' at the sky but all
    you see is gray
Why can't you see the rainbow
    through the rain
(Don't you know)

CHORUS:
You're more than your fancy clothes
More than the friends you know
More than your make up, you better
    wake up
And this is crazy
Forget about this fantasy
Cuz you got personality
I love you for who you are
Underneath

Wear your inside
On the outside (Yeah girl)
Show your true colors to the world
(Underneath, underneath)
You're standing out cuz
    people are different
    (Underneath, underneath)

Wouldn't it be boring if everyone
    was the same

Don't let the boys who don't love
    you for your inner beauty
Start to love you
Oh, you don't need to be your body

CHORUS

Be the star you already are
You know you're precious you've
    come so far (Be the star)
Be the girl you wanna be
Cuz everything else is
    a waste of time
It's your heart and its your life
    (Girl it's your life)

CHORUS

CHORUS

UNSCRIPTED

I got my hair did all for you
Cleaned up my prettiness
'Cause you said I had to

I broke my favorite shades in a mad rush
'Cause all your rules and orders upset me so much

Girl you better hurry up
But I'm feeling like shit
Girl you better dress up
But I'm wearing what I feel
Girl you better act nice
But I act like a clown
And just 'cause you don't want me to, yeah

CHORUS:
'Cause this is my life
This ain't no movie
If I can't do what I wanna do I
I'm going crazy
'Cause all you're doing
Is getting me conflicted
Gotta live, gotta live, my life
Unscripted

Do what I want to when I want to
When I want to
How I want to
When I've got to

I wanna wake up and spread my wings
Put up a smile and let the day begin
Life's a contradiction; so am I
Unpredictable and sometimes shy

You tell me to shut up
But I wanna talk loud
You tell me to give up
But I wanna push hard
You tell me to stop trying
But I wanna go far
Just to prove you wrong, yeah

CHORUS

You think that you've got me, yeah
Know what's going on inside my head
Size me up in just one look
Ain't nothing about me textbook
Do your thing
Whatever makes you happy
Sit it back and let me do me
And maybe you'll know me

Just keep the negative stuff in the streets
You will not control me
Not now, nor ever

CHORUS

CHORUS

What I want to
When I want to
How I want to
When I've got to, etc.

UNTOUCHED

I go ooh ooh, you go aah,
   aah, lalalala, etc.
I wanna get what I want don't stop
Give me give me give me
   what you got
Cause I can't wait any more
Don't even talk about
   the consequence
Cause right now you're
   the only thing that's making
   any sense to me
And I don't give a damn what
   they say, what they think
Cause you're the only one that's
   on my mind
I'll never ever let you leave me
I'll try to stop time for ever never
   wanna hear you say goodbye

CHORUS:
I feel so untouched
And I want you so much
That I just can't resist you
It's not enough to say that I miss you
I feel so untouched right now
Need you so much somehow
I can't forget you
I've gone crazy from the moment
   I met you

Untouched
And I need you so much

See you breathe you I want
   to be you

Llalala, etc.
You can take time
To live the way you gotta
   live your life

Give me give me give me all of you
Don't be scared
To see through the loneliness of
   one more moment
Don't even think about what's right
   or wrong or wrong or right
'Cause in the end it's only
   you and me and no one
   else is gonna be around
To answer all the questions
   left behind
And you and I are meant to be so
   even if the world falls down today
You've still got me to hold you up
   and I will never let you down

CHORUS

Untouched, etc.

CHORUS

365

URLY MORNING GURL

CHORUS:
I'm not an early morning girl
Don't you know
If you hit me up before 11 AM
I won't open the door
The answering machine's gonna
    give you company
While I finish my dreams
I need time for my hair and for my
    thoughts to clear
So please be patient with me

I need a minimum of eight hours
    of beauty sleep
Anytime before
Don't talk to me
And if you've gotta wake me up
It's a essential to be gentle
'Cause there's potential that
    I'll go mental

It helps if someone brings
    breakfast to me
Hot croissants and a cup of Rosalee
Don't rush me
I'll be ready whenever I'm ready

CHORUS

I'm in a lazy phase with my
    crazy ways
Too many rainy days give me
    a hazy gaze
I've gotta naturally rise

Strict rules apply
Don't open the blinds 'cause it
    hurts my eyes

And if I'm in the bathroom give
    me two hours
I need to find myself in the shower
Don't rush me
I'm ready whenever I'm ready

CHORUS

You've gotta be patient with me
Please stay out of my way
'Cause I won't be any good
If I'm not in the mood

CHORUS

CHORUS

366

V.A.C.A.T.I.O.N.

I'm starting to feel invisible
Waiting for the light to shed on
Everything I want and more
Run right past these times I dread
Been feeling this way for so long
Insensitive even when I'm wrong
Getting claustrophobic
    by these walls
Got to get my problems solved

I need to get away now
I need to get away now

CHORUS:
Vacation's just what I need
Get away, holiday just for me
I want to feel warm sand
    under my feet
Blue skies, nice breeze and
    palm trees
Vacation's just what I need
Get away, holiday just for me
I want to feel warm sand
    under my feet
Blue skies, nice breeze and
    palm trees
Vacation's just what I need
Get away, holiday just for me
I want to feel warm sand
    under my feet

Now breathe, chill, relax
Take all the burdens off my back
I'm done, finite, I'm packed

Ready to go, don't know when
    I'll be back
Don't wait for me to return
No, I'll call as soon as I've learned
How to deal with all this bullshit
    around me
And sadly it's a little cloudy in
    my head all day
Never can find the right
    words to say
When these haters step in my way
I'm always the one who pays
Emotional punching bag
I'll never go back to that
Got my self esteem on track
I'm out don't miss me too bad

CHORUS

You can take one look at me
And see that I'm a little disturbed
No one can help me but myself
And no one else that's my word
It's long past due
Allow myself to be consumed
Rewind, recharge and reconnect to
My soul, sanity, my life and you, etc.

CHORUS

Rewind, recharge and reconnect to
My soul, sanity, my life and you, etc.

VINDICATION

Endless nights I lie awake thinking what went wrong
I'm afraid that it's too late but I'm still hanging on
Where have you gone, Mother
It's been so long since I've seen you
Can someone take me home I can't take this anymore
Mama

CHORUS:
Are you thinking of me
Do your days feel empty
Do you look at the photographs
The ones that used to make us laugh
Is it worth a lifetime of bitter separation
How can we forgive when all we want is vindication

I shut you out of my life erased you from my mind
Changed my number went to hide but I still feel you inside
Where have you gone, Mother
Do you know how much I love you
Can someone take me can you take me home
Where I belong

CHORUS

CHORUS

THE VOID

They think they have the answers
For questions you don't ask
They think they know your future
By judging from their past
They tell you of your problems
And you buy right in
Inside you know they're full of it
They need you more than you need them

CHORUS:
It doesn't really matter
What they see in you
They think they know you better
But don't believe it's true
Don't listen to these people
They don't know what they say
Don't listen to their noise
You're better off this way
'Cause it all goes down the void

They say that you're not perfect
But no one is
But really you are special
And they're a bunch of kids

CHORUS

It doesn't really matter
What they see in you
They think they know you better
But don't believe it's true
'Cause it all goes down the void

WAIT A MINUTE

Sitting in my room reading messages I got from you
Seems like forever since I last had you
Over and over again I know every word by heart now
I picture you waking up in an empty bed
How I wish you were here with me instead
But I guess the distance makes the heart grow fonder

CHORUS:
I can't wait to get home
I can't wait to be in your arms
The days are killing me without you
Every thought I have surrounds you baby
Wait until I get home
Save your kisses, save your love
For the moment when I see you and it's only you and me
And I surrender, I surrender, I surrender to you

I can't believe I found myself doing all these silly things
Press my lips against your picture
And I sing the song I wrote for you
I know every word by heart now
Call me in the morning, in the afternoon, and at night
If I don't hear from you it just don't seem right
Something about your voice makes me feel so safe oh darling

Wait a minute, wait until I get home, etc.

CHORUS

Wait a minute, wait until I get home, etc.

CHORUS

WAITING FOR YOU

I miss you
I miss you
So much, etc.

Got to be strong
But I believe
You said that all was up to me
When you come back
Back to me
I will be
I will be here, etc.

WAKE UP CALL

Hey, just givin' you a wake up call

CHORUS:
I'm giving you a wake up call
Wake up, wake up
Just to say I love you
And that I'm thinking of you
Let you know that you've got friends
I'm giving you a wake up call
Wake up, wake up
It's a beautiful day
Don't let it slip away
And live it like it's the first day
Of the rest of your life

Just stopping by
To let you know what's up
Give you a call to see what you're doin'
I got somewhere to go today
I wanted to know if you would come and have fun with me

I know you got some plans
But we can hang with friends
Just wanna chill with you
So what'cha gonna do
Baby, it's up to you

CHORUS

Wake up, wake up, etc.

It's me and my friends
At the crib, eatin' pizza
Coolin' it down while we watch a movie
Don't need no moms and dads

We got it covered
'Cause we know exactly what we doin'
You don't wanna miss out
Hanging home all alone
While we're sittin' here havin' a party
You know the location
So here's my invitation

CHORUS

You know it's party time
All hatin' left behind
It's the party of the year
I'm so glad it's mine
Ladies ride through
Fellas come too
You see the videos
You know what I'm about to do
Set the roof on fire
Got the rhythm wire
Got'cha singing like the Harlem boys' church choir
Yeah, you know what's up
I see you gettin' buck
But before we get started
You gotta wake up

CHORUS

Wake up, wake up
I'm giving you a wake up call
Wake up, wake up

THE WALL

The mirror always said I was an ugly child
Even when my Momma said "That is a lie"
When I went to school I couldn't find my place
Dreaming every day that I could switch my face
Now I'm all grown up and it feels so absurd
That I'm still fetching for attention to confirm my world

CHORUS:
Oh, why do I need you to love me to love myself
Need you to validate how I feel
If God made every one of us the same
Why can't I love me the way that I am
Are you prettier standing next to me
Are you really better than I'll ever be
Every time I believe that you are
I just add another brick to the wall

I'm staring in the mirror putting makeup on
I don't know who the fuck it is I'm hiding from
You always need to tell me that I'm beautiful
And even when you do I don't believe it no more

CHORUS

You say all I should do is take one day at a time and I'll feel much better
And that this shit is all in the mind that I've built over time I'm my own
biggest hater
The trophies that I could receive will never make me believe that I really
deserve them
If I'm not at a peace with myself and keep competing with everyone else

CHORUS

To the wall, to the wall

THE WALTZ

The touch, the rush, oh, etc.

You turn around and make me
Wanna make you think I'm into you
An easy catch, the perfect guy
With perfect lines, it's nothing new
I guess I'll let you have a little taste
'Cause I have nothing here to lose
And if nothing's better than this
Then I guess that's better
   than nothing
What you think I'll do?

The more you play hard to get
The more I think I could
   get into you
The way you dance, and walk away
I can't believe you're getting
   me confused

CHORUS:
You make me feel so - oh
You make, etc.
You make me feel so - oh
Let's go, you know, take it slow

You say you don't want me
You've got it all under control
And I'm like
Yeah, all right, you Casanova, I'm
   gonna waltz right over you
You play your petty games
And I have to admit it's sorta
   kinda cute

But it won't be enough to make me
   fall in love
With a shallow guy like you

You're so naïve if you believe
I'd fall under your spell just
   'cause you snap
What's wrong with me, could you
   tell me please
How did you ever manage
   to do that?

CHORUS

The touch, the rush, etc.

CHORUS, etc.

WE COMIN' UP

CHORUS:
Wherever it's going down we're coming up
All my ladies photogenic, hot and glamorous
We're ruling the spot
Shaking our sexy hmm, like what
Checking if it's sexy what you got
Moving in the spotlight, dress skintight
Party all night boys that's right
Wherever it's going down we're coming up

We shake it up how we like to do
Making them magic 'cause they like how we move
Can't touch it I'm a natural baby
Look around ain't seen a finer lady
Hopping, rocking, ain't no stopping
Now that we got this party hopping
Let's change it up, change the scene
Take it slow or else you know what I mean

CHORUS

Let's move to the next location
VIP information
Don't need no conversation
Sneaking out the back door
Let's crash another party
We never stop until we find the hotter ladies
Let's go
Let's sneak out that back door ladies

CHORUS

CHORUS

WE DA CHAMPIONS

Pull my hair back in a ponytail
So fresh, laced up in my pink
    and white Nikes
Gotta stretch before we hold it down
That's when I'm feeling
    double-dutchy
There ain't no stoppin'

Tiptoe when I do my dance
Get up or get out, hey
Show 'em your stance
One a baby
Two a baby
Three a baby
Jump
Gonna show 'em how we get crunk
Throw your hands up

CHORUS:
And we're jumpin', jumpin'
Early in the morning
Ain't no stoppin', stoppin'
'Till the break of dawn
We da champions, champions
Everybody know
Get it crackin', crackin'
Let the speakers blow
If you wanna get in line
Better be on time
When the school bell rings at a
    quarter of nine
We're da champions, champions
Everbody know
Here we go, jump

Here we jump one time

Pull tricks like you've never seen
Ain't nobody gonna challenge me
'Cause when it comes to the rope
    on the block
Everybody wish they could
    be like me

Wanna see me do the butterfly
Everybody gonna step aside
'Cause what I'm about to
    show you now
Is for sure gonna blow your mind

When it comes to freestyle
    double-dutch
Always live is the Missi
    doing the buck
Harlem shaking the place down and
    doing toe-touch
All night we get it crunk
Throw your hands up

CHORUS

Uh uh, uh uh uh uh, uh uh uh uh,
    uh uh uh
Do the tip-toe, etc.

Do the helicopter
Let the chopper fly
C'mon, let it rise
Take you way up high

Swing it real fast
Give some good thrust
Take it low to the ground
Everybody jump

Jump, jump, jump, jump, etc.
Everybody jump

We da champions, champions, etc.
Everybody love
If you don't believe it, believe it
Give you what you want
And we're jumpin', jumpin'
Early in the morning
Get it crackin', crackin'
Let the speakers blow

If you wanna get in line
Better be on time
When the school bell rings at a quarter of nine
We're da champions, champions
Everybody know
Here we go, jump
Here we jump one time

We da champions, champions
Everybody know

WE HAVE COME TOO FAR

All these years in this relationship
And now you say that you're
    not feeling it
At first you wanna go, now you
    wanna stay
What did I do to make you do
    me this way

I don't know what's going
    on with me
We're making love but it's him I see
You're my family but the
    thrill is gone
And it's driving me crazy

I can't believe it's going
    down like that
I live for you you stab me
    in my back
Don't need this drama from you
Why am I hurting instead of you

I could never forgive myself
If I lied to you
You're my best friend
The only one I can talk to
I got to tell the truth

CHORUS:
We have come too far
To walk away from this
We have come to far
We'll end up regretting this
You know I love you
And what we got is good

But I've lost the passion
Don't want to be misunderstood
We have come too far
To just give up like this

Found a letter in your diary
I didn't read a single word
    about me
You're talking in your sleep calling
    out his name
I hope it's just a fantasy

What you doing going
    through my stuff
Without trust we got no love
I can't control my thoughts
    only what I do
And I've never betrayed you

Baby I don't want to clip your wings
I love you so much I will
    set you free
But before you fly away let me
    hear you say
That this is what you really want

I know I need to be alone
Don't know anymore what's
    right or wrong
Can't keep you hanging on
Don't want to lead you on

CHORUS

I've never been this close to anyone before
If it's true why do I feel like I'm loosing you
If we're meant to be together
We'll find each other
We'll come out of this stronger than ever

We have come too far
To walk away from this
We have come to far
We'll end up regretting this
You know I love you
And what we got is good
Times like these
We got to hold on
We have come too far
We have gone too far
I don't want to lose you
We have gone too far
I don't want to leave you
Don't want to give up, baby

WELCOME TO THE REAL WORLD

Said you like my eyes but
   you love blue
So I changed my brown just for you
I don't miss a thing, you think I care
You call me when your life's a mess
You've made it clear I'm
   second best
When I want you, you're never there
It's cloudy in your misty eye
You burning up deep inside
It's funny how you're trying to hide
You can't handle this

CHORUS:
Welcome to the real world
That's not how you treat a girl
Tell me I'm your first love
Make me feel I'm not enough
I used to walk around you
Now I walk all over you
Something's cutting strings
Come say bye-bye baby girl
Welcome to the real world

You love to revel in my misery
But I'm not where I used to be
And now you need me, it's
   a little late
You had your chance to be
   a good boy
Now be a man you made the choice
To misbehave, get it straight
I'm not here to pat you down
You're the one that's losing ground

Karma's coming back around
   to bite you

CHORUS

When you had me you didn't
   want me
Now you want me you can't have
   me too bad
Thought you knew me and
   I knew you
Now you know you didn't know
   what you had
When I loved you didn't need me
Now you need me and I'm not
   looking back
When you had me didn't want me
Now you want me you can't have
   me too bad

CHORUS

CHORUS

WHAT A WONDERFUL DAY

Staring at the lines in a bitter
    woman's face
Her daddy owned the world and
    he gave her everything
She loves, she hates
She loves, she hates

Living on the streets there's a man
    without a home
Sleeping through the day and
    at night he's all alone
And he loves, he hates
He loves, he hates
I said he loves, he hates
He loves, he hates

PRE-CHORUS
Sometimes you got it good, and
    you got it bad
And you lose it all and the
    world's gone mad
And you hate to love and you don't
    know what to do
You gotta feel the happy, feel the sad
Breathe every bit of life you have
Live every day God gave you
    like your last

CHORUS:
What a wonderful day
Take a deep breath and let the sun
kiss my worries away
I close my eyes and smile,
    all I can say

Is what a wonderful day

Man behind the bars dreaming
    of the sun
Missing his family because of
    what he's done
He loves, he hates
He loves, he hates

Little girl cries at night asking
    'bout her dad
Wondering why he left her and
    when he's coming back
She loves, she hates, etc.

PRE-CHORUS

CHORUS

She loves, she hates, yeah
He loves, he hates
I'm saying she loves, she hates
We love, we hate

WHAT DO YOU STAND FOR

Strangers without faces slowly
   passing me by
I won't give up searching for
   the sun in the rise
Labels on their shirts turn them
   into walking signs
What's in their mind
What's on your mind

CHORUS:
Everybody stands for something
Yeah there's got to be one thing
Tell me where do you fit in
What do you stand for
If you can only choose A or B
But none of them is what you
   want to be
What do you stand for

Greedy corporate monsters
   sweeping everything clean
Used to have more choices now
   there's no in between
I refuse to stand for something if
   it's not in my heart
Maybe you should try it sometime

CHORUS

Don't you want to free yourself from
   uniforms in every day routine
You know you can break free and
   just follow your soul

CHORUS

Yankees, Mets
Bloods, Crips
Hershey's Kiss
Micky D's, KFC
Mini cooper, GMC
Universal, BMG
CNN, NBC
VH1, MTV
Coke and Pepsi
Atheist, protestant
Lesbian, republican
Trendy, healthy
Democrat, just playin'
Hard to get

What do you stand for

What If

I know I've known you for
   quite some time
And as long as I remember you said
   you should be mine
But all the while my hands were tied
Always wanted to say yes but
   I had to deny
What I feel inside is so hard to hide
I give up the fight tonight

CHORUS:
What if I told you
Me and my boo are finally through
Free to do what I want to do
What if I told you
I got my eyes on someone new
What if I said that someone was you

Every night I picture you with me
But still I don't know where
   this will lead
I'm sure this may come
   as a surprise
I only hope your feelings
   haven't changed over time
I'm through with holding back
Don't know how you'd react
Now it's do or die tonight

CHORUS

What would you do if I came to you
And told you that I really had
   thought things through

That I dumped the one that
   I came here with
And it's you I want I'm sure of it
I'm sorry that it took so long to see
But now I truly know that you're
   the one for me
Everything about you just
   makes me crazy
I got to have you baby

What would you do
If I told you that I wanted you
Got my eyes on you

CHORUS

WHAT IT BOILS DOWN TO

This is it you know I had enough
I'm tired of you pushing luck
It's all the stupid things that you do
That makes me so fed up with you
Here you go talk talk talking again
Need to cut the act out 'cause it's just pretend
What you say is not fair
And if you knew me better
Then you'd realize that I don't care
But when you don't think you do thoughtless things
I'm just giving you fair warning
About the hurting pain
I'm fine with not caring don't try to scare
Your words don't mean shit to me
So I won't let it get to me, no
But who will be your friend that day when you fall
And when you need someone to talk to who can you call
No, I don't need no body else but me and myself
Don't mean to seem selfish but I can't help it

CHORUS:
What it all boils down to
Through all the haze, she still loves you
Wait a minute we're out of line
It doesn't matter who's wrong or right
By the end of the damn day
It's not about what you had to say
So put it over your shoulders make up
Let the past be gone
So you can move on

Stop listen up
No I ain't trying to hear it now
So why am I wasting time if you're being childish
We're just two women conversing so why you so upset

You're not a woman yet
Silly me how could I forget
So what's the deal with you and your man friend
When are you going to break it off with him
It's over (Whatever)
Go mind your own
I think it's best that I leave you alone (leave me alone)

CHORUS

Can't stand the things you say
And the choices that you make
Why do you keep hating on me
Girl you're so clueless, you're foolish, you don't understand
You could never be me
When will you understand I can't change who I am
You're too damn stubborn to receive a hand
So what, what's your problem
Can I help you
Please

CHORUS

WHAT'CHA KNOW ABOUT LOVE

So you think you're smooth
Hot like fire
Are you thinking I desire you
Well I do
Player play it cool
Whenever I'm watching
Trying to find a way of butt-touching me
But I disagree
I hate you more
Shut up you never listen
Looking fly but you're not complimenting me
You sure know how to play the fool

What'cha know about, what'cha know about, etc.

CHORUS:
What'cha know about love
Burn like fire
Touch another girl's butt
When you're rocking the club
You're thinking I don't know
But I know what you're thinking
What'cha know about love
You call me a chick
When you're chillin' with your dogs
Pointing out my flaws
But when we're face to face
You're all over me
What'cha know about

When you want to get your freak on
You won't stop trying
Get me with your sweet lies
But I'm not freaking you
So you calling me a church girl

Always teasing, why I got to justify
Stupid things you say make me mad
But you somehow always win me back
I hate you will you stop manipulating
Got me first in line but I'm still waiting
And you think you know it all

CHORUS

Player play it cool
'Cause I ain't that kind of chick
That you can just control, hit, fool around
Why don't you quit playing games with me
Stop acting like a child
Why don't you tell me how you feel?
Stop acting like you know who I am
Don't need a man who don't know
Faith from the real thing

What'cha know about, what'cha know about, etc.

CHORUS

What'cha know about love
You call me a chick
When you're chillin' with your dogs
Pointing out my flaws
But when we're face to face
You're all over me

WHATEVER

I got a new boyfriend he was
    Joey's best friend
Broke up with his ex-girlfriend
And that's when I knew I had to tell
    him that ever since I met him
I kinda liked him, but Michele
    was in the way
Michele was broken hearted though
    we already started
The second that they parted things
    was not fair
Cause everyone else told him
    Joey must have told him
What he thought I felt when they
    were still together
But I'm like

CHORUS:
Whatever, whatever
Get over it he's done with you
Whatever, whatever
Cause I would never lie to you

Everything is perfect, it would
    be so perfect
If I was sure my friends were wrong
They said we won't last like my
    boyfriends in the past
And Michele's not completely gone
She showed up at his driveway
    late last Friday
I was trying to call when he's alone
She doesn't seem to get it, why can't
    she forget it

What do I have to do to prove that
    we're together

CHORUS

Shut up, shut up, shut up, shut up
Leave him alone and find your own
Shut up, shut up, shut up, shut up
Stop pushing, etc.

CHORUS

Shut up, shut up, shut up, shut up
Leave him alone and find your own
Shut up, shut up, shut up, shut up
Stop pushing, etc.

WHEN GOD CREATED WOMAN

You dance like tonight is your last night on earth
Dressed like a gypsy, you smile and you turn
Dangerously close to losing my mind
You softy kiss me for the first time
Prayed for a woman that had more than I need
God wasn't joking when he brought you to me

CHORUS:
He took the stars from the sky and took the blue from the sea
Put it in your eyes to torture me
He took the heat from the sun and put it in your touch
Made me desire you way too much
Gave you legs as long as the lonely night
He knew he got it right
When god created woman he must've been thinking of you
When god created woman

Virgin Maria, please save me from sin
I can't control this desire from within
I prayed for a woman that had more than I need
God wasn't joking when he brought you to me

CHORUS

You dance like I imagine angels do
Make me tremble with every graceful move
I want to spend the rest of my life with you
My heart it won't stop pounding
I can barely breathe
God wasn't joking when he brought you to me

CHORUS

WHEN IT'S OVER

Don't be such a stupid, stupid boy
You don't know what you're
   about to destroy
I saw the way you looked
  at her in the backyard
  (I know what you were thinking)
I thought that I could trust you
  with my heart

PRE-CHORUS:
When it's broken, it's broken
It's never gonna heal again
When my trust is betrayed
You'll never make me feel safe again

CHORUS:
When it's over, it's over
It's never gonna be the same
When it's gone, then it's gone
And it's never coming back again
There's no such thing as a mistake
If you go then go all the way
When it's over, it's over
You'll never know if it could have
  been the real thing

Just the thought of seeing
  you with her
Thinking you might think of her
  makes my stomach turn
If it's true, if it's true
Then don't say it's gonna be alright
'Cause you owe me the truth
And I don't want to find out you lied
  (tell me the truth now)

CHORUS

Don't say that I'm oversensitive
Don't make me believe I'm naive
Don't turn this around on me

PRE-CHORUS

CHORUS

WHEN U FALL IN LOVE

One thing they never called me
   was a shy girl
'Cause when it came to them boys,
   I thought I ruled the world
Whatever I wanted them to do for
   me they would gladly do
Now I'm sitting here trying to
   figure out why that shit
   don't work with you
You walk by so cavalier
I could flash a nip and it's like you
   wouldn't even stare
Ain't no way you ain't feeling me,
   I got proof
But you won't take a chance unless
   I make my move
And I'm

CHORUS:
So scared, afraid you won't care
If I really show my face to you
Something I don't know how to do
You leave me no clue how to act or
   what to say to you
Making me break every one
   of my rules
Is that what they say that you
   got to go through
When you fall in love, when you
   fall in love

I'm wondering what the hell you're
   always running from
The more you run the more with
   you I want to come

Do I want you so bad 'cause you're
   so hard to get
Or are you so hard to get 'cause
   I want you so bad
Is this ego of mine just so
   hard to please
Will I bounce on you once
   you're achieved
No 'cause I knew just by how
   you looked at me
That's how I wanted to be
   looked at baby
And when you'd walk away I'd be
   like, "Please baby come back"

CHORUS

Me not going to say that you're
   not worth the chance it might
   take to get in your life
But what me can't deal with is
   me not know what words
   might not be right
You is a different kind of man,
   the kind me not understand
The kind who not chat no shit,
   the kind me just can't resist
Me body trembles with the thought
   of you not being in my life
So stay, stay, stay

CHORUS

When You Find Your Voice

I know you wanna speak but there's no sound
Can't say what's going on inside right now
Silent tears give away what you cannot reveal
You let your fear take control of what you feel

CHORUS:
When you find your voice inside your heart
I will be there for you wherever you are
When you find the strength to speak
The words will come to you
When you find your voice you'll be silent no more
And like a thundering waterfall
All that you held back so long will pour out of you
When you find your voice

Sometimes you've got to fall to rise again
To find a rhyme or reason for the pain
And when your time has come you'll know how to begin
You'll tell the world all you've held deep within

CHORUS

Even if it takes a hundred days for you
The quiet will be shattered when you finally come through

CHORUS

WHEN YOU WALK AWAY

Hey princess, how you doing
Are you all alone
Are you thinking about me
   holding you
And smelling my cologne
I picture you in the
   hooded sweatshirt
The one you stole from me
I wish I was there next to
   you watching TV
Whenever I'm with you
Time just seems to fly
The world turns into a circus ride
And everything spins by
It feels like the beginning
Of a never-ending dream
And I don't want to wake up
As long as you're with me, but

CHORUS:
When you walk away
It's like my sunshine disappears
When you walk away
Baby then it's clear
What I want to say to show you
   how I feel
When I'm with you all my words
   just feel cliché
Until you walk away
When you walk away
When you walk away

Hey princess it's killing me
To think of yesterday
When I took you out we ended up

In food fights with our
   chocolate cake
We laugh until we cry
About every little thing
And I get so used to being with you
That it tears me up within

CHORUS

Oh, baby, baby how can I explain
Oh, baby, baby tell me do you
   feel the same
Oh, baby, baby why is it so hard
To show what you and
   I already know

CHORUS

Just to see you go
I just want to run up to you and
   just hold you
I want to tell you I love you
And sometimes I just feel so stupid
So cliché until you walk away
And then it becomes real

WHEN YOU'RE IN LOVE

Six AM in the morning I jump out of bed
Can't sleep any longer I can't get you out of my head
Gotta tell my friends what's been going on with me
Well you and me still can't believe but I'm

CHORUS:
Walking down the street with a bounce
Singing songs all day
Hugging strangers, putting smiles on every face
The rain is pouring but I'm feeling warm in my heart
It's crazy all the things you do
When you're in love

Tiny little hearts with our initials in the sky
I can't imagine a day without you by my side
They say it's just a phase but it gets stronger everyday
I hope this feeling is never gonna go away

CHORUS

With you everything feels so much better
With you life seems so much brighter
It's like I got a little bit of sunshine with me
And I'm

CHORUS

WHERE DID ALL THE MONEY GO?

See, I wanna know where did all your money go

Girls, do you know the guys I'm talking about
Making all the money and throwing it down
For all the nice cars and blinging it out

When it comes to being good to the girl
And making her feel like she's his world
It's all about what he wants
It's all about he, himself, and him

Takes you out for dinner
Makes you feel like a queen
But when that check comes
He doesn't pay a thing
When you're at the club
He won't buy you a drink
And you wanna know

CHORUS:
Where did all the money go
Denaros, pesos, dollars, and euros
And you wanna know
Where did all the money go
Armani, Dolce Gabanna
Where did all the money go
Jewels, clothing, Rolex
That's how you roll
Acting like he's making big dough
But when it comes to me

He's broke
Broke ass motherfucker

Guys, you know we're not all material girls
But once in a while gotta show us you care

Don't have to buy us pearls and furs
And don't need to pimp your ride

We're not saying we all depend on you
We make our own money
And we spend it too
But every now and then you've gotta treat me
Treat me like your boo

Birthdays, holidays
Don't wanna spend a thing
It doesn't even have to be a diamond ring
Don't even know where to begin
And we wanna know

CHORUS

Monday, Tuesday, Wednesday, Thursday
Keeps saying he'll take me out
Friday night you come home drunk
And you pass out on the couch
Saturday you wake up late
And it's another lame excuse
Sunday....

See boy, what I really wanna know is
Why you're runnin' on my pimpin' like you've got that dough
Acting like you're wining and dining till you bullshit
You need to step off
I'm getting tired of your noise

When we get down to it
You can't even get a girl a drink
Forget all that rings I deserve
You need to a get clue
I'm gonna find a real dude that for sure is gonna know

CHORUS

WHILE YOU WERE SLEEPING

So far away
From the place where I feel safe
I can't recall
The beauty in your face

PRE-CHORUS
The distance between us
Sews its dirty seeds
Spreading inside of me
With every breath I breathe

CHORUS:
While you were sleeping
I was wandering with
    the lonely people
While you were sleeping
Trying to fill the void you've left
Life is short and the nights are long
And tonight, I moved on
While you were sleeping

A stranger for the night
So I don't wake up alone
To fake what we had
But it doesn't feel like home

PRE-CHORUS

CHORUS

Don't look for me
Don't wait for me
I've found my path
While you were sleeping

Over sticks and stones
Over broken bones
I won't look back
While you were sleeping

There's a place for you
Somewhere in my heart
But that's the past

CHORUS

WHO AM I TO YOU?

Something started
Sometime a while ago
You've grown close to me
And I wonder how much closer
    it could go

We always joke around
What it would be like
You and I together

Try to read between the lines
Easy what you didn't say
I'm wasting all this time
Waiting for you to come my way

It's so frustrating
'Cause I want more from you
I can't go on like this forever

CHORUS
If you only knew
Every night I lay awake
    in bed thinking
What am I gonna do
If you only knew
How it feels when I see you walk by
And I wonder if you feel it too
If you only knew
How I drive myself crazy everyday
'Cause you just don't make a move
It's killing me
I've gotta know the truth
Who am I to you
Who am I to you

You love to ask me out
And I hate to let you down
We always have a good time
But that's all you care about

It's so frustrating
It should be obvious by now
I can't go on like this forever

CHORUS

And I don't want that you come
    to meet your problems
But one is always gonna be around
And I don't mind that you're gonna
    take for granted
When I'm coming with you'd wish
    you'd never let go

CHORUS

WHO DO YOU LOVE?

I feel it in my bones
Feel it 'til I turn green
Getting me all pissy 'cause I see
   you watching
The vixen in the black,
   the seductive girl
Crawling on them fours
Dominating your world

You look at her, you talk to me
I talk to you, you're not listening
You never listen
God, you're so obviously stuck
I can't sit in front

CHORUS
Oh baby, who do you love
I gotta know
Baby, baby if you want my love
I gotta know
Baby, baby who do you love
I wanna know

Can I ask you what exactly
   you are doing
She is foxy but I see you drooling
All over yourself watching your
   little Siren
In the shadows like an evil lion

I look at her
I want her to disappear
   into the mirror
I want to claw her, I want to bite her
I want to tear her to pieces, ah

CHORUS

Jealousy, anxiety
Is eating me from the inside out
You got me foaming at the mouth
Girls, can I hear you shout

We're gonna kick your ass, beat it
If you go and look at another lady
Keep your eyes off her 32 C
We're the motherfuckin' bosses

Who do you love, etc.

WHOLE

Standing on the cliffs
So close to the edge
With every breath, I'm letting go
Of the thoughts that are holding me down

When's the freedom call
I can't wait anymore
There's a fire that's burning within
Far too long, I've held it in

CHORUS
I wanna live
I wanna love someone
Keep on pushing for all I can go
I don't wanna lay down my soul
'Til I'm whole

I need to feel the rush
Flowing through my veins
Feel the happiness when I succeed
Feel all of the pain when I bleed

Need to prove my worth
Prove it to myself
No one can do this for me
It's my time to rise and break free

CHORUS

CHORUS

I wanna breathe
I wanna hold someone
When I stand at the end of my road
I wanna be able to say
I am whole

WHY

If we can make diamonds out of stones
Talk to someone a thousand miles away by phone
Build a house that touches the sky
And build machines to let us fly
Then why can't I love you

If we can find the grave of Jesus
Find a cure to man's most dirty diseases
Out of rocks, clay and some dirt
Build seven wonders of the world
Then why can't I love you

If we can build a spaceship

WHY DOES IT TAKE A BROKEN HEART

Never had time to even think about it
Just didn't mind, took it all for granted
Didn't ever notice how good I really had it
Until I knew what it was like to have it all so bad

CHORUS:
Why does it take a broken heart
Before you say I love you
Why do things have to fall apart
Before they have a value
Why does it have to take so long
'Til you appreciate all the little things
What they really mean

It's such a waste to breathe in not feeling life
Sit there and wait until it's lost, didn't realize
This was your chance, had it in your hand
But you let it slip away
And now it's all too late

CHORUS

If I could rewind the time
And then do everything
I'd make sure you know all the things
That I never had a change to say

CHORUS

Why does it take a broken heart
Before you say I love you

WHY NOT

I like, I like what I see
I want to take you down
To the sycamore tree

Let's hitch a ride
I'll slip on my jeans
Wear that Nirvana shirt
Baby let's live the dream

CHORUS
Don't you know that some things are too good to deny
Don't you know if you feel it you should give it a try
You say why and I say
Why not
I say why not

I say let's have some fun
Let's go crazy like
Hippies on the run

I'll play Bonnie
You can play Clyde
Let's get lost in the riverbanks and hide

CHORUS

'Til the sun comes up, oh yeah
All night long, don't stop, yeah

Don't you know that some things are too good deny
Oh yeah

CHORUS

WHY WORRY

I'm on my way
But I'm not there
Stuck in between these
    words somewhere
I try so hard but I can't
Get to where I wanna be

Say it takes time
But I want you now
Feel everyday I let myself down
Can't figure out how to make
Everybody happy

PRE-CHORUS:
Why worry,etc.
Worries it don't make it better
Why worry

PRE-CHORUS

CHORUS:
Don't worry your life away
Don't worry your life away

Patience will come to
    those who wait
You're in control of your own fate
Sounds like the words inside
A birthday card from Hallmark

I am my own worst enemy
Drenching my soul in misery
I got it so good
But I can't seem to find
    my happiness

PRE-CHORUS

CHORUS

So the time alone, I don't
Know where I'm going
Because I'm in love, in love
To love to die to feel tonight

CHORUS

CHORUS

WHY WOULD I LIE

If you only knew where I was
  coming from
You'd be holding me instead of
  making me feel bad for things
  I haven't done
And if you only knew how
  I feel inside
You wouldn't be mad at me I'm
  trying to get home to you tonight
Rest assure I adore you,
  do anything for you
You're the best thing I have
  in my life

CHORUS:
So why would I lie to you
Why would I lie, why would I lie,
  why would I lie to you
Why would I lie, why would I lie,
  why would I lie to you
'Cause you're precious to me
And I don't want to see anything
  come between us
You're all that I have
Always making me laugh when
  I'm feeling blue
So why would I lie to you
Why would I lie, why would I lie,
  why would I lie to you
Why would I lie, why would I lie,
  why would I lie to you

You think you only gotta
  watch you're back

Yeah you've been hurt before,
  but now you think you know
  me better than that
I must admit, sometimes I get
  a little out of my head
But baby I would never
  let you down
Yeah I'm yours don't forget
Rest assure I adore you,
  do anything for you
You're the best thing I have
  in my life

CHORUS

Why do I have to act a fool when
I'm all the way across
  the country it's cool
But I'm not waking up to you and
  I'm missing you what
  am I supposed to do
You drive me crazy and
  I call you 20 times a day
I'm texting you wishing I was
  counting you
Every second of my life is about you
  how could you think baby
  that I'm not into you

CHORUS

So why would I lie to you
Why would I lie, etc.

WITH ALL MY HEART

Some people fall for every chance
Call it love when it's just romance
Then wind up like two strangers in a battlefield
People are out there just for fun
Afraid to commit to only one
And when it gets too deep they move on
But I can't do that
'Cause when I fall

CHORUS:
I fall with all my heart
I love with all my heart
'Cause I believe that promises are made to last forever
So I love with all my heart
With all my heart

Some people reach for anyone
Get way too close so they're not alone
Then leave somebody crying 'cause the thrill is gone
I see the world through different eyes
Don't ever want to compromise
If it's not the real thing
It's a waste of time
And I can't do that
'Cause when I fall

CHORUS

It takes time before I trust somebody
But when I do I'll hold on with all my heart
Hold on with all my heart
'Cause I believe that promises are made to last forever
So I love with all my heart, with all my heart
With all my heart, with all my heart

All of my

WITHOUT LOVE

Did I say something wrong
Why are you mad at me
Is there something you don't like about me
Baby it's the way I think

You go behind my back
Telling all my friends that you hate the way I look
You really can't stand me
You try to bring me down when I'm reaching out my hand
Do you really think that its worth it in the end

CHORUS:
Without love without love
Without love without love
We're never gonna make it
No, we're never gonna make it
No, no

If I met you face to face
Maybe we could talk it out
If you put yourself in my place
Would you like it if I pulled you down

Show me who you are
You don't even know me
When I turn my back you always talk about me
Pretending you don't hear me when I set it straight
Make it loud and clear I'm the one you love to hate

CHORUS

How do you sleep at night
When you know it isn't right
Be careful what you say
Got to think before it's too late

CHORUS

WITNESS

I've been with some
Sweet talking, heart breaking,
    love faking, money making men
I've done seen my share of
Good looking, thrill seeking,
    pussy fiending, body steaming

What a waste of so much time
Chasing a feeling all my life
Now I've come to realize
That you ain't got nothing without

CHORUS:
Someone who can, who can roll
    with you, grow with you,
    read between your lines
Someone who can, understand
    where you're coming from,
    walk by your side
Who's happy for you when you're
    on top of the world
Sees your joy, sees your hurt
Someone who can be a witness
    to your life

Will he wanna be there if I'm sick
    or if I'm lonely
Call my mother mommy wanna
    know about me, can I
    tell him everything
I know where I'm coming from,
    the bad things I've done
The good things I wanna do
    something so beautiful

There really ain't nothing like
    someone to hold you tight
I need to find

CHORUS

More than driving a fancy car
More than dropping all your
    dough at the bar
More than spending all your
    money on me
More than coming over for
    just one thing
More than telling me what you
    think I want to hear
More than your ice more
    than your gifts
Takes so much more to
    find real love

CHORUS

CHORUS

Someone who can read
    between your lines
Someone who can walk by your side
Who's happy for you when you're
    on top of the world
Sees your joy, sees your hurt
Someone who can be a witness
    to your life

WONDERFUL DAY

Staring at the lines in a bitter
   woman's face
Her daddy owned the world
And he gave her everything
She loves, she hates,
   she loves, she hates
Living on the street
There's a man without a home
Sleeping through the day
And at night he's all alone
He loves, he hates,
   he loves, he hates, etc.

PRE CHORUS:
Sometimes ya got it good
Ya got it bad
Ya losing all
The world's gone mad
You hate to love and you don't
   know what to do
Ya gotta feel the happy
Feel the sad
Breathe everything of life you have
Everything I gave you like your last

CHORUS:
What a wonderful day
Take a deep breath
And let the sun kiss my
   worries away
I close my eyes and smile
Oh I can say
What a wonderful day

Men behind the bars
Dreaming of the sun
Missing his family
Because of what he's done
He loves, he hates,
   he loves, he hates
Little girl cries at night
Asking bout her dad
Wanting to know why he left her
And when he's coming back
She loves, she hates,
   she loves, she hates, etc.

PRE CHORUS

CHORUS

THE WORDS

It's the fifth time of day that I thought of you
I'm giving my best but I can't help myself
I'll never stop trying to search for you
But I'm pretty sure it's much too late now
When I had the chance to get your name
I lost my nerve thinking I could wait

The minutes went by 'til I was ready to try
But you were already gone

CHORUS:
It's the words I didn't say when we were face to face
It's the risk I didn't take when I watched you walk away
The emptiness inside is torturing my mind
It's the thought that I will never know
What it's like to be with you

I keep coming back to the place wasting all my time
Hoping I will catch you walking by someday
All these images of you are running through my head
What would I do to get a second chance

Now I'm moving in circles
And I'm growing desperate for any traces of you

CHORUS

CHORUS

THE WORDS (LOVE U)

Come here a little closer
Sit with me and see
If you can find one single reason not to be with me
If it's just for this moment
Whisper in your ear
The sweetest ah, the sweetest nothings that you'll need to hear

CHORUS:
But the words get in the way can't you see it on my face
Want to tell you my sweet babe, I love you I love you I love you
But the words get in the way, it happens every day
All I really want to say is that I love you I love you I love you I love you

Listen to the birds outside while they sing a lullaby
And know that when the time is right
I'll make love to you, make it last all night
Light the candles baby while I run my bubble bath
Join me with your skin so soft, you know I want you bad

CHORUS

I love you more than any star that fell
More than any fame or wealth
Because of you I love myself
So get a little closer baby

CHORUS

This is no crush this is no ordinary love
I love you babe, etc.

WORK OF ART

From your legs to your thighs
It's just plain perfection
Strong chest, steel as ice
I feel the attraction
V-shaped bags shoulders wide
Built like a warrior
Skin is smooth, muscles tight
I'll make you my soldier

CHORUS:
Oh my hands what to touch you
Just can't resist you
Wanna mess up your hair
Feel you everywhere
Driving me crazy
Your body is a work of art,
    your body is a work of art, etc.

Run with me to the night
Take me away from here
Come alive hold me tight
Whisper something in my ear
Shivers run down my spine
Makes me wanna scream
Baby be mine be mine
Your giving me what I need

CHORUS

What are you doing to me baby
All my friends say I'm crazy
I don't care what they're thinking
As long as I know that you'll
    be with me
Is it my mind going crazy

I don't care what they're thinking
As long as I know that you'll
    be with me
It's like a description
    from a textbook
From your toes to your hair

CHORUS

THE WORLD AIN'T READY

She had a mind of a woman
And the body of a man
No one she talked to
Would wanna understand
Spent her lonely days pretendin'
Somehow fittin' in
But at night she'd put her
   high heels on
Showin' her sexy skin
She'd tear up the dance floor
Breakin' every rule
Drivin' every guy crazy
No one really knew
The struggle she was goin' through
Playin' different roles
Wouldn't let you get too close
Afraid to be exposed

CHORUS:
Be you, the real you
Love who you are
Don't let nobody confuse your
   precious heart
Somebody's right might be
   you're wrong
But you know where you belong
Do what you gotta do
Even if the world ain't ready for you

Guy at the corner store
Got a daughter who likes girls
No matter how he tries
Daddy can't change her morals
So he buys her pretty dresses
Instead of baseball caps

And he hand picks her flowers
And kisses her while she naps
The girl loves her daddy
And wants to see him happy
Says "I do" to a man
Hugs her family at the wedding
But underneath the veil she feels
   she deceived
Herself, her man, her lover and
   the daddy she wanted to please

CHORUS

So easy to laugh at somebody
   (without given a chance)
Single out the stranger
   (not tryin' to understand)
People come in different sizes,
   colors and beliefs
So quick to point the finger until
   the finger points at you

CHORUS

CHORUS

Come on, you gotta love you

WORTH THE WAIT

Just give us a chance
And stop being so afraid
Just hold my hand
Everything will be okay

If you give me your heart
I will handle it with care
I know you've been hurt before
But baby it's not fair

Don't take it out on me
'Cause someone else was too blind to see
That they let go a most precious thing

They never should have been so lucky
To have ever had your love
And I promise you this
I'm not like the rest

CHORUS:
And I will put all my strength
Into breaking down these walls
And if you still don't believe in us
I'll slave to earn your trust
And if you feel like giving up
I won't let you fall
A thousand years could pass my way
But you're worth the wait

Every night I am waiting for your call
I tell you I love you
But at times you say nothing at all

I can feel your insecurity with me
But just give me your pain
And I will gently kiss it away

CHORUS

Don't take it out on me
'Cause someone else was too blind to see
That they let go a most precious thing

They never should have been so lucky
To have ever had your love
But I promise you this
I'm not like the rest

And I will put all my strength
Into breaking down these walls
And if you still don't believe in us
I'll slave to earn your trust

You're worth the wait
If you don't believe, etc.

I'll be here
Until the sun and the moon don't shine
You're worth the wait
If that's what it takes to call you mine
You're worth the wait

I'll be here
Until the sun and moon don't shine
A thousand years could pass my way
But you're worth the wait

YOU

Waited so long for this feeling
Almost gave up on love
All by myself, always dreaming
That love belonged to everyone but me
You were waiting somewhere out there
Guess I always knew that everything I'd been wishing for
Would finally come true

CHORUS:
You give meaning to my life
And you have opened up my mind
You bring out the best in me since we've been together
I finally found a reason to believe in dreams

No looking back
There's no reason
Some things are worth waiting for
It all makes sense now
If you wish for something long enough
Your wishes will come true
Now I've found my happiness in everything you do

CHORUS

Feels like a new life has begun
Every day I love you more
And you make me believe
The best is yet to come

CHORUS

YOU BETTER LEAVE

It's wrong you should know better
I get weak when we're together
It is irresistible undeniable
And I wish life would be that simple

CHORUS:
You better leave me now
'Cause I'm gonna break your heart
Go, get out, don't you make me fall in love
Just walk away let's just pretend we never met
You better leave me now
Cause I don't want to fall in love

I'm scared, scared of what you do to me
Shivers, shivers I can barely breathe
But it's not the time and it's not the place
So turn around 'cause I don't wanna have to say goodbye

CHORUS

Don't give me a reason to stay any longer
Don't give me a reason to stay any longer
Give me a reason to stay a little longer
Give me a reason to stay

CHORUS

Don't give me a reason to stay any longer
Don't give me a reason to stay any longer
Give me a reason to stay a little longer
Give me a reason to stay

You Don't Know What You're Missing

I'm really not the kind of girl who's making the first move
And all my friends are telling me I need to wait three days to call you
But what I felt with you last night made me change my mind
The moment we kissed good-bye I was sure there was a sign

When I texted you in the morning and I didn't hear back by 2
I left a message on your voicemail "hey, it's me, I wanna see you"
Now it's 6pm and still no word I've been checking my phone all day
Every minute that I don't hear from you my hopes fade away

CHORUS:
You don't know what you're missing
Boy, call me I'm waiting
You don't know what you're missing
Thought we had something going on
You don't know what you missing
Thought it was mutual it felt natural
Now I'm sitting here wondering what to do
Driving myself crazy over you

Damn I hate this feeling when I don't know where I stand
Wish my phone would just ring now cuz I won't call again
I thought all guys like to play games and when we talked last night
You said it wouldn't be that way please don't prove me right

CHORUS

Could it be that you lost my number
Or that you texted me and I didn't get it yet or that your phone is dead
Could it be that you have a girlfriend
By the way you kissed me I know you feel the same

CHORUS

YOU FOOL

It's in your eyes; it's in your smile
You couldn't hide it if you tried
You can't deny; it's all in your mind
And I won't lie to you, I feel it, too

CHORUS:
Just close your eyes and
Kiss me, you fool
What are you waiting for?
It's just me and you
This moment is yours
You know what to do
Just pull me close to you
You fool

Without words, without a sound
I can still hear you speak
Don't be afraid, there's no doubt
There's something between us to believe in

CHORUS

It's all in your hands
So hold me while you can
Don't let this go
You fool, you fool,
What are you waiting for

Kiss me
You know what to do
Just pull me close to you
You fool

Kiss me

YOU MAKE ME FEEL SO SEXY

I'm watching you watching me
And I can't deny this feeling
I'm feeling you feeling me
And I know you want to give in
I'll be your fantasy
Tell me your sweetest dreams
There is nothing to worry
Don't be shy baby

Won't you come talk to me
Don't matter what you say
Whatever is on your mind
It will be okay
Don't you waste no time
I'm all you've waited for
It's written in your eyes
We can't stop this anymore

CHORUS:
You make me feel so
You make me feel so
You make me feel so sexy, etc.
I just can't keep my hands
    off you baby

Just move along with me
Let's do it how they do it
I'll let you touch my body
Oh I know you want it
Baby you make me weak
I can't resist your moves
Everything's telling me
That what I want is you

CHORUS

Feels so good falling into your arms
When you're holding me this way
Baby I can't get enough of you

Baby let's find a place
Where we can be alone
We don't have to behave
We'll keep it on the low
Let's be spontaneous
No one will ever know
It's just between you and me
So baby come on
Put it on me

CHORUS

Things you're doing to me just
    make me crazy

YOU SMILE

I woke up and the sky is gray
Got no place to go today
It all feels wrong no matter what I do
Maybe some days are colored blue
I don't know where I belong
I'm tired of having to be strong
It's like the clouds struggle with the sun
Sometimes I feel so alone

CHORUS:
When you smile
You smile
You always paint a rainbow in my sky
When you smile

Baby when it rains it pours
Let me lay my hand in yours
Can't explain, I can't find the words
But I know you feel the way I hurt

CHORUS

There was sadness in my eye
Now it's joy that makes me cry
Felt so bad but I can't remember why

CHORUS

YOUR DREAM

I know it seems unreachable
But you won't let it go
Afraid they'll laugh about you
You let nobody know
So you keep imagining
That someone you look up to
Will someday be you

CHORUS:
But nobody can dream your
    dream for you
Nobody can say it won't come true
Even if it seems impossible
With every breath you take
    you'll feel that
This is what you were born to do
Laughable unthinkable
Even if no one believes in you,
    pull through
'Cause nobody can dream your
    dream for you

They say it's just a fantasy
Too big for even you
But when you close at night
The dream comes alive
And you feel invincible
Imagine all your friends
Wishing they could be just like you

CHORUS

One day you'll look back
And see how far you've come

Got back up when you've
    fallen down
Cried a little when you left
    your hometown
Wondering where you
    found the strength
To push aside the embarrassment
To stand tall through it all

CHORUS

Nobody

YOUR LIES ARE THE TRUTH

I tell myself that I'm strong enough
I can make it through on your
   partial truth
Anything to keep me around
I hate it when you make me smile
'Cause it's just nothing but
   a temporary high for now
It's obvious you bring me down

And just for a moment I fall
   for your touch
You love me, I get it, but
   love's not enough

CHORUS:
It's almost perfect
But under the surface I know
That it's wrong to go on
With such a sweet illusion
'Cause your lies are the truth
That I just can't get used to
'Cause your lies are the truth
That I just can't get used to

I've pulled a string from the tapestry
And I can't believe it's unraveling
But still I try to put it back up
All I need is you to lie to me
And make me see what I want to see
I play along
I just can't give up

So don't tell me you're sorry it
   won't work anymore

Don't sell me your story I've
   heard it before

CHORUS

You opened the door when you
   know I won't go
I'm trapped in denial, you lied
   to my soul
You swear on your life I'm wrong
But I know you, I know you
Don't go
I don't wanna hurt anymore

CHORUS

Fuck you

PERMISSIONS AND CREDITS

Copyright © CHERRY LANE MUSIC PUBLISHING COMPANY, INC. (ASCAP)/ LIEDELA MUSIC (ASCAP)/ GAD SONGS LLC (ASCAP)/ STILL WORKING FOR THE WOMAN MUSIC INC (ASCAP)/ KDB MUSIC PUBLISHING (ASCAP)/ STONESVILLE MUSIC (BMI). Worldwide rights for Liedela Music and Gad Songs LLC administered by Cherry Lane Music Publishing Company, Inc. All Rights Reserved. Used By Permission: **"5th Avenue"** (Toby Gad, Kaci Brown and Madeline Stone) (2009).

Copyright © CHERRY LANE MUSIC PUBLISHING COMPANY, INC. (ASCAP)/ LIEDELA MUSIC (ASCAP)/ GAD SONGS LLC (ASCAP)/ KILKEA PUBLISHING (SESAC). Worldwide rights for Liedela Music and Gad Songs LLC administered by Cherry Lane Music Publishing Company, Inc. All Rights Reserved. Used By Permission: **"9 to 5"** (Toby Gad and Lola Zadeline) (2009); **"Between Those Legs"** (Toby Gad and Lola Zadeline) (2009); **"Crushed"** (Toby Gad and Lola Zadeline) (2009); **"Damn (Be Your Girl)"** (Toby Gad and Lola Zadeline) (2009); **"Goosebumps"** (Toby Gad and Lola Zadeline) (2009); **"I Touch Myself"** (Toby Gad and Lola Zadeline) (2009); **"If It's with a Girl"** (Toby Gad and Lola Zadeline) (2009); **"No Strings"** [a/k/a "No Strings (Let's Have Sex)"] (Toby Gad and Lola Zadeline) (2005); **"Porn"** (Toby Gad and Lola Zadeline) (2009); **"Pure"** (Toby Gad and Lola Zadeline) (2009); **"Sleep With Me"** (Toby Gad and Lola Zadeline) (2009); **"Sleepless"** (Toby Gad and Lola Zadeline) (2009); **"So Simple"** (Toby Gad and Lola Zadeline) (2009); **"Solitary Soul"** (Toby Gad and Lola Zadeline) (2009); **"Surrender"** (Toby Gad and Lola Zadeline) (2009); **"That Thing"** (Toby Gad and Lola Zadeline) (2009); **"Unconditional"** (Toby Gad and Lola Zadeline) (2009).

Copyright © CHERRY LANE MUSIC PUBLISHING COMPANY, INC. (ASCAP)/ LIEDELA MUSIC (ASCAP)/ GAD SONGS LLC (ASCAP)/ A.J. GUNDEL PUBLISHING DESIGNEE (BMI). Worldwide rights for Liedela Music and Gad Songs LLC administered by Cherry Lane Music Publishing Company, Inc. All Rights Reserved. Used By Permission: **"Absolutely Adorable"** (Toby Gad and A.J. Gundel) (2009).

Copyright © CHERRY LANE MUSIC PUBLISHING COMPANY, INC. (ASCAP)/ LIEDELA MUSIC (ASCAP)/ GAD SONGS LLC (ASCAP)/ JEEJ PUBLISHING (BMI). Worldwide rights for Liedela Music and Gad Songs LLC administered by Cherry Lane Music Publishing Company, Inc. All Rights Reserved. Used By Permission: **"Admit It"** (Toby Gad and Esmee Denters) (2009); **"A Little Craziness"** (Toby Gad and Esmee Denters) (2009); **"When You're in Love"** (Toby Gad and Esmee Denters) (2009); **"Who Am I to You"** (Toby Gad and Esmee Denters) (2009).

428

INDEX

LaVergne, TN USA
13 January 2010
169817LV00004B/78/P